The Innocent and the Criminal Justice System

By the same author

Rethinking Miscarriages of Justice: Beyond the Tip of the Iceberg (Palgrave
 Macmillan, 2007)
The Criminal Cases Review Commission: Hope for the Innocent? (ed.,
 Palgrave Macmillan, 2009)

The Innocent and the Criminal Justice System

A Sociological Analysis of Miscarriages of Justice

Michael Naughton
Reader in Sociology and Law, University of Bristol, UK

First published 2013 by
PALGRAVE MACMILLAN

Palgrave Macmillan in the UK is an imprint of Macmillan Publishers Limited, registered in England, company number 785998, of Houndmills, Basingstoke, Hampshire RG21 6XS.

Palgrave Macmillan in the US is a division of St Martin's Press LLC, 175 Fifth Avenue, New York, NY 10010.

Palgrave Macmillan is the global academic imprint of the above companies and has companies and representatives throughout the world.

Palgrave® and Macmillan® are registered trademarks in the United States, the United Kingdom, Europe and other countries

ISBN: 978–0–230–21690–7 hardback
ISBN: 978–0–230–21691–4 paperback

This book is printed on paper suitable for recycling and made from fully managed and sustained forest sources. Logging, pulping and manufacturing-processes are expected to conform to the environmental regulations of the country of origin.

A catalogue record for this book is available from the British Library.

A catalog record for this book is available from the Library of Congress.

Contents

Acknowledgements   viii

List of Cases   ix

List of Statutes   xii

1 **Introduction**   1
   Aims   5
   Structure   7

**Part I   The Nature and Causes of Miscarriages of Justice and
            Abortions of Justice**

2 **Perspectives and Definitions**   15
   Introduction   15
   Competing perspectives   16
   The need to be semantic about 'miscarriages' of justice   27
   Conclusion   31

3 **The Key Causes of Abortions of Justice**   34
   Introduction   34
   Internal factors   35
   External factors   54
   Conclusion   68

4 **The Key Causes of Miscarriages of Justice**   70
   Introduction   70
   Internal factors   72
   External factors   82
   Conclusion   109

Part II   The Limits of the Criminal Justice System in Dealing with Claims of Innocence

5   **The Parole Board**   **113**
Introduction   113
The key obstacles to progression and release for
   indeterminate prisoners maintaining innocence   116
The Parole Board's response   123
A possible way forward   127
Conclusion   137

6   **The Court of Appeal (Criminal Division)**   **140**
Introduction   140
The history of the law on criminal appeals – from innocence
   to safety   143
What is unsafe for the CACD?   151
Is a test for unsafe a better protection for the factually
   innocent?   157
Conclusion   159

7   **The Criminal Cases Review Commission**   **162**
Introduction   162
How the CCRC deviates from what the RCCJ envisaged   167
'Success' rate   173
The CCRC's response   177
A due process defence   182
Conclusion   186

Part III   The Harmful Consequences of Wrongful Convictions and the Limits of Redress

8   **Victimology**   **191**
Introduction   191
Exceptional successful appeals   193
Routine successful appeals   197
Mundane successful appeals   202
An alternative perspective   204
Conclusion   206

9   **Compensation**   **209**
Introduction   209
The ex-gratia scheme   210

Eligibility for the statutory scheme   212
Only certain successful appeals will do   213
Amount   220
Conclusion   225

Part IV Conclusion

10 **Troubleshooting the Black Spots of the Criminal
    Justice System**   **231**

References   238

Index   261

Acknowledgements

I would like to express my gratitude to Gabe Tan for acting as a critical sounding board throughout the process of researching and writing this book and who gave detailed feedback on the various draft chapters and on the first full draft. I am also thankful to Patrick Capps, Aneurin Morgan Lewis and to the three anonymous reviewers who also read the first full draft of the book and gave me their feedback. The feedback that I received contributed to the formation of my thoughts and the firming up of my arguments. I would like to thank Anna Reeve of Palgrave Macmillan for her enthusiasm for the project and her constant encouragement throughout the process. Finally, thank you to Martin Barr who saw the book from copy-edit to press.

List of Cases

Brown and Isaacs v The State [2003] UKPC 10   131

Chan Wing Siu v The Queen [1985] AC 168   131

Davies v DPP [1954] AC 378   131

DPP v Majewski [1977] AC 443   129

DPP v Shannon [1974] 59 Cr App R. 250   20

Folker v Chadd [1782] 99 ER 589   101

General Medical Council v Professor Sir Roy Meadow [2006] EWCA Civ
   1390   73, 102–104

Livingstone v Rawyards Coal Company (1880) 7 R (HL) 1   221

Millar v Dickson [2002] WLR 1615   40

Murray v UK [1996] 22 EHRR 29   40

R v Andrew Adams [2007] EWCA Crim 1   196, 216

R v Barry George [2007] EWCA Crim 2722   75–77, 219

R v Basil Anthony Williams-Rigby and Michael James Lawson [2003]
   EWCA Crim 693   60–61

R v Blackburn [2005] 2 Cr App R 30   41

R v Blackwell [2006] EWCA Crim 2185   58–59

R v Bonython [1984] 38 SASR 45   102

R v Brown [2002] EWCA Crim 2804   28, 41, 115, 195

R v Cannings [2004] EWCA Crim 1   74–75, 199–200

R v Clark [2000] EWCA Crim 54   48

R v Clark (Sally) [2003] EWCA Crim 1020   103

R v Clarke and McDaid [2006] EWCA Crim 1196   171

R v Clarke and R v McDaid [2008] UKHL 8   171

R v Clarke; R v Hewins, Court of Appeal (Criminal Division), 15
   February 1999   48

R v Cooper [1969] 1 All ER 32   155–156

R v Criminal Cases Review Commission, ex parte Pearson [2000] 1 Cr
   App R 141   151–152, 154–155, 169, 172

R v Cummiskey [2003] EWCA Crim 3933   43

R v Davis, Johnson and Rowe [2001] 1 Cr App R 115   152–153

R v Day [2001] Crim LR 984   62–63

R v Devlin [1997] CLY 1152   89

R v Downing [2002] EWCA Crim 263   114, 115, 126, 138, 195, 209

R v F [1999] Crim LR 306   156

R v Fotheringham (1988) 88 Cr App R 206   129

R v Gee [2006] EWCA Crim 2271   59–60

R v Giles [2009] EWCA Crim 1388   54

R v Graham [1910] 4 Cr App R 8   56

R v H; R v C [2004] UKHL 3   52

R v Hadley and Others [2006] EWCA Crim 2544   53

R v Henry; R v Manning [1969] 53 Cr App R 150   57

R v Hickey and Others [1997] EWCA Crim 2028   21–22, 23, 43, 219

R v Hodges and Another [2003] EWCA Crim 290   102

R v Hodgson [2009] EWCA Crim 490   30, 181, 217

R v Hoey [2007] NICC 49   98

R v Hyde [1991] 1 QB 139   131

R v Irvin (Kenneth Anthony) [2007] EWCA Crim 2701   88

R v Kamara (John) [2000] EWCA 37   28, 51

R v Kenyon [2010] EWCA Crim 914   150

R v Kingston [1994] 3 All ER 353   130

R v Latif [1996] UKHL 16   154

R v Lawless (Ian) [2009] EWCA Crim 1308   94

R v McIlkenney and Others [1991] 93 Cr App R 287   67

R v Maynard and Others [2002] EWCA Crim 1942   61–62

R v Mullen [1999] EWCA Crim 278   153–154, 213

R v North (Robert) [2006] EWCA Crim 915   88–89

R v O'Brien and Others [2000] EWCA Crim 3   222, 224

R v Palmer [1971] AC 814   133, 134

R v Paris, Abdullahi and Miller [1993] 97 Cr App R 99   27, 30, 63, 64

R v Pendleton [2001] UKHL 66   151

R v Powell (Anthony); R v English [1999] 1 AC 1, 12   132

R v Puaca [2005] EWCA Crim 3001   105–106

R v Rahman [2008] 3 WLR 264   132

R v Richardson, Conlon, Armstrong and Hill EWCA 20 October 1989   2, 41–42

R v Richardson (Nigel John) [1999] 1 Cr App R 392   129

R v Robb [1991] 93 Cr App R 161   102

R v Secretary for the Home Department and the Parole Board, *ex parte* Owen John Oyston [unreported] (see *The Independent*, 15 October 1999)   124

R v Secretary of State for Home Department, *ex parte* Hepworth, Fenton-Palmer and Baldonzy and R v Parole Board, *ex parte* Winfield [1997] EWHC Admin 324   124

R v Shirley [2003] EWCA Crim 1976   126

R v Silcott, Braithwaite and Raghip (1991) The Times, 9 December, CA   92

R v Silverlock [1894] 2 QB 766   101

R v Simpson (Thomas William) [1909] 2 Cr App R 128   146–147

R v Spencer and Others [1986] 83 Cr App R 277   57–58

R v Stanton [2004] EWCA Crim 490   90–91

R v Turnbull and Others [1976] 63 Cr App R 132   85, 87–90

R v Turner [1975] 1 QB 834   101

R v Twitchell [2000] 1 Cr App R 373   28, 31, 32, 72, 91

R v Vernett-Showers and Others [2007] EWCA Crim 1767   54

R v Ward [1993] 2 All ER 577   28, 51–52, 67, 108

R v Williams (G) 78 Cr App R 276   133

R v Williamson [1908] 1 Cr App R 3   146

R (Adams) v Secretary of State for Justice [2009] EWCA Civ 1291   216–217

R (Mullen) v Secretary of State for the Home Department [2004] UKHL 18   153, 214–215

R (on the application of Adams) (FC) (Appellant) v Secretary of State for Justice (Respondent) [2011] UKSC 18   219

R (on the application of Guittard) v Secretary of State for Justice [2009] EWHC 2951   113

Reed v Wastie [1972] Crim LR 221 (DC)   134

Salduz v Turkey (2008) 49 EHRR 421   40

Skuse v Granada Television Ltd [1996] 1 WLR 1156   67–68

Woolmington v DPP [1935] AC 462   71

List of Statutes

Crime and Punishment (Scotland) Act 1997) (c. 48)   163
Criminal Appeal Act 1907 (c. 23)   1, 18, 143–145, 146, 147, 148, 149, 159
Criminal Appeal Act 1966 (c. 31)   147, 155, 156
Criminal Appeal Act 1968 (c. 19)   142, 148, 149, 151, 155, 156, 163, 168, 218
Criminal Appeal Act 1995 (c. 35)   21, 142, 149, 154, 156, 163, 166, 169, 173, 174, 205, 213, 218
Criminal Evidence (Witness Anonymity) Act 2008 (c. 15)   219
Criminal Justice Act 1948 (c. 58)   63
Criminal Justice Act 1967 (c. 80)   133
Criminal Justice Act 1988 (c. 33)   11, 56, 205, 210, 211, 212, 215, 220
Criminal Justice Act 2003 (c. 44)   17, 19, 52, 78, 183, 232
Criminal Justice and Immigration Act 2008 (c. 4)   133, 134, 209, 220, 221, 222
Criminal Justice and Public Order Act 1994 (c. 33)   56, 113
Criminal Law Act 1967 (c. 58)   133
Criminal Procedure (Insanity and Unfitness to Plead) Act 1991 (c. 25)   173–174
Criminal Procedure and Investigations Act 1996 (c. 25)   25, 52, 232, 237
Dangerous Dogs Act 1991 (c. 65)   176, 186
European Convention on Human Rights   26, 34, 40, 46
Human Rights Act 1998 (c. 42)   26, 34
Magistrates' Court Act 1980 (c. 43)   202
Mental Health Act 1983 (c. 20)   173
Police and Criminal Evidence Act 1984 (s. 66)   1, 3, 6, 22, 25, 30, 32, 38–41, 46–49, 72, 87, 89, 154, 183, 232, 237
Prosecution of Offences Act 1985 (c. 23)   49
Senior Courts Act 1981 (c. 54)   141
Sexual Offences Act 1967 (c. 60)   135
Sexual Offences Act 2003 (c. 42)   19
Supreme Court Act 1981 (c. 54) 217   21

1

Introduction

Miscarriages of justice, used interchangeably in this introduction with the term wrongful convictions, and defined simply as the conviction of those believed to be factually innocent of the criminal offences that they were convicted of, are a perennial problem that plagues the criminal justice system. Yet, despite the devastation that they undoubtedly cause to victims and their families (discussed in Chapter 8), they can act as pointers to the flaws of the criminal justice system in need of corrective reform. Indeed, certain successful appeal cases that exemplify new 'errors' in how miscarriages of justice are caused or in the criminal justice system's ability to overturn alleged miscarriages of justice have been influential in shaping the safeguards that exist to attempt either to prevent them from occurring and/or in introducing the mechanisms for them to be overturned when they do.

A pertinent example of a key landmark in the history of the criminal justice system is the establishment of the Court of Criminal Appeal in 1907, which was intended as creating an opportunity for innocent victims of miscarriages of justice to overturn their convictions (also discussed in Chapter 6). It is intrinsically linked with the case of Adolf Beck who was twice wrongly convicted of larceny in the late nineteenth and early twentieth century due to erroneous eyewitness identification evidence (see Coates, 2001; *The Times*, 1904). Another example of a defining moment in the history of the criminal justice system is the abolition of capital punishment in the UK and the link to the case of Timothy Evans, who was wrongly executed for the murder of his baby daughter Geraldine (see Eddowes, 1955; Kennedy, 1961). The introduction of formal guidelines on police investigations under the Police and Criminal Evidence Act (1984) (PACE) is another relevant illustration that is connected to a high-profile miscarriage of justice case. This time the wrongful convictions of three youths, Colin Lattimore, Ronald Leighton and

Ahmet Salih, for the murder of Maxwell Confait (see Fisher, 1977; Price and Caplan, 1976; Price, 1985). A final example here is the establishment of the Criminal Cases Review Commission (CCRC), the first independent public body in the world with the role of reviewing alleged miscarriages of justice and sending cases back to the relevant appeal court if it is believed that the conviction will be overturned. It took over the role of reviewing alleged miscarriages of justice from the Home Secretary, following revelations that potentially meritorious alleged miscarriage of justice cases, mainly involving convictions for Irish Republican Army (IRA) bombings that killed and seriously injured scores of innocent people (see for instance, Woffinden, 1987), were not being referred back to the Court of Appeal (Criminal Division) (CACD) for political as opposed to legal reasons. The key cases linked with the setting up of the CCRC are the infamous Guildford Four (see Conlon, 1990) and the Birmingham Six (Hill and Hunt, 1995). The case of the Guildford Four relates to Gerry Conlon, Paul Hill, Carole Richardson and Patrick Armstrong who were convicted and given life sentences in 1975 for the IRA pub bombings in Guildford, Surrey, which killed five people and injured over 100 others. The case of the Birmingham Six relates to the convictions of Paddy Joe Hill, Hugh Callaghan, Richard McIlkenny, Gerry Hunter, Billy Power and Johnny Walker for two IRA pub bombings in Birmingham in 1974 that killed 21 people and injured 162 others.

It is crucial to note, however, that the foregoing examples of notorious miscarriages of justice and momentous reforms that have shaped the criminal justice system were not overturned by the normal machinations of the criminal justice system. On the contrary, they were hard fought for. And a salient feature of all of the cases cited is that they were able to generate national and even international campaigns which were able to induce widespread public crises of confidence in the workings of the criminal justice systems at the time. It was those campaigns that were able to force the governments of the day to intervene and introduce the subsequent reforms of the criminal justice system to correct the apparent failings. In the Beck case, the furore caused by the press coverage of his wrongful convictions led to public demands for an investigation into how such a gross miscarriage of justice could occur. This prompted the government of the day to launch an official commission of inquiry (see *The Times*, 1904). It concluded that the responsibility lay primarily with the trial judge and that the problem could have been rectified had Beck had an opportunity to appeal against his ruling (Whiteway, 2008). The problem at the time was that the only way to appeal against an alleged miscarriage of justice was through the Royal Prerogative of Mercy by a petition to the Home Office, the success of which often depended upon whether it was supported by an influential person who had taken an interest in the case (see Pattenden, 1996: 30; discussed further in Chapter 6 in this book). As Risinger (2006) noted, the most significant consequence of the Beck case, then, was that it firmly established 'the necessity of providing a judicial forum to consider new evidence of actual innocence, since executive clemency through the Home Office was too political and unpredictable'.

The campaign for Timothy Evans was also widespread and included notable supporters such as Michael Eddowes, a high-profile lawyer who wrote *The Man on Your Conscience* in 1955 following his investigation into the case. In it he argued that Evans could not have been the killer of his daughter and the most likely murderer was his landlord, John Christie (see Eddowes, 1955). Eddowes' book was followed by another book about the case by Ludovic Kennedy, an influential television journalist and public figure. In *Ten Rillington Place*, Kennedy (1961) further developed the thesis that a man of subnormal intelligence had been used as a scapegoat by the police and had been a 'fall guy' who had been hanged for Christie's crimes. This fuelled a widespread concern among the public that an innocent person had been executed in error and consolidated the campaign for the abolition of capital punishment. It led to a vote in Parliament in 1965 to suspend the death penalty for five years when Sidney Silverman's private member's bill was passed. The following year Timothy Evans received a posthumous pardon from the Queen. And in 1969 capital punishment was totally abolished in the UK.

As for the convictions in the *Confait* affair and the cases of the Guildford Four and the Birmingham Six, the campaigns in both episodes were so successful that they led to various official inquiries and royal commissions. More specifically, the *Confait* affair spawned an official inquiry that was conducted by Sir Henry Fisher (see Fisher, 1977), which found that the police investigation was geared simply to manufacturing an incriminating case against the three accused. The Royal Commission on Criminal Procedure (1981) (RCCP) followed the Fisher Report (Fisher, 1977), which recommended the introduction of PACE (see Royal Commission on Criminal Procedure, 1981). The case of the Guildford Four invoked three inquiries by Sir John May (see May, 1990, 1992, 1994). These were extended by the Royal Commission on Criminal Justice (RCCJ), announced on 14 March 1991, the day that the Birmingham Six overturned their convictions in the CACD, which recommended the establishment of the CCRC (see Royal Commission on

Criminal Justice, 1993; for an extensive discussion of the foregoing examples and the link to reforms of the criminal justice system, see also Naughton, 2007: ch. 4).

As such, there is a discernible vital link between reforms to the criminal justice system from the lessons learned from an analysis of successful appeals to determine the causation of miscarriages of justice or the obstacles to them being overturned. Such reforms have improved the safeguards against similar occurrences in the future for all members of society and/or provided the appeal mechanisms to overturn them if and when they do occur. Despite this, those individuals and/or organisations that assist alleged victims and/or strive to reveal the wrongs of the criminal justice system when convictions are overturned have often been depicted as 'troublemakers' and even as 'enemies of the state'. Ludovic Kennedy, for instance, was involved with numerous campaigns for high-profile victims of miscarriages of justice, apart from the Timothy Evans case, for almost 50 years before his death in October 2009 (for some of the most significant cases that he supported, see Kennedy, 2002). In his book, *Thirty-Six Murders and Two Immoral Earnings* (Kennedy, 2002), he described the theme of much of his work as an examination of police corruption and judicial complacency. In 1994 he was knighted for his services to journalism and came to be seen as something of a national treasure towards the end of his life. Yet, his obituary observed that his efforts were regretted by some in the establishment as the effect was often to undermine public confidence in the police and criminal justice system in general (see *The Telegraph*, 2009). Similarly, for his part in helping to find the true perpetrators of the IRA bombs that killed and injured the victims in the Birmingham Six case (see Mullin, 1986), Chris Mullin, the investigative journalist turned Labour MP who went on to establish the Department of Justice within the Home Office, found himself on the front cover of *The Sun* newspaper alongside the headline: 'LOONY MP BACKS BOMB GANG'. The list goes on and includes notable figures such as Paul Foot, the editor of the *Daily Mirror* at the forefront of the campaign for the Bridgewater Four (see Foot, 1986, 1997). It includes Gareth Peirce, the solicitor who helped to overturn the convictions of the Guildford Four and the Birmingham Six, and who was immortalised when played by Emma Thompson in the film about the Guildford Four case, *In the Name of the Father*. It includes, David Jessel, the producer of the BBC television series *Rough Justice* and then Channel 4's, *Trial and Error*, which contributed to overturning around a dozen miscarriages of justice (see Naughton, 2007: 197). It includes Bob Woffinden, the investigative journalist who has devoted much of his professional life to revealing miscarriages of justice. In short, all of whom have been seen at some time or other as trouble-makers who were somehow against the criminal justice system due to the orientation of their concerns.

For some who strive to overturn or reveal miscarriages of justice to be seen as in some way anti-establishment or in some way against the crim-inal justice system is not seen as necessarily problematic and such a depiction has even been embraced. Michael Mansfield QC, for instance, perhaps the most high-profile criminal barrister of his generation who acted for the Guildford Four and Birmingham Six, is, apparently, quite happy to refer to himself as a 'radical' lawyer in his memoirs. In it he recounts how he was aware that members of the judiciary had regard-ed him as a 'dangerous radical' throughout his working life, based on the controversial cases that he took on (see Mansfield, 2009: 150). On the back cover of his book, Mansfield celebrates the review by the *Sunday Times* that declared: 'The Establishment loathes him'. Similarly, Shami Chakrabarti, Director of the leading human rights organisation, Liberty, which has a long history of assisting victims of miscarriages of justice, embraced Jon Gaunt's description of her as the 'most danger-ous woman in Britain' in his column in *The Sun* newspaper on 19 June 2007. In a keynote speech to the Police Foundation John Harris Memorial Lecture in July 2008, she even went so far as to describe her-self in positive terms as a 'professional troublemaker' (Chakrabarti, 2008: 367).

Aims

Against this background, an analogy with factory maintenance engi-neers seems apposite as a way of framing the various analyses of this book. Indeed, it would be bizarre to think of factory maintenance engi-neers who respond to reported failures with factory plant or machinery breakdowns as troublemakers or somehow 'enemies of their factories'. The whole *raison d'être* of factory maintenance engineers is, rather, to troubleshoot and/or address reported failures in the machinery of their factories so that the manufacturing process runs smoothly. Similarly, and whether those so labelled reject or accept the idea that they are troublemakers, this book puts forward the alternative thesis from a sociological perspective that the endeavour to unearth miscarriages of justice is better seen as part of the overall *troubleshooting* of the criminal justice system. Troubleshooting the criminal justice system is conceived here as a necessary part of a diagnostic enterprise of critical sociological interrogation to identify the nature, causes and extent of the problematic termed miscarriages of justice and the capabilities of the existing mechanisms for dealing with them. Conceptually, it is part of the overall maintenance of the criminal justice system that seeks to help to better understand the failings, or what I term as the 'black spots' of the criminal justice system that can either cause miscarriages of justice or prevent them from being overturned. It is a necessary precursor to fixing the flaws of the criminal justice system that are revealed in analysis of miscarriage-of-justice cases.

Indeed, like any social system, the criminal justice system has many known black spots that render it vulnerable to accidental mistakes or even intentional transgressions. For instance, PACE was introduced to provide safeguards for suspects of crime and to prevent wrongful convictions from occurring by requiring, for instance, that interviews are tape-recorded. Yet, we know that miscarriages of justice are still possible when suspects are 'verballed' 'off the record' and by other forms of negotiation and coercion on the way to the police station and when they are in the holding cell prior to the formal tape-recorded interview (see for instance, Eades, 2010: 237). Such forms of critical knowledge are useful as they can assist in devising strategies and reforms that can guard against possible miscarriages of justice from being caused by such black spots. In response to the problem of off-the-record verballing, to stay with the same example, a possible solution could be that police officers are no longer permitted to enter into conversations with suspects unless they are tape- or video-recorded, which could easily be enabled with portable recording devices. This would not only act to protect police suspects from miscarriages of justice, but would also protect the police from possible false allegations of malpractice and misconduct, thereby contributing to promoting public confidence in the criminal justice system and the rule of law.

More specifically, this book is a sociological exploration of the criminal justice system through the lens of how it deals with claims of innocence by alleged victims of miscarriages of justice. It considers:

- the different perspectives and definitions of 'miscarriages of justice';
- the causes of wrongful convictions in terms of whether they were caused intentionally or unintentionally;
- the limits of how the criminal justice system deals with claims of innocence by alleged victims of wrongful convictions, with a focus on the Parole Board, the Court of Appeal (Criminal Division) (CACD) and the Criminal Cases Review Commission (CCRC);

- the likely scale of the problem and the harm suffered by primary and secondary victims; and
- the limits of state relief in the form of statutory compensation available to victims of miscarriages of justice who overturn their convictions on appeal.

This diagnostic endeavour of the black spots of the criminal justice system is a necessary precursor to devising strategies on how to respond to the causes of wrongful convictions and the barriers that currently exist in terms of overturning alleged wrongful convictions.

In troubleshooting the criminal justice system, however, this book does not indulge in speculations about miscarriages of justice or unsupported critiques of the limits of the criminal justice system in dealing with them. On the contrary, the analyses presented here are all drawn from already achieved successful appeal cases, which represent an official, systemic acknowledgement that the criminal conviction that was overturned by the appeals system was erroneous or wrongful in some way (see also Naughton, 2007: ch. 2). As such, this book barely touches on the subject of alleged miscarriages of justice. That said, the miscarriages of justice that can be/are caused by social actors working both inside and outside of the criminal justice system, as well as by the structures and procedures of the criminal justice system itself, will be an ever-present spectre in the chapters that follow. This is especially the case in those chapters covering the different approaches to defining miscarriages of justice, understanding how they are caused and the limitations of the official mechanisms that exist for alleged victims to overturn them.

Structure

The book is structured into four parts: Part I deals with the nature and causes of 'miscarriages of justice' and 'abortions of justice', with the latter being a new concept for this book to distinguish between intentional wrongful convictions from those that were unintentional; Part II with the limits of the criminal justice system in dealing with claims of innocence by alleged victims of wrongful convictions; Part III looks at the harmful consequences of miscarriages of justice and the limits of the redress in the form of state compensation provisions for victims of miscarriages of justice; and Part IV provides a conclusion to the book that reflects on the critical diagnoses in the preceding chapters to suggest reforms to improve the existing black spots that have been identified.

In more specific terms, the next chapter shows that the term 'miscarriages of justice' is problematic as a catch-all term for the diverse phenomena that the phrase is employed to include. Structured into two parts it, first, explores three identifiable perspectives in miscarriages of justice studies: (1) a lay perspective that sees miscarriages of justice as relating to either factually innocent victims of wrongful convictions or factually guilty offenders who escape justice; (2) a criminal-justice-system perspective that sees miscarriages of justice in an altogether different way, relating simply to breaches of the prevailing rules and procedures of the existing criminal justice system; and (3) a due process perspective that sees any breach of due process or enacted human rights as examples of miscarriages of justice. It then distinguishes between 'miscarriages of justice' and 'abortions of justice' in terms of whether there is evidence that the wrongful convictions was intentional or not intentional in the successful appeal. It considers how these two distinct phenomena relate (or do not relate) to the lay perspective and wrongful conviction of the factually innocent, emphasising the different normative assumptions underpinning each of the different identifiable categories.

From this starting point, Chapters 3 and 4 look deeper into the causes of abortions of justice and miscarriages of justice, respectively. These chapters are each structured into two broad parts in terms of how the causation of abortions of justice and miscarriages of justice relate either to agents that are internal or external to the criminal justice process and to the forms of evidence that are admissible in criminal trials. More specifically, in terms of abortions of justice, Chapter 3 shows how police officers and Crown prosecutors intentionally breach their governing statutes and regulatory codes and how witnesses make false allegations to secure convictions. As for miscarriages of justice, Chapter 4 shows how the legislative framework of the criminal justice process is stacked against suspects and defendants, meaning that factually innocent individuals are vulnerable to conviction without intent by police officers, prosecutors who work within their guidelines and by witnesses who give inherently unreliable evidence in good faith that the courts accept as admissible.

Chapter 5 looks at the vital role of the Parole Board in the wrongful conviction problematic as it, generally, makes the decisions about whether prisoners maintaining innocence serving convictions for serious criminal offences can be progressed through the prison system and be possibly released safely back into society. It highlights the 'parole deal', a form of coercion akin to a plea bargain which means

that prisoners who maintain innocence and refuse to complete specified accredited offending behaviour programmes that are listed on
their sentence plans may never be recommended to be released by the
Parole Board. It presents the findings of survey research on the key
obstacles to progression and release that confront prisoners maintaining innocence who require a recommendation from the Parole Board.
It considers the justifications that the Parole Board put forward to support its continuation with its current method of risk assessment based
on cognitive psychology and the perspective that if prisoners are
taught to think differently then they will reduce their risk of reoffending. Finally, the chapter considers a possible way forward that moves
beyond a mere psychologically oriented perspective on why prisoners
maintain innocence with the application of a socio-legal perspective.
More specifically, it engages with claims of innocence by prisoners
maintaining innocence to reveal a range of different reasons for why
prisoners say they are innocent when they are not, and which cannot
be attributed to psychological denial. It also establishes that some prisoners maintaining innocence may, in fact, be innocent, a possibility
that the Parole Board has not acknowledged or made accommodation
for in its risk assessments and decisions.

Chapter 6 traces the origins of the criminal appeals system. Focusing
on the CACD and appeals against serious criminal offences given in the
Crown Court, it details the various statutes that have governed its operations since it was established in the early years of the twentieth century. It shows that the current CACD criteria for quashing convictions on
the basis that they are 'unsafe' means that factually guilty appellants
can be successful on appeal while factually innocent victims of wrongful conviction may not have admissible grounds of appeal; they may be
procedurally barred. This stems from a concern that trials are 'fair' and
with breaches of due process and points of law and not with whether
appellants are factually innocent or guilty. A particular conflict with a
lay perspective on how the criminal appeals system should operate is if
the evidence that alleged factually innocent appellants want to present
to the CACD was or could have been available at the time of the original trial such evidence may not be accepted as admissible. This is far
removed from the concern for potentially factually innocent victims of
wrongful convictions that lay at the heart of the introduction of the criminal appeal system just over a century ago. Despite this, there is a discernible due process perspective in the literature that will be evaluated that
appears to have lost sight of the original intention that the appeals system
should provide relief to factually innocent victims of wrongful conviction.

Chapter 7 looks at the CCRC, the last resort for alleged factually innocent victims of wrongful conviction who fail to have their convictions overturned in the normal appeals system. It considers the ability of the CCRC to assist applicants who claim that they are factually innocent of Crown Court convictions for serious criminal offences in two broad parts. First, it compares how the CCRC differs from what was recommended by the RCCJ, that is, a focus on whether there is a 'real possibility' that the CACD will see the conviction as legally unsafe rather than the question of whether applicants are factual innocent or guilty. It shows that the CCRC's 'real possibility test' means that the factually innocent may not have their convictions referred to the CACD while the convictions of the factually guilty will be referred by the CCRC (and overturned by the CACD) if they are believed to fulfil the test. Second, the type of cases that the CCRC reviews are considered in the context of its claimed 'success' rate. This reveals the wide range of matters that the CCRC deals with which the previous system for dealing with alleged wrongful conviction post-appeal did not. It shows that the CCRC's contribution to overturning Crown Court convictions is actually less than its predecessor, despite having a greater budget and staff cohort. Finally, the chapter provides a critical analysis of four dominant lines of defence that are routinely deployed in attempts to counter critiques of the CCRC's structural limitations in assisting the factually innocent.

Chapter 8 explores the harm caused by wrongful convictions to direct and secondary victims through case studies of successful appellants in the various appeal courts. As such, the analyses in this chapter are not intended to be definitive, nor is it claimed that all direct and secondary victims will experience the impacts of successful appeals in the same or even similar ways. Rather, the aim is to develop a holistic victimology of successful appeals that takes into account the harms that can befall all successful appellants in whichever appeal court the conviction is overturned and whether it is within or outside of the normal appeals process. Finally, an alternative perspective is critically analysed to show that the criminal justice system and its advocates operate within a restrictive analytical framework that is narrowly focused only on successful appeals that are overturned following a referral by the CCRC. This means that the harmful impacts that can occur to the overwhelming number of successful appellants who overturn their convictions within the normal appeals system and to any associated secondary victims are totally excluded from their gaze and their general concerns.

Following on from this, Chapter 9 evaluates the statutory compensation scheme for victims of miscarriages of justice in England and Wales under s.133 of the Criminal Justice Act 1988. In three parts it, first, considers the now terminated ex-gratia scheme to show the important part that it played in providing financial redress to factually innocent successful appellants who overturned their convictions through the normal appeals process and for the harm caused to victims of police misconduct and other public officials more generally. Second, it shows that due to the narrow definition of what constitutes a miscarriage of justice under the statutory compensation scheme most successful appellants who have their convictions quashed in an appeal court will not be eligible for compensation. Finally, it assesses the caps that now apply and the deductions routinely taken from the awards to eligible applicants. This reveals that those who do receive compensation from the statutory scheme may not be adequately compensated for the harms and losses that they suffer.

The book concludes with a critical reflection of the black spots that were identified in the preceding chapters and with ideas for how they may be eliminated. Overall, it is concluded that there needs to be a more sincere commitment from the criminal justice system and agents who work for it to protect the innocent from wrongful convictions and to assist the innocent to overturn their convictions when they occur.

PART I

The Nature and Causes of
Miscarriages of Justice and
Abortions of Justice

2

Perspectives and Definitions

Introduction

A crucial issue to be addressed at the outset of any sociological enquiry is the matter of defining the problematic under consideration. As this relates to the term miscarriage of justice, it is a particularly nebulous concept. It is used to cover a range of differing situations and scenarios that are often lumped together under the same euphemism. This clouds the very different meanings that miscarriages of justice have in social and legal reality and how they are understood and articulated in the different and competing discourses that exist. In particular, there is much confusion about what precisely constitutes a miscarriage of justice, how the term miscarriage of justice relates to intentional and or unintentional acts by those that cause them, and how notions of miscarriages of justice relate (or just as importantly, do not relate) to the wrongful conviction of the factually innocent. As will be shown, a conceptual muddle exists in the area of miscarriages of justice studies stemming from a conflation between lay discourses based on lay aspirations on what the criminal justice system should (at least attempt to) deliver and what it actually delivers through its statutes and its operations. This needs emphasising before the book gets under way, proper: 'miscarriages of justice' are problematic, not just in terms of the harm to victims and the loss of faith in the system that they can engender but, equally, in terms of the need to distinguish clearly just what is meant when articulations about miscarriages of justice are made.

For instance, even if the term miscarriage of justice is restricted to quashed criminal convictions as in this book, and not just used as a general metaphor for any kind of apparent unfairness and/or subjective expression of injustice, it is variously used as synonymous with at least the following four scenarios:

1. the wrongful conviction of the factually innocent;
2. the wrongful acquittal of the factually guilty;
3. convictions quashed by the appeals system because they are deemed to be unsafe; and/or
4. convictions thought to have been obtained in breach of due process or human rights, regardless of whether the convicted are innocent or guilty.

This has significant implications for the sociological study of what are commonly called 'miscarriages of justice', as the way in which they are defined determines, crucially, how they are understood; the conceptualisation of the harm that they can cause and, importantly, what can be done politically with such data in terms of how it can be acted upon (Naughton, 2007: 162; Hillyard and Tombs, 2004: 13; Pearce and Tombs, 1992).

With this in mind, this chapter, structured into two broad parts, provides the conceptual lenses through which the remainder of the book will be framed. First, it begins the exploration of miscarriages of justice by distinguishing between a lay perspective deriving from public and political utterances on what would constitute a miscarriage of justice, how the criminal justice system sees as a miscarriage of justice and a further competing discernible due process perspective. Then, the chapter distinguishes between three different phenomena which are often conflated under the general rubric of 'miscarriages of justice': 'miscarriages of justice', 'abortions of justice' and 'the wrongful conviction of the innocent', highlighting the different normative assumptions underpinning each of the different identifiable categories.

Competing perspectives

A lay perspective

A lay perspective on what constitutes a miscarriage of justice can be discerned from newspaper reports, television programmes, films and music, autobiographical/biographical accounts by victims, radio broadcasts, statements by politicians, from campaigning and victim support organisations, and so on. From these sources, a miscarriage of justice is straightforward, chiefly concerned with the truthful and moral correctness of the outcomes in the criminal justice process, relating either to the wrongful conviction of the factually innocent or the wrongful acquittal of the factually guilty.

Charles Clarke (cited in Travis, 2006) the then Home Secretary, succinctly summed up a lay perspective on miscarriages of justice in the following terms:

> What individuals want to see is a legal system which correctly finds guilty those who are guilty and acquits those who are innocent, with respect to what they did or didn't do rather than whether or not the legal process was or was not correctly followed.

This view of how the criminal justice system should operate prioritises the question of factual guilt or innocence over procedural justice. It also expresses the lay perspective on what would constitute a miscarriage of justice: it is either the wrongful conviction of the factually innocent or the acquittal of the factually guilty (see Naughton, 2007: 14–26; 2009c: 17–22; Kyle, 2004: 664). The governmental White Paper *Justice for All* (Home Office, 2002: 13), which led to the introduction of a plethora of reforms to the criminal justice system under the Criminal Justice Act 2003 (discussed below), emphasised lay aspirations for the criminal justice system in the following terms:

> We have an absolute determination to create a system that meets the needs of society and wins the trust of citizens, by convicting the guilty … [and] … acquitting the innocent.

Lay concern with factual innocence and guilt has underpinned public portrayals of miscarriages of justice and attempts to rectify them throughout history. Television programmes such as BBC's *Rough Justice* or Channel 4's *Trial and Error*, were concerned with unearthing evidence to prove (or disprove) the claims of factual innocence of alleged victims of miscarriages of justice. Similarly, human rights and civil liberties organisations such as JUSTICE and Liberty were concerned with assisting individuals who were thought to be factually innocent of the crimes that they were convicted of. Both of these however ceased giving assistance to alleged victims of wrongful conviction when the Criminal Cases Review Commission (CCRC) was established on the mistaken belief that their services were no longer necessary. More recently, the establishment of the Innocence Network UK (INUK) and its network of member innocence projects to investigate claims of factual innocence by alleged victims of miscarriages of justice in the UK has revived the concern that the criminal justice system, despite the establishment of the CCRC, cannot guarantee that factually innocent victims of wrongful conviction will be able to overturn their conviction (see Naughton, 2006a, 2009b, 2009c).

On the other hand, the acquittal of people thought to be factually guilty of crimes has equally sparked public outrage and a widespread sense that a gross miscarriage of justice has occurred (see for instance, discussion of the case of Stephen Lawrence as an example of this kind of miscarriage of justice in Savage *et al.* 2007: 84–85; also Savage, 2007: 201; Goodhart, 2012). Indeed, political utterances on miscarriages of justice in recent times are frequently centred on the failure of the criminal justice system to convict the factually guilty, allowing them to escape punishment. For Tony Blair (2002), when he was the Prime Minister, such instances represent possibly the greatest miscarriages of justice of all:

> It's a miscarriage of justice when the police see their hard work and bravery thrown away by courts who let a mugger out on bail for the seventh or eighth time to offend again; or when courts don't have the secure places to put people. And it's perhaps the biggest miscarriage of justice in today's system when the guilty walk away unpunished.

Lay discourses on miscarriages of justice, whether they relate to the wrongful conviction of the factually innocent or the wrongful acquittal of the factually guilty, are important as they are often the driving force behind reforms to the criminal justice system. As outlined in Chapter 1, cases thought by the public to be genuine instances of innocent people being wrongly convicted and unjustly punished have led to some of the most significant reforms of the criminal justice system to prevent them from occurring or to provide the means of challenging them if and when they occur. These include the case of Adolf Beck which was instrumental in the establishment of the Court of Criminal Appeal in 1907 (discussed further in Chapter 6); the case of Timothy Evans, believed to have been wrongly executed for the murder of his daughter, which is linked to the abolition of capital punishment in the UK; and the 'Irish' cases of the Guildford Four, the Maguire Seven, the Birmingham Six, as well as other wrongful convictions associated with IRA bombing campaigns, which caused a widespread public crisis of confidence in the entire criminal justice system amid evidence of widespread police misconduct that led to a royal commission and the setting up of the CCRC (for further discussion, see Naughton, 2007: ch. 4; Chapter 7 in this book).

Conversely, cases where factually guilty individuals are believed to have evaded justice have also prompted radical reforms aimed at tightening the criminal justice system to ensure the conviction of the guilty. For instance, the aftermath of the *Stephen Lawrence* affair not only led to changes in police practices aimed at weeding out institutional racism, perhaps just as crucially it led to reforms to the 800-year-old double jeopardy rule (Law Commission, 2001: 1) that were introduced under the Criminal Justice Act 2003, which now allows acquitted individuals to be tried again for certain serious offences if there is new evidence of guilt (see Part 9, Criminal Justice Act 2003). The Criminal Justice Act 2003 also introduced a series of legislative reforms aimed at making convictions of the factually guilty easier to obtain, such as allowing 'hearsay' evidence and widening the channels in which 'bad character' evidence is admissible in criminal proceedings. Similarly, the real concern that too few rapists are brought to justice has led to a shift in the burden of proof under the Sexual Offences Act 2003, so that those accused are now required to show that they had a reasonable belief that consent was obtained, which is something that cannot so easily be proven. More recently, the legitimate concern with gang and organised crime ushered in the Criminal Evidence (Witness Anonymity) Act 2008 allowing evidence to be given anonymously, undermining the ability of defendants to cross-examine their accusers effectively (see Naughton, 2012).

It seems morally correct to see miscarriages of justice in these lay terms. Both the factually innocent who have been wrongly convicted and victims of crime who watch their perpetrators getting away scot free are harmed in a multitude of ways by a criminal justice system that is supposed to protect them (Naughton, 2007: ch. 8). Legislative reforms to protect the factually innocent and convict the factually guilty are therefore necessary to restore public faith in the criminal justice system and to minimise the occurrences of such injustices in the future.

However, the lay morality that underpins public and political views on miscarriages of justice does not correspond with how the criminal justice system sees a miscarriage of justice. Rather, the criminal justice system operates on an altogether different plane, or in a different paradigm or sphere, that possesses a rationale and internal self logic on what constitutes a miscarriage of justice that differs sharply from lay understandings (for an analysis from the perspective of autopoietic theory, see Nobles and Schiff, 2000).

A criminal justice system perspective

Miscarriage of justice, as it relates to the criminal justice system, is detached from the lay notion of factual innocence and guilt. Contrary to the desire at the heart of lay discourse to know the truth of whether alleged victims of miscarriages of justice are, in fact, innocent or guilty, criminal trials are better understood as a more pragmatic enterprise. They seek to determine, instead, whether there is a sufficiency of admissible evidence to find defendants guilty or not guilty of the specific criminal offences that they are charged with. As Doreen McBarnet (1981a: 12–13) critically observed:

> What is involved is not a philosophical or scientific concept of proof but a much less demanding *legal* concept. The justification lies not in any idealism that 'the truth the whole truth and nothing but the truth' results, but in pragmatics. The courts are there not to indulge in the impossible absolutes of philosophy or science but to reach decisions – quickly. So the courts have drawn a line at what will do as proof. Prosecutors do not have to prove everything a jury might want to know, they only have to produce a *sufficiency* of evidence. The law defines how much evidence constitutes 'sufficient' to prove a case and it is the judge's role to decide and to persuade the jury that the required legal standard has been met. (original emphasis)

The following quotation from Lord Simon in the House of Lords' ruling in DPP v Shannon (p. 736) is a good example of case law to emphasise the divide between lay discourses and how the criminal justice system actually operates in social reality:

> The law in action is not concerned with absolute truth, but with proof before a fallible human tribunal to a requisite standard of probability in accordance with formal rules of evidence.

The problem with such a pragmatic approach to obtaining criminal convictions in a criminal justice system that is officially acknowledged to be fallible is that it risks convicting the factually innocent. Indeed, it is important here to make a distinction between the *sufficiency* and *reliability* of evidence. As mentioned above, legitimate lay fears that factually guilty criminals are not being convicted have resulted in legislative changes that render admissible inherently unreliable and/or highly circumstantial forms of evidence, such as bad character, hearsay, anonymous witness testimony, and so on. Magistrates and juries can, therefore, decide that there is a legal sufficiency of evidence to infer guilt and give guilty verdicts despite the unreliability of such evidence and the possibility of convicting the factually innocent.

This problem is well illustrated in the area of wrongful convictions for historical sexual or physical abuse. Those accused of such offences, which may be claimed to have occurred many years or even decades before the allegations are made, have been shown to have been convicted on nothing more than the testimonies of the accusers. For instance, in 2004 George Anderson and Margaret Hewitt were convicted of abusing children at a Barnardo's home some 20 years earlier on nothing more than the testimonies of their accusers (see BBC News, 2005c). Anderson was given an 18-year prison sentence for offences including rape, sexual assault and gross indecency, which he had allegedly committed against five children between 1979 and 1981. Hewitt was sentenced to 11 years' imprisonment after she was convicted of a total of 53 charges, including physical and sexual assault and gross indecency, which she was said to have committed against eight children between 1977 and 1981. However, their convictions were quashed in June 2005 after one of the complainants admitted that he had lied (see Palmer 2006).

Despite such examples, and as will be the focus of the analysis in Chapter 6, the question of factual innocence or guilt does not feature in criminal appeal legislation. Appeals in the Crown Court against convictions given in magistrates' courts are governed by the terms of s.79 of the Supreme Court Act 1981, which permits a full rehearing of the case in the Crown Court. In line with criminal trials, rehearings in the Crown Court do not seek to determine if appellants are factually innocent or guilty but whether they are guilty or not guilty of the offence(s) that they are accused of on the basis of the evidence presented at court. In more serious cases, appeals to the Court of Appeal (Criminal Division) (CACD) do not attempt to determine factual innocence or guilt either. Rather, s. 2 of the Criminal Appeal Act 1995 instructs that it (1) shall allow an appeal against conviction if it thinks that the conviction is unsafe; and (2) shall dismiss such an appeal in any other case (the criminal appeal system is discussed in detail in Chapter 6).

The following extract from the successful appeal judgment that quashed the convictions of the four men wrongly convicted for the murder of 13-year-old Carl Bridgewater (Patrick Molloy, Jim Robinson, Michael Hickey and Vincent Hickey – the Bridgewater Four), illustrates how the criminal appeals system is not concerned with whether appellants are factually innocent or guilty:

> This Court is not concerned with the guilt or innocence of the appellants, but only with the safety of their convictions. This may, at first sight, appear an unsatisfactory state of affairs, until it is remembered that the integrity of the criminal process is the most important consideration for courts which have to hear appeals against conviction. Both the innocent and the guilty are entitled to fair trials. If the trial process is not fair, if it is distorted by deceit or by material breaches of the rules of evidence or procedure, then the liberties of all are threatened. (R v Hickey and Others, part 4)

Although the Bridgewater Four are widely believed to be factually innocent of the murder of Carl Bridgewater (see for instance, Foot, 1986, 1997), it is significant to note that such successful appeals against criminal convictions are not acknowledgments of factual innocence and both the factually innocent and the factually guilty who satisfy the required criteria of the appeal courts can have their convictions overturned.

For instance, Michael Weir was convicted in 1998 for the murder of 79-year-old Leonard Harris when a DNA profile extracted from the victim's gloves matched Weir's profile on the National DNA Database (NDNAD). Weir's conviction was overturned a year later, however, when it was ruled that the DNA evidence, the only evidence linking him to the murder of Mr Harris, was inadmissible. It transpired that Weir's DNA profile was loaded onto the NDNAD as a result of an earlier charge for a drug offence which was later dropped, meaning that his profile should have been removed from the NDNAD under the terms of PACE (National DNA Database, 2004: 5). It is interesting to note that the House of Lords subsequently ruled that such evidence obtained in breach of PACE is not necessarily inadmissible and that it should be left to the discretion of the trial judge as to whether or not to admit evidence in these circumstances. Despite this, Weir's conviction was not reinstated as the Crown Prosecution Service (CPS) missed the deadline to take the case to appeal by a day (see Steele, 2000).

Despite such cases, and returning to the Bridgewater Four appeal judgment, Roch LJ further reasoned in quashing the convictions that those successful appellants who have their convictions overturned because they are unsafe should have the presumption of innocence restored to them:

The unhappy conclusion that we have reached is that the criminal justice process did not operate fairly in this case as it should have done ... We shall consequently allow these appeals and quash the convictions ... in respect of all four appellants ... Consequently the presumption of innocence in respect of the four appellants will be re-established. (R v Hickey and Others, part 4)

This demonstrates a need to distinguish between lay notions of *factual innocence* and the criminal justice system's notion of *legal innocence*, concepts which are not synonymous. Moreover, the judgment in the Bridgewater Four case shows that the lay concern with factually guilty offenders escaping justice for their crimes cannot be conceptualised as a miscarriage of justice from the criminal justice system's perspective. The presumption of innocence at the heart of the criminal justice process mandates that those accused of committing criminal offences are to be treated as legally innocent if they are acquitted in criminal trials, because there is insufficient evidence to show that they are legally guilty, or if they have their convictions overturned on appeal because their convictions are deemed to be unsafe (for a critical analysis, see Naughton, 2011a). Put simply, criminal justice is governed by strict adherence to procedural propriety and sufficiency of evidence, which is distinct from social justice and moral concerns about factual innocence and guilt.

A due process perspective

Another identifiable approach to defining miscarriages of justice is one that can be termed the due process perspective. Exemplified in the work of Clive Walker (1999), this perspective focuses the critical lens on the issue of 'justice' in attempts to illuminate what might count as 'miscarriages of justice'. For Walker (1999: 31):

A 'miscarriage' means literally a failure to reach an intended destination or goal. A miscarriage of justice is therefore, *mutatis mutandis*, a failure to attain the desired end result of 'justice'. The meanings of justice and the ways in which it may be denied need to be dissected further, since the desired ends will inherently affect what counts as a miscarriage.

From this starting point, Walker (1999) constructed a perspective from existing due process safeguards and enacted human rights legislation to forward a normative framework that contained a variety of different scenarios in which miscarriages of justice can be said to occur (hereafter the due process perspective). From such a due process perspective, Walker (1999: 33–37) asserted that there are at least seven different types of miscarriage of justice along the following lines:

> [W]henever suspects or defendants or convicts are treated by the state in breach of their rights, whether because of, first, deficient processes or, second, the laws which are applied to them or, third, because there is no factual justification for the applied treatment or punishment; fourth, whenever suspects or defendants or convicts are treated adversely by the state to a disproportionate extent in comparison with the need to protect the rights of others; fifth, whenever the rights of others are not effectively or proportionately protected or vindicated by state action against wrongdoers or, sixth, by state law itself ... it may be possible to derive from their infliction a seventh, indirect miscarriage which affects the community as a whole.

As far-reaching as this analysis appears to be of the different ways in which justice may be miscarried, there are a number of acute problems with such an approach from a sociological perspective. First, a problem with defining miscarriages of justice in terms of a definition of 'justice' sets subjective criteria for when miscarriages of justice can be said to have occurred. Different perspectives on what 'justice' is would each conceptualise 'justice' and, therefore, 'miscarriages of justice' very differently (for discussion, see, for instance, Greer, 1994).

Second, seeing miscarriages of justice as infractions of due process or enacted human rights produces a conceptual confusion that includes very different phenomena under the same rubric. Alternatively, a sociological perspective would want to distinguish, both in descriptive terms and in analyses, between the different things that Walker (1999) amalgamates. The matters highlighted, such as deficient processes, the laws which are applied to them, the lack of factual justification for the applied treatment or punishment of suspect, defendants or prisoners and the various issues pertaining to the proportionate or disproportionate treatment of citizens, whether they are factually guilty or innocent, puts forward a catch-all notion of miscarriages of justice. This obscures a more nuanced analysis of the diverse problematics identified and, just as crucially, what can be done in response.

Third, seeing miscarriages of justice as breaches of due process and human rights subordinates the concept to the vagaries of the criminal justice process and to the state's determinations on those human rights that it wants to afford its citizens. It means that when the procedures of the criminal justice system are changed or reformed, such as the rules of disclosure of evidence between prosecution and defence (for example, under the Criminal Procedure and Investigations Act 1996) or changes to the procedures for interviewing suspects in police stations (for instance, under PACE), that definitions of miscarriages of justice will also have to shift. Similarly, if the state derogates from aspects of enacted human rights or reforms the procedures for dealing with terrorist suspects so that they can be detained for longer periods without charge, for instance, then notions of miscarriages of justice would, again, have to change as well. In short, the due process perspective puts the state in the driving seat on determining what constitutes due process in the first place and when it can be said to have been breached.

Finally, a due process approach also conflicts with the lay and criminal justice system perspectives outlined above. As Walker (1993: 4) argued:

> Some observers attempt to distinguish between those who are really 'innocent' and those who are acquitted on a 'technicality'. However, a conviction arising from deceit or illegalities is corrosive of the state's claim to legitimacy on the basis of due process and respect for rights ... Accordingly, *even a person who has in fact and with intent committed a crime could be said to have suffered a miscarriage if convicted on evidence which is legally inadmissible.* (original emphasis)

Contrary to this, John Rawls (1971: 75), for instance, in the landmark *A Theory of Justice*, a central starting point for discussions on law and social justice, is unequivocal in his analysis on what would constitute a miscarriage of justice which fits perfectly with a lay perspective:

> Even though the law is carefully followed, and the proceedings fairly and properly conducted, it may reach the wrong outcome. An innocent man may be found guilty, a guilty man may be set free. In such cases we speak of a miscarriage of justice.

From a lay perspective, then, miscarriages of justice do not require breaches of due process or enacted human rights. On the contrary, the conviction of the factually innocent or the acquittal of the factually guilty on breaches of due process will always be considered to be miscarriages of justice from a lay perspective. As this relates to the criminal justice system perspective, a miscarriage of justice is about whether convictions are unsafe and even acknowledged breaches of due process or such things as the European Convention on Human Rights (ECHR) and/or the Human Rights Act (1998) does not automatically render criminal convictions unsafe in law (see Naughton with Tan, 2010: 33–35). In this light, defining miscarriages of justice in terms of how the concept justice is conceived renders miscarriages of justice as perspectival, or entirely in the subjective eye of the beholder. If a different perspective of justice were adopted, then a different notion of a miscarriage of justice would be derived.

Overall, then, the due process perspective can be conceived as working against lay/social justice and to be contra common sense. First, it implies that the wrongful conviction of the factually innocent will not occur if due processes are complied with (see for instance, Spencer, 1989: 203; 2006: 683). This fails to account for wrongful convictions that cannot be attributed to breaches of due process, as evidenced, for instance, by DNA exonerations that prove factual innocence in cases where due process was adhered to (see Naughton and Tan, 2011; also discussed further below in the case of Sean Hodgson).

Second, it leads to the perverse conclusion that no miscarriage of justice has occurred even if a factually innocent person is convicted so long as due process was adhered to. This neglects the numerous examples of wrongful convictions caused by mistaken evidence by forensic science expert witnesses or mistaken eyewitness identification given in good faith which do not act against due process or the right to a fair trial (discussed in Chapter 4).

Third, instead of a more discriminating understanding of the causes of miscarriages of justice, the due process perspective sees a single monolithic cause, breaches of due process and enacted human rights, albeit with many different instances and types of alleged injustice conceptualised under this heading. This fails to account for the procedures of the criminal justice system that can cause miscarriages of justice or obstruct them from being overturned. It also neglects critical scrutiny of the structures of the criminal justice system that act to protect some individuals and groups from conviction while rendering other individuals and groups vulnerable to conviction (for a detailed discussion, see Naughton, 2007: ch. 3; Greer, 1994).

Finally, the due process perspective fails to note that until the criminal justice system officially acknowledges that alleged breaches of due process or human rights have occurred and determined that the breach is sufficiently serious to render a conviction to be deemed to be unsafe, then a miscarriage of justice cannot be said to have occurred from a criminal justice system perspective. This renders the study of miscarriages of justice, as opposed to *alleged* miscarriages of justice, an entirely legalistic endeavour, operating entirely in the realm of criminal convictions and successful appeals against criminal convictions as decided by the criminal appeals system (see Naughton, 2005b: 165).

The need to be semantic about 'miscarriages' of justice

Beyond the foregoing discussion on the incompatibility, or one might say incommensurability, between lay discourses on miscarriages of justice, the workings of the criminal justice system and a due process perspective, this section further dissects the term 'miscarriages' of justice as it relates to convictions overturned by the CACD. Adopting a more semantic approach, it further highlights the inadequacy of the term 'miscarriages' in covering cases of wrongful conviction caused by the intentional and deliberate acts of agents of the criminal justice system, a phenomenon termed here as 'abortions of justice', and how these two concepts relate (or do not relate) to the wrongful conviction of the innocent.

Miscarriages of justice versus abortions of justice

The term 'miscarriage' is not restricted to its relations to the workings of the criminal justice system. It is also commonly used in medical science as a euphemism to distinguish the spontaneous abortion of a pregnancy from an abortion of a pregnancy that derives from an intended or deliberate act. Miscarriages of pregnancy, then, denote unprompted, unplanned and unfortunate occurrences that cannot be avoided.

In the same way, it seems that a clear distinction also needs to be made between those unintended wrongful convictions and those that were caused by intentional acts, whether by actors internal or external to the criminal justice system. There is a marked difference between wrongful convictions that derive from mistaken eyewitness identification given in good faith as in the case of Adolf Beck (discussed above and in Chapter 2) and when police officers manufacture incriminating cases against suspects, such as extracting false confessions and obtaining fabricated witness statements such as in the case of the Cardiff Three (see R v Paris, Abdullahi and Miller; Sekar, 1997); or when prosecutors intentionally withhold evidence from the defence team that shows that a defendant may be factually innocent of the alleged offence, such as the cases of Judith Ward (see R v Ward; Ward, 1993) and John Kamara (see R v Kamara; Shorter, 2010); or when alleged victims of sexual abuse make false and malicious allegations, such as in the case of Anderson and Hewitt (cited above).

As such, the term miscarriage of justice is profoundly problematic as a universal signifier of the very different scenarios that emerge in analyses of successful appeals against criminal conviction, especially those that stem from intentional acts to subvert the criminal justice process; the procedures of the criminal justice system that exist to safeguard against wrongful convictions. In short, miscarriages of justice is not only problematic as a term to capture the different perspectives that utilise it, it is too mild a term to attach to all types of 'error' and/or forms of malpractice and misconduct that are shown in successful appeals. It presents an image of a phenomenon that is unintended and unavoidable and one in which no one is to blame.

However, notorious cases such as that of Keith Twitchell (see R v Twitchell) and Robert Brown (see R v Brown) were not unavoidable or inevitable accidents of the criminal justice system. On the contrary, they were the result of the intended actions of criminal justice system personnel who consciously chose to transgress and subvert the procedures of the criminal justice system that are expressly meant to protect against such occurrences and forms of behaviour. Twitchell was tortured into signing a confession for his alleged part in an armed raid on a local factory in 1980 in which a security guard was killed and £11,500 stolen. When he was arrested, eight or nine police officers handcuffed Twitchell's wrists to the back legs of the chair upon which he was sitting. Then, a plastic bag was placed over his head and pressed against his nose and mouth until he lost consciousness (Burrell and Bennetto, 1999). This suffocation procedure was repeated until he could no longer resist and signed the statement that the police put in front of him. For his confession, Twitchell served 13 years of his 20-year conviction, being released in 1993 (see R v Twichell). Brown was convicted for the murder of 51-year-old Annie Walsh found bludgeoned to death in her Manchester flat on 31 January 1977 (Hopkins, 2002). Evidence emerged during his appeal that Brown's confession was also obtained after he was seriously assaulted throughout his interviews with the police, which was described in the successful appeal judgment as part of the 'culture of corruption and conspiracy to pervert justice' within the Greater Manchester Police at the time (R v Brown).

It seems that a more appropriate descriptor for such successful appeals against criminal convictions that show that the criminal justice system was *intentionally* transgressed, as opposed to those that can be conceived to occur *unintentionally*, is the notion of an 'abortion of justice'. Abortions of justice, then, occur when actors either internal or external to the workings of the criminal justice process knowingly and intentionally cause wrongful convictions.

By contrast, miscarriages of justice are defined here as wrongful convictions that are due to unintended actions of actors internal or external to the criminal justice system that occur from time to time in any human system. Examples are cases caused by experts giving flawed evidence in good faith that cannot be attributed to any intentional wrongdoings, for instance the cases of Kevin Callan and Patrick Nichols. Callan served three years of a life sentence for the murder of his 4-year-old stepdaughter, Amanda Allman. His conviction was overturned when an alternative forensic report suggested that Amanda most likely died as a result of a fall from a playground slide (see Callan, 1997). Nichols spent 23 years in prison for the murder of an elderly family friend, 74-year-old Gladys Heath. New expert evidence, however, contested this view positing, instead, that she had possibly suffered a heart attack and accidentally fallen down a flight of stairs (see BBC News, 1998a).

The question of innocence

In defining successful appeals as either miscarriages of justice or abortions of justice, as determined by the concept of intent, a crucial question from a lay perspective concerns how they relate to factually innocent and factually guilty successful appellants. Although we can typically discern whether successful appellants are victims of a miscarriage or an abortion of justice from the reasons that led to the quashing of the conviction by the CACD, the terms of criminal trials and the appeals system alike makes it difficult if not impossible to know in most cases if they are, indeed, factually innocent or factually guilty.

As indicated above, neither criminal trials nor appeals seek to determine whether defendants or appellants are factually innocent or factually guilty. Trials determine whether defendants are guilty or not guilty and appeals decide if their convictions are unsafe, all of which is governed in terms of the prevailing rules of evidence, procedures of criminal trials and the criminal appeals criteria. The result is that evidence of factual innocence will not be available in most cases of successful appeal, save those rare cases that are overturned when DNA evidence establishes factual innocence, for instance.

Two such examples are the cases of the Cardiff Three and Sean Hodgson, in which factually innocent individuals confessed to crimes that they did not commit. The Cardiff Three, Stephen Miller, Tony Paris and Yusuf Abdullahi, were convicted when Miller confessed to the murder of his girlfriend, Lynette White, who had been stabbed at least 50 times (see Sekar, 1997). Two years later, the Cardiff Three had their convictions overturned when they were able to show that Miller's police interview was oppressive and contrary to guidelines under PACE (see R v Paris, Abdullahi and Miller). Perhaps not surprisingly, the Cardiff Three continued to face public doubts about their guilt for the murder until the case made British legal history as the first wrongful conviction case to be vindicated with the conviction of the real murderer, Jeffrey Gafoor, when DNA found at the crime scene matched his (see BBC News, 2003; Bennetto, 2003). It transpired that South Wales Police had coerced witnesses to give false testimonies against the Cardiff Three to improve the chances of conviction (see Sekar, 2011). Similarly, Sean Hodgson confessed to a Catholic priest that he raped and murdered Teresa de Simone and later repeated his confession to two police officers. Hodgson spent 27 years in prison until DNA completely exonerated him of the murder as his profile did not match that of the semen sample obtained from the victim (see R v Hodgson, paragraph 43).

However, a crucial distinction can be made between the Cardiff Three and Hodgson. As the Cardiff Three were intentionally wrongly convicted by South Wales Police they are an example of factually innocent victims who suffered an abortion of justice. Alternatively, no police officers or prosecutors can be reasonably blamed for the wrongful conviction of Hodgson, as he voluntarily confessed to the crime. Indeed, additional attempts were made at the time to verify Hodgson's confession by conducting blood group analysis on the semen found at the crime scene (this was before the advent of DNA profiling) which duly matched Hodgson. This was, thus, seen as confirmatory evidence of his guilt (see R v Hodgson, paragraph 10). In this sense, Hodgson can be characterised as a factually innocent victim of a miscarriage of justice.

At the other end of the spectrum to miscarriages of justice and abortions of justice where factual innocence is established are those rare successful appeals that are obtained by factually guilty offenders when a clear abortion of justice can be shown. An example is the case of Nicholas Mullen, who had a life sentence overturned in 1999 for terrorist offences on the grounds that the British police intentionally violated international law in securing his extradition from Zimbabwe so that he could stand trial, which amounted to a breach of process that invalidated his conviction.

An example of a factually guilty miscarriage of justice is the case of Weir cited above, as the breach of process was clearly unintentional as the investigating police officers would not have known that his DNA should have been removed from the NDNAD.

Finally, in between the two opposing ends of the factually innocent and the factually guilty are the vast majority of miscarriages of justice and abortions of justice in which the successful appellants' factual innocence or guilt may never be clearly established. This includes victims of abortions of justice such as Twitchell and Brown cited above who, literally, had confessions tortured out of them. It also includes those miscarriages of justice cases such as Callan and Nichols in which the expert evidence that led to their convictions was fundamentally discredited.

From a criminal justice system perspective legal innocence will be restored when the convictions are deemed to be unsafe by the CACD. Yet, the need to know whether successful appellants are factually innocent or whether they got away with it on an apparent breach of process or point of law at the core of the lay perspective will mean that such victims of miscarriages and abortions of justice are likely to continue to suffer ongoing whispering campaigns about their factual guilt and experience discrimination as long as their factual innocence is not confirmed.

Conclusion

This chapter has provided a framework for distinguishing the dominant perspectives and the different categories of wrongful conviction which will be utilised throughout the various discussions in the remainder of the book.

The analysis of the key perspectives on miscarriages of justice emphasises that when miscarriages of justice are discussed the crucial question that must be asked at the outset is what perspective on miscarriages of justice is being employed: are they being discussed in terms of factual guilt or innocence, safety of conviction or breaches of due process? This is not to suggest that the different perspectives do not overlap. The factually innocent, for instance, might claim that they have been wrongly convicted due to a grave breach of due process, which might, in turn, lead to their convictions being seen as unsafe by the CACD. Yet, unless we know what is being referred to in articulations of miscarriages of justice sociological understanding is obscured and it is difficult to target policy responses to deal with the problem.

Table 1   Miscarriage of justice, abortions of justice and factual innocence and guilt

	Miscarriages of justice	Abortions of justice
Factually guilty	e.g. Weir	e.g. Mullen
Factual innocence established	e.g. Hodgson	e.g. Cardiff Three
Factual innocence not established	e.g. Callan, Nichols	e.g. Twitchell, Brown

In terms of definitions, the chapter has distinguished between successful appeals that are miscarriages of justice which derive from the *unintentional* acts that cause wrongful convictions, and abortions of justice which are caused by the *intentional* subversion of the procedures of the criminal justice process that exist to safeguard against wrongful convictions and which give legitimacy to the criminal justice system. The six different ways in which miscarriages of justice and abortions of justice relate to the factual innocence or guilt of successful appellants are depicted in Table 1.

It is important to note that this division between miscarriages of justice and abortions of justice as they relate to the issue of factual innocence, whether established or not, bears no relation to the severity or extent to which victims are harmed by their wrongful conviction. That is, whether wrongful convictions are caused intentionally or unintentionally they each generate harmful consequences on individuals, families and society as a whole (which will be further explored in Chapter 8).

However, the value of the different categories is that they provide a clearer understanding of the different sociological problematics that exist and a more lucid basis upon which research can be framed and strategies can be devised to tackle them. First, it has to be accepted that some miscarriages of justice are inevitable and can never be fully delimited. Human beings, whether internal or external to the workings of the criminal justice system, will always be susceptible to making mistakes which will result in miscarriages of justice that convict the factually innocent.

However, retrospective lessons can be learned from reflecting on the unintentional mistakes that cause miscarriages of justice. This might include better training for police officers on PACE guidelines so that they do not allow the factually guilty to have their convictions overturned through technical loopholes (for example, Weir). It might also include the need for courts to be more cautious about the fallibility of forms of evidence that we learn about from miscarriages of justice cases, such as expert opinions (for example, Callan and Nichols) and eyewitness identification evidence (for example, Beck).

In terms of abortions of justice, we have to accept that there are also people, either internal or external to the criminal justice system, who will intentionally cause wrongful convictions for a variety of reasons. So called, 'noble cause corruption' when police officers fit up suspects that they believe to be guilty in the absence of other evidence is an established feature of deliberate police misconduct (discussed in the next chapter), as is prosecutorial non-disclosure in an adversarial criminal justice system where prosecutors put winning cases before a just outcome (discussed in the next chapter). Likewise, financial motives for making false and malicious allegations of sexual and physical abuse are well established in successful appeals (for example, Anderson and Hewitt). Lessons to be learned from abortions of justice, then, include the need for accountability in the form of criminal sanctions against those who intentionally cause wrongful convictions, whether they are committed by actors internal or external to the criminal justice system.

The overall conclusion that can be drawn is that miscarriages of justice and abortions of justice as evidenced by successful appeals illustrate that the best way to protect the factually innocent from wrongful convictions and the factually guilty from escaping justice is an ever vigilant eye on the methods used to build cases against suspects, on the tactics employed by prosecutors and, crucially, the reliability of the evidence that is claimed to indicate factual guilt for criminal offences.

3

The Key Causes of Abortions of Justice

Introduction

The last chapter observed how the presumption of innocence is officially restored to successful appellants who have their convictions overturned by the Court of Appeal (Criminal Division) (CACD). This applies even to those factually guilty offenders who overturn their convictions on points of law and/or breaches of due process. This reveals just how far the criminal justice system differs from lay discourses and moral concerns about whether those who have convictions quashed are factually innocent victims of wrongful convictions or factually guilty offenders who manage to escape their punishment. Yet, the practice to re-establish the presumption of legal innocence to successful appellants who may not be factually innocent can also be read as expressing a robust commitment by the criminal justice system to compliance with the due process procedures that make up the criminal justice process.

This practice, no doubt, stems from the right for those accused of crimes to be presumed innocent, a long-standing principle at the heart of the criminal justice system in England and Wales. It is enshrined in Article 11 of the Universal Declaration of Human Rights, Article 6 of the ECHR, and it is enacted domestically in the UK in accordance with the Human Rights Act (1998). As such, it is unsurprising that convictions that can be shown to have been obtained in breach of due process procedures or enacted human rights are ideal candidates to be overturned in the appeal courts, even when appellants such as Mullen and Weir discussed in the last chapter are believed to be factually guilty.

Against this background, this chapter analyses the causation of abortions of justice as evidenced by successful appeal cases in two parts.

First, it considers factors internal to the criminal justice process to show a widespread disregard of the presumption of innocence as a safeguard against wrongful convictions. This includes police officers who intentionally cause abortions of justice by manufacturing incriminating cases against suspects of crime and by prosecutors who flagrantly abuse their professional codes and do not disclose evidence that might undermine their own case. The second part looks at factors that are formally external to the criminal justice process that cause abortions of justice. It highlights the problem of witnesses who intentionally make false allegations of sexual abuse, witnesses who give false testimonies to assist the police case against an accused and even cases of forensic scientists who, allegedly, tailor their evidence to fit with the case against an accused.

Internal factors

Police

Official guidelines on the procedures that the police should employ when questioning suspects of alleged crimes have existed for just over a century since the introduction of the Judges' Rules in 1912. The origins of the Judges' Rules are widely believed to be located in a letter dated 26 October 1906 from Lord Alverstone, the then Lord Chief Justice, to the then Chief Constable of Birmingham. It replied to a request for advice on inconsistent judicial decisions in his police force area on the issue of whether suspects should or should not be cautioned before the police obtained their evidence (see Abrahams, 1964: 54). Linked directly with the presumption of innocence and the right of silence for those accused of crime, the Judges' Rules introduced the requirement that the police when making an arrest should inform suspects that that they need say nothing but that anything that they did say might be used in a court against them (Hostettler, 2009: 241).

The Judges' Rules initially comprised four rules that were formulated and approved by the judges of the King's Bench Division in 1912, to which five additional rules were added in 1918. In specific terms, they advised the police as follows:

- Rule 1 permitted police officers to question any person or persons, whether suspected or not, if it was thought that useful information could be obtained to assist in a crime investigation.
- Rules 2–6 related to the circumstances in which cautions should be issued and the precise wording for the caution.

- Rule 7 mandated that prisoners who make voluntary statements must not be questioned about their statement except for the purpose of removing any ambiguities that may exist, for example to clarify if a time cited is a.m. or p.m.
- Rule 8 related to situations in which two or more persons are charged with the same criminal offence and statements are taken separately from each of the persons charged. It advised that in such circumstances police officers should not read these statements to the other persons charged. Rather, each of those persons charged should be given a copy of the statements of their co-charged and if the person charged chose to make a statement in reply, the usual caution should be administered.
- Rule 9 recommended that whenever possible, all statements should be taken down in writing and signed by the person making it after it has been read to them and they have had the chance to make any corrections that they may wish. (abridged from St. Johnston, 1966: 86–87)

Put simply, the Judges' Rules appear to have been an overt attempt to guard against wrongful convictions that derive from false confessions, rendering confession evidence admissible at a trial only if it was given voluntarily, under caution, and without any interference from interviewing police officers. However, the Judges' Rules as originally devised in 1912 and 1918 were superseded with new Rules in 1964. The new Rules were approved by all of the Queen's Bench judges at the time under a Home Office Circular in response to major criticisms by judges and the legal profession that they were too loosely written and could even hamper the detection and punishment of crime (for a critical analysis of the original Judges' Rules, see Abrahams, 1964: 1–38; St. Johnston, 1966: 87–90).

Despite this, and most significantly from the perspective of guarding against false confessions and wrongful convictions, the new Judges' Rules retained the central notion that all confessions should be voluntarily made by suspects. They made it clear that although the Judges' Rules were concerned with the admissibility of confession evidence, it was equally vital that the processes by which confessions were obtained from suspects were fair and not in any way oppressive:

> In giving evidence as to the circumstances in which any statement was made or taken down in writing, officers must be absolutely frank in describing to the court exactly what occurred, and it will then be for the judge to decide whether or not the statement tendered should

be admitted as evidence. The Rules ... should be constantly borne in mind, as should the general principles which the judges have set out before the Rules. But in addition to complying with the Rules, interrogating officers should always try to be fair to the person who is being questioned, and scrupulously avoid any method which could be regarded as in any way unfair or oppressive. (Home Office Circular, 1964: paragraphs 3–4; Home Office Circular, 1978: paragraph 2)

Moreover, the introductory note to the new Judges' Rules of 1964 highlighted that notwithstanding any changes that were made to the original Judges' Rules they do not affect the general principles that should be observed in police questioning of suspects (see Home Office Circular, 1964). Of most pertinence to this discussion of the five general principles that were outlined were:

- Paragraph (c) that stated that suspects 'at any stage of an investigation should be able to communicate and consult privately with a solicitor ... even if ... in custody provided that in such a case no unreasonable delay or hindrance is caused to the processes of investigation or the administration of justice'; and,
- Paragraph (e) that stated that it is a 'fundamental condition of the admissibility' of confession evidence that any oral or written answer by a suspect 'shall have been voluntary', in the sense that it was 'not obtained by fear of prejudice or hope of advantage, exercised or held out by a person in authority, or by oppression'.

However, as the Judges' Rules were not rules of criminal law that were governed by parliamentary statute, evidence obtained in breach of the Judges' Rules could (and was) still be deemed to be admissible in criminal proceedings if the presiding judge deemed it so and police officers who breached the Rules were not liable to criminal sanction. Doreen McBarnet's (1981b) critique of the Judges' Rules is insightful in highlighting how the notion of voluntariness of suspects' confession evidence was routinely interpreted by the courts in ways that failed to protect suspects from wrongful conviction. It cited cases in which prison cells were bugged, phones had been tapped in police stations, police officers had posed as prisoners to illicitly obtain incriminating evidence against a suspect and suspects had been interrogated for seven hours continuously, which the courts had deemed to be admissible voluntary statements from the accused (see McBarnet, 1981b: 110).

Matters came to a head around the fallout from the *Confait* affair (discussed in Chapter 1; see Price and Caplan, 1976; Kettle, 1979; Price, 1985), which exemplified the need for police accountability, both in the interests of greater reliability of evidence and the enhancement of suspect's rights. It led to the replacement of the Judges' Rules with PACE, which came into effect on 1 January 1986, following a recommendation from the Royal Commission on Criminal Procedure (RCCP) (see Royal Commission on Criminal Procedure, 1981). In particular, the inquiry into the case by Sir Henry Fisher (1977), which preceded the RCCP, had been especially critical of the police practices that led to the wrongful convictions of three youths, Colin Lattimore, Ronald Leighton and Ahmet Salih, for the murder of Maxwell Confait, which he argued was geared simply to manufacturing an incriminating case against the accused.

PACE, then, replaced the merely administrative directions of the Judges' Rules in an attempt to find what Beynon (1986: 120) termed the 'fulcrum between police powers and citizen's rights', extending the Judges' Rules in profound ways in an attempt to provide enhanced safeguards against wrongful convictions. In response to the RCCP's call for 'fairness' and 'openness' in police investigations (Royal Commission on Criminal procedure, 1981: paragraph 2.18), PACE was enacted with the aim of 'extending, clarifying and specifying police powers and suspects' right by means of statutory rules (Dixon *et al.*, 1990: 345).

PACE contains 8 codes of practice (A–H) which provide the core framework of police powers and safeguards around stop and search, arrest, detention, investigation, identification and interviewing detainees. Most crucially for this discussion, Code C sets out the requirements for the detention, treatment and questioning of suspects not related to terrorism in police custody by police officers and Code E deals with the mandatory audio recording of interviews with suspects in police stations. More specifically, Code C (3a) details that the normal procedure for dealing with persons brought to police stations or who go to police stations voluntarily is for the custody officer to make sure the person is told clearly about the following continuing rights, which may be exercised at any stage during the period in custody:

- (i) the right to have someone informed of their arrest.
- (ii) the right to consult privately with a solicitor and that free independent legal advice is available.
- (iii) the right to consult the PACE codes of practice.
- All detainees must also be given a written notice setting out the above three rights – the arrangements for obtaining legal advice; the

right to a copy of the custody record; and, they must be given the caution in the terms prescribed in section 10: 'You do not have to say anything. But it may harm your defence if you do not mention when questioned something which you later rely on in Court. Anything you do say may be given in evidence.'

- Additionally, written notice briefly setting out their entitlements while in custody must be given to detainees.
- All detainees shall be asked to sign the custody record to acknowledge receipt of these notices. Any refusal must be recorded on the custody record.

Despite the statutory provisions under PACE that were/are supposed to act as safeguards against wrongful convictions, the academic literature on police misconduct (see for instance, Newburn, 1999) reveals that breaches are routine, arguably creating an environment in which abortions of justice can be said to be inevitable. Bridges and Sanders' (1990) research in ten different police stations, for instance, identified some of the 'ploys' that are used by police officers to deter suspects from accessing free legal advice from a solicitor. This is in direct contravention of PACE, s. 58(1) that provides that suspects are entitled to consult, if they so request, with a solicitor privately at any time. Moreover, paragraph 6.4 of Code C also mandates that: 'No police officer should, at any time, do or say anything with the intention of dissuading a detainee from obtaining legal advice.' The ploys employed by police officers identified by Bridges and Sanders (1990: 498) include comments on the lack of need for legal advice and the likely increase of time in custody if suspects request legal advice. The most common ploy was to read the suspects' rights too quickly, incomprehensively or incompletely, which they found occurred in 43 per cent of cases (Bridges and Sanders, 1990: 498). According to one police officer cited by Bridges and Sanders (1990: 499):

Now under PACE you read them their rights as quickly as you can – hit them with it so quickly they can't take it in – say 'sign here, here, and here' and there you are: nothing's changed, we all know that, though you wouldn't get any policeman to admit it to you.

This is important as a plethora of further research studies shows that the way that custody officers explain the rights that suspects have to them will influence whether legal advice is requested (see for instance, Phillips *et al.*, 1998: 61; Brown *et al.*, 1992; Sanders *et al.*, 1989; Maguire, 1988).

Linked to this, Bucke and Brown (1997) conducted research on the treatment of people in police custody at 25 police stations in ten police forces. They found that only 40 per cent of detainees (those arrested for offences or detained for other reasons) requested legal advice and that 89 per cent of requests resulted in a consultation with a solicitor, meaning that only 34 per cent of detainees got access to legal advice (Bucke and Brown, 1997: 19–24).

More recently, Pleasence *et al.* (2011), in the most extensive study of its kind to date, drew on data extracted from 30,921 custody records, across 44 police stations in four police force areas and found that the problem had not improved in the 15-year period since Bucke and Brown's (1997) research. It found that across all four police force areas 45.3 per cent of detainees requested advice, with 77.5 per cent of requests resulting in solicitor consultations, amounting to 35.1 per cent overall (Pleasence *et al.*, 2011: 10).

This has crucial ramifications for the intentions that led to the introduction of PACE as the denial of legal advice that prejudices a suspect's right to a fair trial may render the police in breach of Article 6 of the ECHR (Murray v UK). This was succinctly stated in Salduz v Turkey (paragraph 55), another ECHR case, as follows:

> The Court finds that in order for the right to a fair trial to remain sufficiently 'practical and effective' article 6(1) requires that, as a rule, access to a lawyer should be provided as from the first interrogation of a suspect by the police, unless it is demonstrated in the light of the particular circumstances of each case that there are compelling reasons to restrict this right.

As such, and generally speaking, only voluntary refusals of legal advice do not constitute a breach of Article 6 as stated in Salduz v Turkey, unless the refusal was involuntary and uninformed as further stated in Millar v Dickson.

On top of this, Mike McConville's (1992: 545) research has profound implications for the protective reach of video-recorded interviews with suspects in police stations under s. 60a of PACE, as well as generally with tape-recorded interviews. It found that when the video recorder was turned off 'a whole exchange of charge bargaining, bail inducements, threats and promises' occurred as the police placed 'continuing pressure on the suspects' while the custody officer recorded that PACE codes had been dutifully complied with (see also Baldwin, 1992: 328; Bridges and Sanders, 1990: 508). Choongh's (1997: 87) research confirmed

McConville's (1992) earlier research citing a custody officer telling a suspect to 'keep your mouth shut because we can do whatever we want to you'.

As this relates specifically to potentially vulnerable suspects, Raynor (2009) highlighted the trend to replace medical examiners with custody nurses to decide whether suspects are fit to be interviewed. Raynor (2009) cited Richard Charlton, Chair of the Mental Health Lawyers Association (MHLA), who warned that:

> The move signals a downgrading of the evidential procedure, with nurses exposed to pressure from hard-pressed colleagues to declare someone mentally fit for interview. It's a backward step and will certainly result in miscarriages of justice.

In the context of the academic research literature it is perhaps not surprising that the police are heavily implicated in successful appeals that fall into the category of abortions of justice under both the Judges' Rules and PACE. In the pre-PACE era, high-profile cases of police misconduct that caused abortions of justice include Robert Brown, discussed in the last chapter as a victim of serious physical assault by Greater Manchester Police to extract a confession for murder (R v Brown).

Paul Blackburn is another notable victim of an abortion of justice under the Judges' Rules. Convicted at the age of 15 in 1978, the police claimed that he had written his own confession to the abduction and attempted buggery of a 9-year-old boy and that they had had no involvement. He had his conviction overturned after serving 25 years in prison, however, when new linguistic analysis evidence proved that the police could not have told the truth about how the confession was written. This revealed that the Judges' Rules had been breached in relation to their prohibition of prompting a person who was writing a statement (see R v Blackburn, p. 441).

No discussion of abortions of justice caused by breaches of the Judges' Rules would be complete without reference to the case of the Guildford Four, Gerry Conlon, Paul Hill, Carole Richardson and Patrick Armstrong, who were convicted and given life sentences in 1975 for the IRA pub bombings in Guildford, Surrey, that killed five people and injured over 100 others. Paul Hill and Patrick Armstrong were also wrongfully convicted for an IRA bomb attack on a pub in Woolwich that killed two people. In 1989, after they had spent 15 years in prison, the Guildford Four had their convictions overturned. An inquiry by Avon and Somerset Police into the records of Surrey

Police found evidence that typescripts and notes of interviews had been tampered with and detention sheets had been falsified. Crucially, this undermined the basis of the prosecution case which had relied on the confessional evidence of the four defendants as it was apparent that certain police officers had lied, which rendered the convictions no longer tenable (see R v Richardson, Conlon, Armstrong and Hill). Gerry Conlon's (1990) account of how his confession was obtained includes the denial of access to a solicitor, to sleep and to food. The following extract from his book firmly implicates Surrey police officers in intentionally causing the abortions of justice:

> I was standing with my feet apart in the search position, leaning against the wall and ... [a police officer] ... grabbed me by the balls and pulled them downwards. They told me I could have it the hard way or the easy way ... then ... [another police officer] ... was feeing for two spots behind my ears, just where the lobes join the skull. For a moment his two middle fingers rested there, and then suddenly he drilled them into my skull and yanked me upwards ... the pain was indescribable. (78–79).

Despite such cases, perhaps, the most notorious group of police officers who were responsible for causing literally dozens of abortions of justice in the era of the Judges' Rules was the West Midlands Serious Crime Squad, which was disbanded in 1989. The inquiry in the early 1990s by West Yorkshire Police revealed that West Midlands Serious Crime Squad had systematically fabricated evidence, tortured suspects and written false confessions to obtain convictions for serious crimes (Burrell and Bennetto, 1999).

The Birmingham Six (Paddy Joe Hill, Hugh Callaghan, Richard McIlkenny, Gerry Hunter, Billy Power and Johnny Walker) who were wrongly convicted for two IRA pub bombings in 1974 was the most notorious West Midlands Serious Crime Squad abortion-of-justice case. The bombs killed 21 people and injured 162 others. The Birmingham Six served almost a hundred years in prison between them until their convictions were overturned in 1991 (see Hill and Hunt, 1995; Callaghan and Mulready, 1993; Mullin, 1986; Woffinden, 1987: 277–301; Kennedy, 2002: 227–247). Central to the evidence against the Birmingham Six were the confessions of four of the six men that were obtained by West Midlands Serious Crime Squad by unlawful means (Gudjonsson and MacKeith, 2005: 54). In his book, Paddy Joe Hill gave an insight into the ordeal that he had gone through at the hands of the police. He revealed that he was subjected to beatings, mock executions, threats that he would be thrown from a speeding police car or off a high building and how he was burnt with cigarettes (Hill and Hunt, 1995: 68–77; see also Peirce, 2011). Hugh Callaghan (Callaghan and Mulready, 1993: 36–46) also wrote of not being allowed sleep, food or water, and of how he was beaten and threatened with dogs and guns. Years later, the investigative journalist Chris Mullin would prove that the Birmingham Six were factually innocent when he tracked down and interviewed the IRA bombers who were responsible for the crimes (see Mullin, 1986: 244–267).

Another high-profile abortion-of-justice case attributable to West Midlands Serious Crime Squad is the Bridgewater Four. Convicted for the murder of 13-year-old newspaper delivery boy Carl Bridgewater, Michael Hickey, Vincent Hickey and James Robinson each spent 17 years in prison, while Patrick Molloy died in prison in 1981 (see R v Hickey). Crucially, there was no evidence of any kind that the four men killed Carl Bridgewater. Moreover, the evidence that the police did have pointed to someone else who was convicted for another murder on a neighbouring farm to where Carl was murdered a year after Carl had been killed and in exactly the same manner (see Foot, 1986, 1997). This was suppressed by West Midlands Serious Crime Squad and the entire prosecution case was based almost solely on the confession of Patrick Molloy that was obtained after ten days of violent interrogation, during which he was denied access to a solicitor and he was not allowed to sleep. Throughout his ordeal, his food was heavily salted and he was denied liquids. In desperation he drank from the toilet (see Regan, 1997).

Other notable West Midlands Serious Crime Squad abortions of justice include the cases of Derek Treadaway who spent nine years in prison for robbery and conspiracy to rob. He alleged that his confession was falsely obtained by the police handcuffing him and placing a series of plastic bags over his head to suffocate him until he felt forced to sign the written confession, which had already been prepared for his signature by West Midlands Serious Crime Squad police officers (see R v Treadaway; also Johnston, 1997); John Cummiskey who spent eight years in prison for armed robbery (R v Cummiskey); and Trevor Campbell who spent 14 years in prison for the murder of 84-year-old Ethel Cawood (see *The Times*, 1999).

Fifteen years after West Midlands Serious Crime Squad had been disbanded abortions of justice were still coming to light as a result of its activities. In October 2003, for example, the convictions of Christopher

Hagans and John Wilson, who spent nine years in prison for armed robbery was quashed by the CACD (Revill, 2003). This brought the total to more than 40 high-profile abortions of justice that were caused by West Midlands Serious Crime Squad amid claims that there were dozens more hidden cases that might never be overturned:

> I have no doubt there are dozens of people who have served time in jail but were innocent. The Serious Crime Squad were operating like the Wild West, they were out of control. (Gareth Peirce, cited in Burrell and Bennetto, 1999)

Maurice Punch's (2003; see also Punch and Gilmour, 2010: 10–12) analysis of police deviance and corruption seems appropriate in thinking about the behaviour of the large number of police officers (over 100) that played a part in the abortions of justice that were caused by West Midlands Serious Crime Squad. Distinguishing between the 'myth system' that organisations present to the outside world and the 'operational code' that governs how things actually get done, Punch (2003: 173) provided a useful framework for explaining how organisations such as police forces can cause what are here termed as abortions of justice:

> On the one hand, organisations ask people to bend and break rules for institutional ends and, on the other hand, people are very creative at getting around rules, regulations and procedures for their own ends. It is that discrepancy – between what is supposed to be happening and *what really goes on* – that leads us to examine the mechanisms and processes by which systems get 'out of synch' and even out of control. (original emphasis)

In a similar vein, Green and Ward (2004: 4–7) also distinguished between 'official' and 'operative' goals to argue that acts and omissions are attributable to state agencies, rather than individuals, when they are performed in pursuit of organisational goals. Official goals are those prescribed by an organisations legal mandate, mission statement, public pronouncements, and so on. Operative goals are goals which are widely shared within the organisation, either being transmitted by management or forming part of a staff occupational culture, which in practice guide the acts which individuals perform in the purported execution of their official duties. In some instances, state agencies, such as police forces or sub-units within them, adopt illegitimate and unlawful goals, that is, goals which are completely at odds with their official mandate and for the pursuit of which no official justification is possible. Thus, corruption of the kind seen in the case of West Midlands Serious Crime Squad can in some instances become an organisational goal of an entire police force (see also, for instance, Reiner, 2010; Davies, 2003).

Punch (2003) engaged critically with the metaphors normally employed to explain how police officers can participate in breaches of police guidelines and even widespread criminal activity to secure convictions as in the case of West Midlands Serious Crime Squad. He argued that the notions of 'rotten apples', which attributes the problem to individual bad cops who contaminate a force of otherwise good, honest officers, and of a 'rotten barrel' of 'illness and of contagion in a particular area or unit', with the implicit analogy that the offending part (unit or squad) of an otherwise healthy police force can be clinically removed and the problem will be resolved, are inadequate (Punch, 2003: 172). Indeed, for Punch, such analogies are part of the damage limitation exercises that police forces deploy when defending against revelations that police deviance is systemic and endemic and which ought to be seen as illustrative of a police service that is a more akin to a 'rotten orchard':

> What usually cannot be admitted … [in examples such as West Midlands Serious Crime Squad] … is that deviance had become *systemic* – in some way encouraged, and perhaps even protected, by certain elements in the system … [Instead] … the metaphor of 'rotten orchards' … [is better] … to indicate that it is sometimes not the apple, or even the barrel, that is rotten but the *system* (or significant parts of the system). (2003: 172, original emphasis)

Penny Green and Tony Ward's (2004: 3) uncomplicated definition of state crime fits well with the foregoing analyses:

> [A] state is legitimate to the extent that (1) it acts in accordance with the rules that it sets for itself and its citizenry, and (2) those rules are seen as justified by shared beliefs.

The obvious limit of such a definition is that it gives primacy to the state on what will count as a state crime. It means that unless and until the state, a state agency or an actor working for a state agency can be shown to have departed from the state's own rules and procedures or is not justifiable in terms of the values the rules of the state purport to serve a state crime cannot be said to have occurred (Green and Ward, 2004: 1). Yet, from this perspective on state crime, any intended breaches of the codes of conduct contained in the Home Office (state) requested and sanctioned Judges' Rules (and PACE below) on how suspects of crime should be detained and interviewed can be conceptualised as firmly locating this analysis of abortions of justice caused by West Midlands Serious Crime Squad as unquestionable crimes of the state.

This analysis is strengthened by reference to the further breaching of enacted statutes at the time by West Midlands Serious Crime Squad, such as the ECHR and the Universal Declaration of Human Rights which are also, arguably, intended to govern the actions of state agencies and agents with the overall aim of protecting against abortions of justice. In the West Midlands' cases a number of fundamental rights and freedoms are shown, albeit retrospectively, to have been intentionally breached by police officers who sought to obtain evidence that might secure convictions by means not proscribed in international law. These include Article 3 of the ECHR (right not to be subjected to torture or to inhuman or degrading treatment or punishment); Article 5 of the ECHR (right to liberty and security); Article 6 of the ECHR (which includes the right to a fair trial and to be presumed innocent until proved guilty according to law). As for the Universal Declaration of Human Rights, a raft of fundamental and inalienable rights that are afforded to UK citizens and which overlap with the rights contained in the ECHR were breached in the abortions of justice caused by West Midlands police officers. These include Article 3 (right to life, liberty and security of person); Article 5 (no one shall be subjected to torture or to cruel, inhuman or degrading treatment or punishment); Article 9 (no one shall be subjected to arbitrary arrest, detention or exile); Article 10 (everyone is entitled to a fair hearing); Article 11 (everyone charged with a penal offence has the right to be presumed innocent until proved guilty according to law).

In this context, despite the apparent limit of Green and Ward's (2004: 3) definition of state crime, the possibility of holding the state to account even on its own terms can be conceived as providing a key site of struggle for justice, however that concept is defined and/or understood. That is, without such things as the Judges' Rules or the enactment of domestic statutes such as PACE and international statutes such as the ECHR and/or the Universal Declaration of Human Rights, the possibility of conceptualising the abortions of justice that stem from breaches of state rules and statutory codes of conduct would be greatly impeded.

The abortions of justice caused by West Midlands Serious Crime Squad occurred under the Judges' Rules which, as discussed above, were replaced by PACE and came into effect in 1986. At the time, it was widely reported that PACE would render wrongful convictions a thing of the past by putting statutory requirements, rather than informal guidelines, on how the police should deal with suspects of crime (see for instance, Steele, 1997). Despite this, abortions of justice have continued to be caused by police officers, working either individually or together, who put the quest for incriminating evidence that might aid convictions above the letter and the principles of the rights of suspects (see Sanders and Young, 1994; Coleman *et al.*, 1993; Sanders and Bridges, 1983).

A notable example is the ongoing call for a public inquiry into the string of abortions of justice caused by South Wales Police (see BBC News, 2001; Livingstone, 2003; ITV Wales, 2010), which also highlights that disbanding troublesome police units or squads, such as West Midlands Serious Crime Squad, does not necessarily eliminate systemic police deviance in other police force areas. The campaign for a public inquiry into South Wales Police, described as 'Britain's worst case of institutionalised corruption involving a single police force' (McVeigh, 2000), was supported at its height by some 30 MPs and Members of the Welsh Assembly (see for instance, Lewis, 2002; O'Brien, 2005). Moreover, in the period between 1982 and 2000, which bridges the Judges' Rules and PACE eras, up to 30 officers from South Wales Police had been subject to temporary suspensions, although no disciplinary action had resulted, with some senior officers opting to take early retirement on full pensions to avoid disciplinary proceedings, despite there being a list of complaints against them (see McVeigh, 2000). More generally, Freedom of Information Act requests from the BBC to the 53 police forces in the UK between 2008–2010 revealed in a Panorama programme that was aired in October 2011 that at least 489 officers from 47 police forces that were facing misconduct charges were allowed to retire discreetly in the two-year period without having to face disciplinary proceedings (see Fallon, 2011).

Included in the dossier of 12 cases spearheading the campaign for a public inquiry into South Wales Police are nine murders, which remain unsolved following successful appeals. They involve accusations of fabricated police interview notes, false or missing evidence, non-disclosure of evidence, and bribes and intimidation. A number of the successful appeals can be conceived as abortions of justice that occurred post-PACE. This would indicate that the introduction of PACE made little difference to police officers who are prepared to intentionally break the prevailing rules even when they are enshrined in statute.

In the case of the Cardiff Newsagent Three, for instance, Michael O'Brien, Ellis Sherwood and Darren Hall were convicted in July 1988 of the murder of Cardiff newsagent, Philip Saunders, found lying unconscious in the front garden of his home in the Canton area of Cardiff on the night of 12 October 1987. Their convictions were overturned in December 1999, however, after they had each spent 11 years in prison. The successful appeal was based largely on new forensic psychology evidence that undermined the reliability of Hall's confession and guilty plea. The successful appeal judgment also listed multiple infractions of PACE by South Wales Police officers who sought to 'improve' the evidence against the three men to help to secure the convictions: all three men were denied access to solicitors; they were interviewed 'off the record', two were handcuffed to hot radiators and other objects in the police station; they were all subjected to oppressive treatment by the police; and prosecution witnesses claimed that they were pressured by South Wales Police officers and offered inducements such as having criminal charges dropped to give evidence against the three men at their trial (see R v O'Brien, Sherwood and Hall).

Another clear post-PACE abortion of justice that is included in the dossier of cases put forward in support of the demand for a public inquiry into South Wales Police is the conviction of Annette Hewins. Along with her niece, Donna Clarke, she was convicted of an arson attack that resulted in the death of Diane Jones and her two daughters, 2-year-old Shauna and 13-month-old Sarah Jane, in a house fire at their home on the Gurnos housing estate in Merthyr Tydfil, South Wales, in October 1995. At Cardiff Crown Court in June 1997, Hewins was sentenced to 13 years' imprisonment and Clarke to 20 years. However, their convictions were overturned in February 1999 with the CACD concluding that there was no sufficient evidence to prove the case against Hewins. A retrial was ordered for Clarke that was later abandoned by the prosecution as it would have been a breach of the double jeopardy rule that was in place at the time (BBC, 2002c). It transpired that the main prosecution witness had been pressured by South Wales Police officers to implicate Clarke, and in so doing, also implicated Hewins who was with Clarke at the time of the offence (see R v Clarke; R v Hewins). A rarity in such cases, Hewins received a public apology from South Wales Police in March 2006 who admitted that she was innocent and had nothing at all to do with the fire (BBC, 2006c).

Prosecution

In addition to recommending the statutory formalisation of codes of practice on police investigatory powers and safeguards for suspects of crime that came into being under PACE, the RCCP was also highly critical of the role of the police at the time as both investigators of alleged criminal offences who also decided whether to prosecute. As already mentioned, the case against the three suspects in the investigation into the murder of Maxwell Confait focused on constructing an incriminating case to assist in obtaining a strong prosecution case in the hope of securing a conviction. The concerns that the case raised about the possibility of further wrongful convictions by prosecution-oriented policing led to the implementation of another of the RCCP's main recommendations, namely the establishment of a new independent prosecution authority under the Prosecution of Offences Act 1985, which created the Crown Prosecution Service (CPS).

Since 1986, the CPS is the principal prosecution service that deals with all serious and complex criminal prosecutions in England and Wales. It is headed by the Director of Public Prosecutions (DPP), who is overseen only by the Attorney General who, in turn, is accountable to Parliament for the work of the CPS. Like the police under the Judges' Rules and now PACE, prosecutors are also governed by their own guidelines in the form of the Code for Crown Prosecutors (see Crown Prosecution Service, 2010a), which provides the general principles to be applied when making decisions about prosecutions. The following extract from the General Principles of the Code for Crown Prosecutors highlights the extent to which it is intended to protect against prosecutors causing intentional abortions of justice:

> 2.1 … It is the duty of prosecutors to make sure that the right person is prosecuted for the right offence and to bring offenders to justice wherever possible … 2.2 … Prosecutors must ensure that the law is properly applied; that all relevant evidence is put before the court; and that obligations of disclosure are complied with … 2.4 … Prosecutors must always act in the interests of justice and not solely for the purpose of obtaining a conviction … 2.5 … Prosecutors are bound by the duties set out in this legislation. (Crown Prosecution Service, 2010a: 3)

More specifically, the Code for Crown Prosecutors outlines the Full Code Test to be applied by prosecutors when deciding whether or not to charge a suspect(s) with a criminal offence, although in exceptional circumstances the CPS may apply what is termed the Threshold Test. This permits the detention of suspects in custody after charge in cases where the suspect is thought to present a substantial bail risk if released and the evidence required to apply the Full Code Test is not available and requires further investigation (see Crown Prosecution Service, 2010a: 15–18). The Full Code Test, which must be applied as soon as is reasonably practicable and in any event before the expiry of any applicable custody time limit or extended custody time limit, has two stages: (1) the evidential stage, to be followed by (2) the public interest stage. At the initial evidential test stage, prosecutors must be satisfied that there is 'sufficient evidence to provide a realistic prospect of conviction against each defendant on each charge' (Crown Prosecution Service, 2010a: 7). They must consider whether the evidence is reliable and would be admissible at trial. In their deliberations they must also consider what the case for the defence may be and how it might affect the prosecution case against the accused. Crucially, if the case is not thought to pass the evidential stage, prosecutors must not proceed with a prosecution, no matter how serious or sensitive the alleged crime may be (Crown Prosecution Service, 2010a: 7–9).

If a case is thought to pass the evidential stage, prosecutors must then decide whether a prosecution would be in the public interest. In so doing, prosecutors are required to consider a range of different factors for and against prosecution (see Crown Prosecution Service, 2010a: 11–15) 'carefully and fairly' and are only supposed to commence or continue a prosecution if a case is thought to have passed both stages (Crown Prosecution Service, 2012).

Finally, the underlying guiding principles that govern the operations of the CPS are stated as including the following:

> Our decisions will be independent of bias or discrimination ... We will act with integrity and objectivity and will exercise sound judgment ... In our dealings with each other and the public we will be open and honest. We will show sensitivity and understanding to victims and witnesses and treat all defendants fairly ... We are accountable to Parliament and to the public; we will work together with our colleagues to maintain public trust and to provide an efficient criminal justice system. (Crown Prosecution Service, 2012)

Despite this governing framework, critical analysis of successful appeals also implicates prosecutors as an internal cause of abortions of justice when they intentionally choose not to disclose evidence that may be favourable to the defence. This is apparently because prosecutors are more interested in obtaining convictions over and above the duties that they have according to the CPS's governing codes and principles.

In the pre-CPS era, cases such as R v Kamara exemplified further to the Confait case the kinds of abortions of justice that could be caused under the old system when the police decided the charge against suspects of crime and instructed private prosecutors to act for them at trial. John Kamara was convicted of the murder of John Suffield Jnr in December 1981, a Liverpool betting shop manager who had been tied up had been stabbed 19 times in a robbery in March of that year. A total of £176 was stolen (see R v Kamara). However, after he had spent almost 20 years in prison, while maintaining his innocence, the CACD overturned Kamara's conviction following a referral by the CCRC. In particular, the CCRC found that other than having to wear prison clothes on the identification parade (see *Liverpool Echo*, 2000), the non-disclosure of 201 witness statements that could have been favourable to Kamara's defence that had been 'hidden' by the police (see BBC, 2000) was a breach of the Attorney-General's Guidelines which were in place at the time (see R v Kamara, paragraph B). Citing a crucial comment from Glidewell LJ in the earlier successful appeal judgment in the case of Judith Ward, Otton LJ in Kamara emphasised the importance of full disclosure of all of the evidence by prosecutors to safeguard against wrongful convictions in the following terms:

> Non-disclosure is a potent source of injustice and even with the benefit of hindsight, it will often be difficult to say whether or not an undisclosed item of evidence might have shifted the balance or opened up a new line of defence. (R v Kamara, paragraph B)

Ward had also been a victim of an abortion of justice that was caused in large part by prosecutorial non-disclosure in the pre-CPS period, as well as non-disclosure by the police and forensic and medical experts. Convicted in November 1974 for a series of IRA bombings, one of which on an army coach which killed nine soldiers, a woman and two children, Ward spent 18 years in prison until the CACD overturned her conviction in May 1992. In quashing Ward's conviction, the CACD's judgment highlighted the systemic non-disclosure by the prosecution, the police and by government forensic science experts and medical experts who worked with the police and the prosecution acting in concert to secure a conviction (see R v Ward, paragraphs 1–2).

The most significant consequence of Ward's landmark successful appeal was the introduction of the Criminal Procedure and Investigations Act 1996 (CPIA), which gave statutory force to the prosecution duty of disclosure. Prior to Ward, there was no statutory duty on prosecution disclosure. Rather, under guidelines issued by the Attorney-General in December 1981 the duty of the prosecution was to make available to the defence any evidence thought by the prosecution and prosecuting counsel to have some relevance, that is 'has some bearing on the offence(s) charged and the surrounding circumstances of the case' (see R v H; R v C, paragraph 15). Glidewell LJ in Ward highlighted the limited nature of the existing disclosure duties on prosecutors at the time of her conviction in the following terms:

> An incident of a defendant's right to a fair trial is a right to timely disclosure by the prosecution of all material matters which affect the scientific case relied on by the prosecution, that is, whether such matters strengthen or weaken the prosecution case or assist the defence case. This duty exists whether or not a specific request for disclosure of details of scientific evidence is made by the defence. Moreover, this duty is continuous: it applies not only in the pre-trial period but also throughout the trial. (at 626)

This was enshrined in the CPIA 1996, as amended by s. 37 of the Criminal Justice Act 2003, with s. 3(1) requiring that prosecutors must:

(a) disclose to the accused any prosecution material which has not previously been disclosed to the accused and which might reasonably be considered capable of undermining the case for the prosecution against the accused or of assisting the case for the accused; or,

(b) give to the accused a written statement that there is no material of a description mentioned in paragraph (a).

CPIA 1996, s.7(A) further requires that prosecutors have a continuing duty to disclose, with the most crucial section specifying that:

(1) This section applies at all times –
    (a) after the prosecutor has complied with section 3 or purported to comply with it, and,
    (b) before the accused is acquitted or convicted or the prosecutor decides not to proceed with the case concerned.

(2)   The prosecutor must keep under review the question whether at any given time … there is prosecution material which –

  (a)   might reasonably be considered capable of undermining the case for the prosecution against the accused or of assisting the case for the accused, and,

  (b)   has not been disclosed to the accused.

(3)   If at any time there is any such material as is mentioned in sub-section (2) the prosecutor must disclose it to the accused as soon as is reasonably practicable.

The current leading legal authority on prosecution disclosure is the successful appeal in the case of R v Hadley and Others. It outlines when prosecution non-disclosure is likely to result in a conviction being seen as unsafe by the CACD. The case concerned three successful appellants who had been convicted of supplying heroin. The prosecution had failed to disclose video material to the defence relating to surveillance of the appellants' business premises. It was held that the undisclosed information, which was capable of assisting the defendants' case and of undermining the prosecution case against them, ought to have been disclosed. Significantly, *Hadley* outlined the CACD's two-stage test in deciding whether convictions were unsafe as follows: first, it has to determine whether the material should have been disclosed; then it has to decide whether the failure to disclose the materials in question makes the conviction unsafe. It noted that it does not necessarily follow that if it is found that material should have been disclosed, then the conviction will always be deemed unsafe. It made clear that the CACD will not regard a conviction as unsafe if the non-disclosure can be said to have little significance in relation to any real issue in the case, with individual items of evidence being seen in the context of other evidence in the case.

However, *Hadley* clarified that appellants do not have to show categorically that the disclosure of the non-disclosed materials would have affected the outcome of the proceedings. Rather, they need only show that the non-disclosed material would have been capable of affecting the decision of the jury at trial, not that it must have done so. Overall, *Hadley* emphasised that, given the importance of full disclosure of all relevant material in ensuring a fair trial, the CACD is unlikely to accept that the safety of a conviction is unaffected where a substantial volume of material is not disclosed to the defence (R v Hadley and Others).

Despite this, abortions of justice such as R v Hadley and Others that are caused by prosecution non-disclosure are not uncommon. In the case of R v Giles, for instance, Toulson LJ indicated that prosecution non-disclosure is widespread in the following terms:

> Nondisclosure of material information has been a constant source of trouble over recent years. The principles applicable are entirely clear and there is no need for us to restate earlier authorities on the subject, but it is always a matter of concern when a material nondisclosure occurs and, as in this case, a conviction has to be quashed as unsafe at a time when the appellant has completed the sentence passed upon him ... but [the prosecution] has been unable to explain to the court why it is that there was not proper disclosure of this material, especially in circumstances where the point had been noted by somebody in the CPS on the sensitive material log as a matter which would require consideration if the trial took the course that it did. The question of disclosure of that material may well have been a matter which ought to have been considered in any event. (paragraphs 12–13)

A final example of a recent abortion of justice that was caused by intentional prosecution non-disclosure is the case of R v Vernett-Showers and Others. The case concerned ten appellants of the 11 defendants who had been convicted of various offences relating to the alleged controlled delivery of heroin into the UK from Pakistan. The appellants had their convictions referred back to the CACD by the CCRC, and four had their convictions quashed. At the appeal, the prosecution conceded that undisclosed material could have been of potential assistance to three of the appellants at trial that showed that there had been a substantial breach of process in two of the prosecutions and that the other successful appellant had been set up by a police informant. The fourth successful appellant also had his conviction overturned on the basis that he had been set up by police informants, a fact that surfaced only in the post-trial disclosure material (see R v Vernett-Showers and Others).

External factors

False allegations of sexual offences

False allegations of sexual offences are a common feature of the criminal justice system and the reasons for making such false allegations are legion. A perusal of the cases cited in national newspapers over the last couple of years includes the following cases:

- Christine Jordan was jailed for two years in March 2012 for perverting the course of justice after making a false allegation of rape against Kevin Percival. She had met Percival on a bus and invited him back to her flat for sex. She made the false allegation after he failed to remember her name when they met five days later in a local pub. (Smith, 2012)
- Kelly Atkins, aged 20, was also jailed for two years in 2012 for making false rape claims against her ex-boyfriend, Wayne Maddox, because he refused to restart their relationship that had ended after ten months. (Editorial, 2012)
- Emma Templeton was sentenced to ten months' imprisonment suspended for a year in 2011 after she admitted that she perverted the course of justice when she falsely accused Father Patrick Udoma, a Catholic priest, of rape after their relationship ended. (Hull, 2011)
- Samantha Morley was jailed for 12 months in 2011 after admitting a false rape claim in an attempt to hide the fact that she had been unfaithful to her soldier fiancé while he was in Afghanistan and that her child was not his. (Ellicott and Kisiel, 2011)
- Nicola Osborne was jailed for 18 months in February 2011 after falsely claiming she had been abducted and raped. She made the false claim because she was worried her husband would find out that she had had a one-night stand. (BBC, 2011a)
- Louise Creighton, an 18-year-old student, was sentenced to 180 hours of community service after admitting making a false rape allegation against a man she had met at a music festival in Scotland. She made the false claim as she had a girlfriend and 'did not feel comfortable' that she had slept with the man. (MacLarty, 2011)
- Leyla Ibrahim was jailed for three years in July 2010 after she falsely claimed she had been raped to her friends. She had slashed her body, hair and clothing to make her rape claim appear more convincing, and even gave herself a black eye to support her claims. She had fabricated the rape to teach her friends a lesson because they had abandoned her at the end of a night out. (Tozer, 2010)
- False allegations can also be made in child custody battles as in the case of Victoria Haigh, the former jockey and racehorse trainer, who coached her 7-year-old daughter to make false claims that her father, David Tune, was a paedophile. (Doughty, 2001)

Against this background, the remainder of this section considers a prominent external causal factor of abortions of justice that emerges in analyses of successful appeals, namely false allegations of sexual offences, particularly false allegations of rape, historic sexual offences when the complainant was a minor and/or allegations of sexual offences against children. Such abortions of justice are facilitated by a criminal justice system that allows uncorroborated witness testimonies to be admissible evidence in criminal trials, despite the inherent unreliability of such evidence. As Doreen McBarnet (1981a: 14) noted, juries are told that there must be corroboration of proof of a charge, but they are not left to decide whether the general idea that two supporting pieces of evidence constitutes proof is valid, they are told it is.

> Corroboration equals legal sufficiency. The only question for the jury is whether they are convinced by the evidence, *not* whether they are convinced by the assumption that such evidence constitutes proof. (original emphasis)

Specifically, s. 32(1) of the Criminal Justice and Public Order Act 1994 abolished the requirement on judges to issue a warning to juries when summing up the 'dangers' of convicting defendants charged with sexual offences on the uncorroborated testimony of alleged victims. This followed s. 34 of the Criminal Justice Act 1988, which abrogated the requirement on judges to give a warning to juries about convicting an accused on the uncorroborated evidence of a child.

The idea of the need for such a warning can be traced to the thoughts of English jurist Matthew Hale who noted in the seventeenth century that allegations of rape 'are easily to be made and hard to be proved, and harder to be defended by the party accused' (cited in Law Commission, 1991: 89). The warning came into effect as a development in common law that had its origins in the early years of the Court of Criminal Appeal, established in 1907. In the case of R v Graham in 1910, for instance, the defendant was charged with unlawfully and carnally knowing a girl of or above the age of 13 and under the age of 16. Setting out the basic framework for what would become the warning for uncorroborated witness evidence in criminal trials, the judge told the jury that they were at liberty, if they thought it right, to act on the uncorroborated evidence of the prosecutrix alone, but that they should scrutinise the case with great care and be quite satisfied that the case for the Crown was made out and that they ought to act upon the girl's evidence (R v Graham).

As the case law developed, the warning was refined to include three categories of 'suspect witness' evidence that required judges to issue a full warning as to the danger of convicting upon uncorroborated evidence: an alleged accomplice, an alleged victim of a sexual offence or a child giving sworn evidence. In essence, the judge was obliged to:

1. warn the jury that it would be dangerous to convict without corroboration, and explain why;
2. direct the jury as to what evidence is and is not capable of providing it; and,
3. explain that if nevertheless, after giving full weight to the warning, they are satisfied without any doubt that the testimony of the witness (complainant) who gave the uncorroborated evidence is truthful, the absence of corroboration does not matter, and they may convict. (Law Commission, 1991: 23)

The appeal judgment in the cases of R v Henry; R v Manning contained important guidance on the kind of wording to be used by judges in issuing the warning to juries, expressed in the following terms:

[T]here is no magic formula or mumbo jumbo required in a direction relating to corroboration. What the judge has to do is to use clear and simple language that will without any doubt convey to the jury that in cases of alleged sexual offences it is really dangerous to convict on the evidence ... alone. This is dangerous because human experience has shown that ... [a] ... false story ... is very easy to fabricate, but extremely difficult to refute. Such stories are fabricated for all sorts of reasons, which I need not now enumerate, and sometimes for no reason at all. (R v Henry; R v Manning, paragraph 153)

Another important moment in the development of the common law practice of dealing with uncorroborated evidence was the House of Lords' judgment in R v Spencer and Others. Although it did not officially extend the categories of suspect witness evidence for which a warning must be given, it accepted the argument that the evidence of other types of suspect witnesses also required judges to warn juries of the inherent danger of convicting on uncorroborated statements. The appellants who had been employed as nursing staff at a secure hospital had been convicted of offences relating to the ill-treatment of patients. The prosecution case at trial had depended entirely on the uncorroborated evidence of patients who had a criminal record and suffered from mental disorder. The case had been referred to the House of Lords by the CACD to consider the following point of law of general public importance:

In a case where the evidence for the Crown is solely that of a witness who is not in one of the accepted categories of suspect witnesses, but who, by reason of his particular mental condition and criminal connection, fulfilled the same criteria, must the judge warn the jury that it is dangerous to convict on his uncorroborated evidence? (R v Spencer and Others)

It was argued on behalf of the appellants at the House of Lords' appeal that common law categories are not static and are never closed but, rather, adapt to new circumstances as they arise in cases before the courts; that whether a judge is obliged to give a warning or not, judges always retain a residual discretion to give such a warning if it is thought that it is plainly required; and that there was an arguable duty on judges in the instant case of mentally ill patients with criminal convictions making uncorroborated allegations against hospital staff to issue a warning about the lack of corroboration on the basis that if a warning was not given, then subsequent convictions could be challenged because no such warning had been given.

In affirming the question that was asked by the CACD and quashing the convictions of Alan Spencer, Kenneth Ball and Michael Mason, the House of Lords' judgment declared:

[W]hile it may often be convenient to use the words 'danger' or 'dangerous', the use of such words is not essential to an adequate warning so long as the jury are made fully aware of the dangers of convicting on such evidence. (R v Spencer and Others)

It seems clear that the issuing of a warning of the inherent dangers of uncorroborated witness testimony was expressly intended to provide defendants with a fair trial and to ward against the possibility of wrongful convictions. A pertinent question that will be addressed in the next chapter is why criminal charges are brought against defendants on evidence that is so obviously problematic as to require a warning in the first place and why was the warning abolished. The evidence from successful appeal cases is equally clear. The abolition of the warning has contributed to abortions of justice that are caused by individuals who intentionally give false testimony of alleged sexual offences that is not supported by any other form of evidence.

Warren Blackwell, for instance, was convicted at Northampton Crown Court in October 1999 for a sexual offence that he was alleged to have committed in the early hours of New Year's Day that year. He served almost three and a half years in prison for the offence. It was not disputed at trial that Blackwell and his complainant had met earlier in the evening at a party at a village social club and that during the evening they had played a game of pool against each other. At around 12.50 a.m. the complainant alleged that she went outside for some fresh air and that she was grabbed from behind by Blackwell who forced her to a grass area where he repeatedly punched and indecently assaulted her (see R v Blackwell). His conviction was quashed by the CACD in September 2006, however, following a review by the CCRC that discovered that his accuser, who had changed her name at least eight times and had a propensity for self-harm, had made at least five other false allegations of sexual and physical assault to police in three separate forces; that she was married twice and made false allegations against both husbands, one of whom was a policeman; had once accused her own father of sexual assault, but police concluded she had made it up; and had accused a boy of rape when she was a teenager, only for a doctor to discover she was still a virgin (see Greenhill, 2006a; R v Blackwell). In October 2006, Lord Campbell-Savours used parliamentary privilege to name the woman (see Greenhill, 2006b; for a response by the named complainant, see Taylor, 2006). A report into the case by the Independent Police Complaint's Commission (IPCC) in June 2010 firmly linked abortions of justice that stem from intentional false allegations that are uncorroborated and no longer protected by a warning of the dangerousness of convicting on such evidence with police non-disclosure. It revealed that police officers were told that Blackwell's accuser was 'unreliable', 'unstable' and craved attention, but they failed to disclose it to the prosecution or the defence teams prior to his trial (Camber, 2010).

In another pertinent case, Timothy Darryl Gee (known as Darryl Gee), a supply music teacher, was jailed for eight years in January 2001 at Bradford Crown Court following allegations of an historic rape and indecent assaults made by a woman aged 23 at the time. He had taught her in school in Huddersfield in 1989 when she was 11 years old. His first appeal was dismissed in July 2002. He died about a month later in prison from blood cancer, which prison doctors had failed to diagnose. Gee's alleged victim had also previously accused her father of rape and indecent assault. He was convicted in November 2000 and had been sentenced to 12 years' imprisonment. He even shared a cell with Gee during their imprisonment. In July 2005, both cases were referred back to the CACD by the CCRC on the basis of new expert evidence that cast doubt on the mental state of the complainant and, hence, the reliability of her evidence in both cases. In particular, since the original trial of her father, the alleged victim's account of his alleged abuse was said to have become 'more florid' and she had made no mention of being abused by Gee in recent psychotherapy and counselling sessions which she had received since the two trials had taken place. This was deemed to be grounds enough for the complainant's father's conviction to be overturned. Gee's successful appeal judgment noted that had the court been furnished with the evidence before the CACD, namely that his accusers' father would likely have been acquitted about two months prior to his trial, the chances of attacking his accuser's credibility would have 'immeasurably stronger' and he, too, would more than likely be acquitted. On this basis, the CACD posthumously quashed his conviction as well (see R v Gee; Paton, 2006).

In another notable joint successful appeal case following false allegations of historic abuse, Basil Williams-Rigby and Mike Lawson were convicted as part of 'Operation Care', a police and social services investigation that began in 1996 into allegations that large numbers of staff at a residential community home near Liverpool had sexually abused boys in their care. More specifically, eight of those who had been at the home during the period when Williams-Rigby had been employed there, 1975 to 1984, alleged that they had been sexually abused by him. There were allegations of buggery, attempted buggery, masturbation, oral sex, other forms of gross indecency and indecent assault, one allegation of taking indecent photographs and two allegations of cruelty to a child. In August 1999, Williams-Rigby was convicted at Liverpool Crown Court of 22 out of 47 counts in the indictment, and was sentenced to 12 years' imprisonment (R v Basil Anthony Williams-Rigby and Michael James Lawson, paragraph 2). Similarly for Lawson, there were allegations of indecent assault, buggery, taking an indecent photograph, and common assault made by eight complainants in relation to the period that he worked at the Home, 1974 to 1997. In June 2000, Lawson was convicted on 17 counts of indecent assault relating to 7 complainants and was sentenced to seven years' imprisonment. As in the case of Williams-Rigby, the prosecution case depended only upon the evidence of the complainants, all of whom by the time they gave evidence had criminal records (R v Basil Anthony Williams-Rigby and Michael James Lawson, paragraph 15). Williams-Rigby and Lawson had their convictions overturned in March 2003. For Williams-Rigby, new evidence from two former residents at the home, one of whom was in prison for murder, who had shared dormitories with the complainants gave him good character evidence and testified that it would not be possible for the allegations to have occurred with the alleged regularity without their knowing about it (R v Basil Anthony Williams-Rigby and Michael James Lawson, paragraphs 8–9). For Lawson, there was new evidence from a witness that he had met while in prison and who had been a former resident at the home. The evidence, which had not been available at the time of Lawson's trial, was that one of his complainants had fabricated an allegation against him in order to finance a sex change (R v Basil Anthony Williams-Rigby and Michael James Lawson, paragraphs 24, 33–36; for an extensive analysis of false historic allegations of abuse in case homes, see Webster 2005).

A final example is the successful appeal of Roger Beardmore at Stafford Crown Court in March 1998 who was convicted of the rape and attempted rape of a girl between the ages of 3 and 6 years old that allegedly occurred in the early 1990s. In December 2001, however, his conviction was overturned after he had served three years in prison when the complainant, who was aged 14 at the time, admitted that she lied to gain her mother's attention. She said that she retracted her allegations because she wanted to correct a wrong which had been 'keeping her awake, crying all night' (see Peek, 2001).

Prison informants

Successful appeal cases also reveal the use of prison informants, or 'grasses', who also intentionally give false testimonies that contribute to abortions of justice. A leading authority on the phenomenon of false testimonies by prison informants is the case of R v Maynard and Others. Robert Maynard, Reginald Dudley, Kathleen Bailey and Charles Clarke were convicted for offences related to the murders of William Moseley and Michael Cornwall in a case known as the Epping Torso Case. One of the main grounds of the successful appeals of the four appellants was the retracted evidence of prison informant, Anthony Wild, who claimed that his evidence against the appellants had been fabricated in collusion with the police (R v Maynard and Others, paragraph 7; see also Campbell, 2002; Dudley, 2002).

Commenting on the case just before the convictions were overturned, James Morton (2001: 234) observed that:

> All informers are dangerous. They rarely give evidence because they have seen the Light. Rather it is a mixture of revenge, money, the opportunity to wriggle out of a difficult position, or a combination

of the three and a number of other reasons which circulate in the cans of worms that are inside their heads. Prison cell informers are particularly dangerous. They say they want to help society when all they really want to do is help themselves to an early release.

Despite this, prison informant evidence that can assist in obtaining convictions is still deemed to be admissible in criminal trials, although evidence from police or prison grasses that support the defence ('I shared a cell with the accused and he swore to me that he didn't do it') is not a feature. Indeed, it is significant that the successful appeals in R v Maynard and Others were not overturned on the retracted evidence of Wild alone, a point that was emphasised by Mantell LJ in the final paragraph of the successful appeal judgment in the following terms:

> We turn briefly to the position regarding Anthony Wild. Over the years the courts have learned to regard post-trial retractions by persons of Wild's character with a degree of cynicism. Wild and his like are particularly vulnerable to pressure both inside and outside of prison and both before and after trial. Even so, the judge had directed the jury that they should treat Wild's evidence with caution and suggested, in terms, that they should only act upon it insofar as it had been supported by other evidence in the case. He particularly mentioned the police interviews. Lacking support from the police evidence it follows that even without the later retractions Wild's evidence standing alone would have been insufficient to support the convictions. We only add that had it not been possible to impugn the interview evidence it is unlikely that Wild's volte-face of itself would have caused us to question the safety of any of these convictions. (R v Maynard and Others, paragraph 58)

Mantell LJ was alluding to the discredited police interview evidence by Dr Hardcastle who had been commissioned by the CCRC to examine the speeds of writing of the photocopied handwritten records of a number of disputed interviews. In particular, it showed that the first police interview of Dudley could not have been recorded contemporaneously in the time and manner claimed, which had so-called 'knock-on effects' on the reliability of all the appellants' police interviews. The convictions were accordingly deemed unsafe by the CACD and were overturned (see R v Maynard and Others, paragraphs 6, 9, 42–57).

Another more recent example is the case of Paul Day, a prison informant who committed suicide only days after he had admitted that he had fabricated evidence in a number of cases and that he wanted to retract his statements. Among the cases Day claimed he had been asked to help with was that of alleged innocent Michael Stone, who was convicted of the murder of Lin and Megan Russell in Kent in 1996 (see Cookson, 2008; Cookson and Campbell, 2006).

False witness testimonies

In addition to coercing suspects into making false confessions as in the cases cited above, witnesses for the prosecution have been known to perjure themselves and give false testimonies that contribute to abortions of justice.

The Perjury Act 1911, s. 1, as amended by the Criminal Justice Act 1948, states that:

> If any person lawfully sworn as a witness or as an interpreter in a judicial proceeding wilfully makes a statement material in that proceeding, which he knows to be false or does not believe to be true, he shall be guilty of perjury, and shall, on conviction thereof on indictment, be liable to penal servitude for a term not exceeding seven years, or to imprisonment for a term not exceeding two years, or to a fine or to both such penal servitude or imprisonment and fine.

In terms of the likely scale of the problem, Soothill *et al.* (2004) found that between 1979 and 2001 4,354 males and 936 females were convicted at least once for perjury, which equates to an average of around 240 convictions per year over the period.

As perjury relates to this discussion of abortions of justice that are evidenced by successful appeals, Michael Watson (2005: 548) argued that it is a serious crime that can lead to the conviction of the innocent. A notable example in the area of successful appeals is the Scottish case of Billy Love who was convicted of perjury and was given a six-year custodial sentence in 1998 for lying under oath and causing Thomas 'T. C.' Campbell and Joseph Steele to spend 17 years in prison (see also Seenan, 2001; Watson, 2002).

More recently, three witnesses, Mark Grommek, Leanne Vilday and Angela Psaila, were imprisoned for 18 months each in 2008 for committing perjury during the trial of the Cardiff Three. It was their testimonies that led to the convictions of the three factually innocent men, Stephen Miller, Tony Paris and Yusuf Abdullahi, for the murder of Miller's girlfriend, Lynette White.

The case is not straightforward, however, in that it was accepted by the prosecution at trial that Grommek, Vilday and Psaila were subjected to the same kind of treatment at the hands of South Wales Police officers that the Cardiff Three had been and that they had been coerced into lying. The tactics used by the police to extract a confession from Miller over five days and some 13 hours of interrogation were brutal, described in the successful appeal judgment of the Cardiff Three by Taylor LCJ in the following terms:

> Short of physical violence, it is hard to conceive of a more hostile and intimidating approach by officers to a suspect. It is impossible to convey on the printed page the pace, force and menace of the officer's delivery. (R v Paris, Abdullahi and Miller, p. 103)

It is also significant that Vilday and Psaila, who were prostitutes at the time, were both acknowledged by the court as having been vulnerable. Vilday had been threatened with jail and losing custody of her young child if she failed to give the police the evidence that they wanted. Psaila claimed that she was 'treated like an animal' when she was interviewed:

> It was disgusting what they did to me. The police knew what they were doing. I felt like a dog being beaten. When I asked to leave [Butetown police station] they said 'no'. When I asked for a solicitor they said 'no'. I didn't feel I could argue with these men. I had no choice … I said to myself, 'You had better do what you are told to do'. (BBC News, 2011a)

As for Grommek, he claimed that Detective Inspector Richard Powell had thrown a chair during an interview and threatened him with a 'blanket job', meaning that he would be beaten with a blanket over him so that the marks would not show. He also claimed that he was threatened with false imprisonment and that the threats and intimidation weakened his will. He claimed that he had no choice but to falsely implicate the Cardiff Three: 'I really think I was on the verge of a nervous breakdown' (Grommek, cited in Sekar, 2008).

In light of the foregoing, the defendants argued for a defence of duress, which would be a full defence to the charge of perjury if successful and the three would have been acquitted. This was denied on the basis that a defence of duress, which is available for all criminal offences except murder, would require the three to show that the threats that they experienced were death or serious injury and that they believed that the threats would be carried out immediately or imminently (Ashworth, 2003: 221–231).

In sentencing the three, Maddison J highlighted the severity of the offence of perjury saying that it 'strikes at the heart of the criminal justice system' and although he also accepted that the behaviour of the police had been of a nature that is 'unacceptable in a civilised society', he ruled that they had nevertheless had ample opportunity to tell the truth, if not to police, then to officers of the court (Maddison, cited in Hirsch and Sekar, 2008; see also, BBC News, 2011b; Sekar, 2008).

Forensic science expert witnesses

Another known cause of abortions of justice from successful appeal cases that also needs to be included in critical analyses is the problem of forensic science expert witnesses who knowingly fail to disclose evidence in favour of an accused, fabricate evidence against an accused or present their evidence in ways that assists the police and/or prosecution in obtaining criminal convictions.

As this relates to the US, Brandon Garrett and Peter Neufeld (2009: 77–79) conducted the first study to analyse the forensic science testimony by prosecution experts in the trials of factually innocent persons, all convicted of serious crimes, who were later exonerated by post-conviction DNA testing. They found that in 13 of the 137 cases reviewed there was either a failure to disclose exculpatory data or analysis, or an outright fabrication of forensic evidence. Examples included withholding laboratory reports, analysis or the existence of further evidence. Other cases involved fabrication, including falsifying or altering laboratory reports.

A high-profile example in the US is Fred Zain, a police chemist whose expert testimony and laboratory tests helped to convict scores of alleged rapists and murderers in two states, West Virginia and Texas, over a 13-year period from 1980. Concerns about Zain's work first emerged publicly in 1992, when tests he had performed five years earlier featured prominently in the quashing of two rape convictions against Glen Woodall when DNA proved that he was factually innocent. He had served 4.5 years in prison of the two life sentences, plus 203 to 335 years that he had been given (see Innocence Project, 2010: 3). Other abortions of justice to factually innocent individuals caused by Zain include Gilbert Alejandro who served 3.5 years in prison, William O'Dell Harris who served 7 years, Gerald Davis who served 8 years and James Richardson who served 9 years (Innocence Project, 2007).

This prompted an investigation by the West Virginia Supreme Court following a petition from William Forbes, Prosecuting Attorney for Kanawha County, requesting whether habeas corpus relief should be granted to prisoners whose convictions were obtained through Zain's wilful false testimony. The Report, which found that Zain had a long history of falsifying evidence in criminal prosecutions, states:

> The acts of misconduct on the part of Zain included (1) overstating the strength of results; (2) overstating the frequency of genetic matches on individual pieces of evidence; (3) misreporting the frequency of genetic matches on multiple pieces of evidence; (4) reporting that multiple items had been tested, when only a single item had been tested; (5) reporting inconclusive results as conclusive; (6) repeatedly altering laboratory records; (7) grouping results to create the erroneous impression that genetic markers had been obtained from all samples tested; (8) failing to report conflicting results; (9) failing to conduct or to report conducting additional testing to resolve conflicting results; (10) implying a match with a suspect when testing supported only a match with the victim; and (11) reporting scientifically impossible or improbable results. (West Virginia Supreme Court, 1993)

The Report concluded that these 'irregularities' were the result of systematic practice rather than an occasional inadvertent error and discussed specific cases that were prosecuted in which Zain gave scientifically inaccurate, invalid or false testimony. Finally, the Report discussed criticisms of Zain's procedural failings, which included:

> (1) no written documentation of testing methodology; (2) no written quality assurance program; (3) no written internal or external auditing procedures; (4) no routine proficiency testing of laboratory technicians; (5) no technical review of work product; (6) no written documentation of instrument maintenance and calibration; (7) no written testing procedures manual; (8) failure to follow generally-accepted scientific testing standards with respect to certain tests; (9) inadequate record-keeping; and (10) failure to conduct collateral testing. (West Virginia Supreme Court, 1993)

Asked why he thought Zain did what he did, Jack Buckalew (cited in Chan, 1994), a former superintendent of the West Virginia State Police, was reported as saying: 'The only possible reason I can speculate on is to enhance his status with prosecutors by saying what he thought they wanted him to say.'

A notorious example in the British context is the Home Office forensic scientist, Dr Frank Skuse, who will for ever be immortalised in the annals of judicial infamy for the part that his evidence played in helping to secure the convictions of the Birmingham Six and Judith Ward (see for instance, Peirce, 2011; Hill and Hunt, 1995: 129–132). Skuse declared that he was 99 per cent certain that Paddy Hill and Billy Power of the Birmingham Six had been handling explosives based on results he had obtained from Griess tests. He retained this view even though the more sophisticated gas chromatography multiple spectrometry (GCMS) tests that he later carried out were negative for Power and contradicted the initial results from the Griess tests for Hill (see Woffinden, 1987: 284–285).

We now know that the Griess test on which Skuse based his near certainty that Power and Hill had been in contact with IRA bombs is merely a preliminary test. It produces the same results for nitroglycerine as an innocent compound such as nitrocellulose. That is, a person handling playing cards or even certain types of soap could give the same readings as someone who had been handing explosives (see R v McIlkenney and Others; Hilliard, 1990: 160). Judith Ward's successful appeal, which quickly followed the quashing of the Birmingham Six convictions, noted further how the Griess test that Skuse had used to link her to IRA bombs was 'valueless', as it could also have given a positive result for black shoe polish as well as other household products (see R v Ward).

In a debate in the House of Commons in 1988 when the Birmingham Six were still imprisoned and the campaign for their release was at its height, Chris Mullin, who revealed the truth of the Birmingham bombings in his book (Mullin, 1986) and who was by now MP for Sunderland South, was adamant that Skuse should not be seen as an incompetent scientist who had made an honest mistake. Firmly implicating Skuse as playing a vital part in the abortions of justice, Mullin said that Skuse had intentionally conspired with police officers to cover up the 'ferocious programme of violence' by West Midlands Serious Crime Squad detectives, which led to the extraction of false confessions that provided the additional evidence needed to secure the convictions (HC Deb, 1988).

In 1994, Skuse brought libel proceedings against a Granada *World in Action* television programme, 'Who Bombed Birmingham?', which aired in March 1985 (see Skuse v Granada Television Ltd; Mills, 1994a). The

Home Office had given him compulsory retirement at the age of 51 for 'limited efficiency' just days after the programme was shown (*New Scientist*, 1991). He claimed that it suggested that he had caused or contributed to the wrongful imprisonment of the Birmingham Six (see Tan, 1993). However, he later dropped his action claiming that the financial risks were too great. It was reported at the time that Skuse, who like Zain did not keep laboratory notes, abandoned his libel case following the failed attempts by forensic scientists representing both sides in the action to reproduce the tests which Skuse said he carried out. Ian McBride, producer of the 1985 *World in Action* programme, said at the time:

> We stand by our programme. We have not apologised to Dr Skuse or paid any damages or costs. We regard his withdrawal as a vindication of our programme. It was very unfortunate that this case raised doubts about the innocence of the Birmingham Six. (see Mills, 1994b)

Conclusion

At the Innocence Network UK (INUK) symposium on the reform of the CCRC in March 2012 (see Innocence Network UK, 2012b), Paddy Joe Hill of the Birmingham Six recounted the following story of when he and Gerry Conlon of the Guildford Four met Maria Eagles, then Under-Secretary of State in the Ministry of Justice, and half a dozen or so other MPs, on 17 December 2007, in relation to the harm caused by wrongful convictions and the lack of aftercare services provided to victims:

> Maria Eagles came through the door and she walked up to me and Gerry Conlon and she put her arms around us and she hugged me and Gerry Conlon and she had tears in her eyes and she turned around and said to me and Gerry Conlon: 'I want to apologise to you two personally for what happened to you. I have just finished reading your files in the back room and I want to tell both of you now, you were not miscarriages of justice, you were something else.'

Maria Eagles may not have had the vocabulary to describe what she meant, but she was clearly trying to articulate that cases like the Guildford Four and the Birmingham Six are abortions of justice. Such cases are not synonymous with accidental miscarriages of justice that derive from the unintentional acts of criminal justice system agents working within the parameters of their statutory and regulatory guidelines.

Defined in the last chapter as abortions of justice, this chapter has looked at how such cases can be caused by actors both internal and external to the criminal justice process. Internally, the academic research literature and successful appeal cases have been utilised to show that police officers and prosecutors can show a total disregard for the presumption of innocence as they intentionally breach statutory safeguards and codes of conduct that are meant to protect against wrongful convictions. It was argued that they commit state crimes as they construct incriminating cases against suspects/defendants in the hope of obtaining convictions. Externally, the abolition of a duty on judges to warn juries of the dangers in finding guilt based on allegations of sexual offences that are not supported by other and more reliable forms of direct evidence was highlighted as a potential cause of abortions of justice. In addition, other forms of false witness testimony from prison informants, other prosecution witnesses, and from forensic science expert witnesses were also shown to be implicated in causing abortions of justice.

A common defence of abortions of justice is to individualise the cause: they are attributed to 'bad apple' police officers who act in unlawful ways to achieve some kind of personal reward; to individuals who make false allegations of a sexual offences for reasons of vengeance, to cover up an infidelity, embarrassment, compensation, and so on; to individual rogue forensic scientists who want to enhance their status; or with individual prosecution witnesses and prison informants who are vulnerable to police manipulation or who give false testimonies in return for the dropping of criminal charges, financial rewards, and so on.

In so doing, the underlying systemic causes of wrongful convictions are shielded and not subjected to critical evaluation. Yet, as the next chapter will show, the causes of both intentional abortions of justice and unintentional miscarriages of justice are systematic in a criminal justice system that allows inherently unreliable forms of evidence to be admissible in criminal trials, which facilitates miscarriages of justice even when no intentional wrongdoing or breach of due process occurs.

4
The Key Causes of Miscarriages of Justice

Introduction

The last chapter showed how abortions of justice are caused by intentional breaches of the safeguards that exist to try to protect against them by agents of the criminal justice system and by a variety of prosecution witnesses who give false testimonies for a range of reasons and motivations. As troubling as abortions of justice are, a 'positive' aspect is that if intentional breaches of the statutory and regulatory guidelines that govern the operations of the police and prosecution services can be shown to have occurred, then convictions are likely to be overturned. This is also true if witnesses can be shown to have given false or unreliable evidence against an accused. In line with this, all of the abortions-of-justice cases cited in the last chapter were successful on appeal.

This was argued to be intrinsically linked with the presumption of innocence, which is widely presumed by the public to be a key safeguard against wrongful convictions (see, for instance, Dennis, 2005). The discourse of the presumption of innocence implies that the overriding aim is an attempt to protect innocent people from being convicted even at the expense of guilty offenders escaping conviction for their crimes or having their convictions overturned if they are found to be in breach of process. This is the thrust of the oft quoted formulation from the famous eighteenth-century English jurist, Sir William Blackstone (1765–1769): 'It is better that ten guilty persons escape than that one innocent suffer.' The belief that the criminal justice system operates in this way is, arguably, even enhanced in public consciousness when the public becomes aware that convictions have been overturned, notwithstanding whether the successful appellants are factually innocent or guilty, because the prevailing procedures of the legal process were not adhered to. This notion is supposedly reinforced by the evidential burden placed firmly on the Crown (the state) to prove guilt beyond a reasonable doubt. In Woolmington v DPP (paragraphs 481–482), a leading legal authority on the presumption of innocence, Lord Sankey went so far as to describe the burden on the prosecution to prove the guilt of the accused beyond a reasonable doubt as a 'golden thread' that ran through the common law of England.

However, as Hamer (2011: 422) recently observed:

> If wrongful convictions were wholly unacceptable the criminal standard of proof would demand absolute certainty ... If absolute certainty were demanded there would be no convictions ... [so] ... in administering criminal justice, 'some risk of convicting the innocent must be run'. A standard below absolute certainty is ... [therefore] ... imposed.

The notion that a lower bar than absolute certainty of factual guilt is the pragmatic foundation of criminal trials would likely be acceptable to the general public who, correctly, see the main duty of the criminal justice system to apprehend criminal offenders so that they may be brought to justice. Yet, I would argue that accepting that wrongful convictions will occur provides a moral defence for them even before they have occurred, which gives a tacit legitimacy to the processes that cause them when they do.

Against this background, this chapter explores the police investigation and prosecution stages of the criminal justice process and the forms of evidence that are deemed to be admissible in criminal trials. It shows that unintentional miscarriages of justice can occur despite a theoretical presumption of innocence that is thought to protect against them. This is because the procedures of the criminal justice system facilitate police officers and prosecutors to construct entirely incriminating cases against suspects so that there is a high chance of obtaining convictions. In this process, defence lawyers are generally unable to provide robust assistance to their clients as they are reliant on forms of evidence that are constructed to imply that their clients are guilty. Moreover, to assist the criminal justice system to achieve its core goal of obtaining convictions against criminal offenders a legislative framework has been created that allows inherently unreliable forms of evidence to be admissible in criminal proceedings, which, in consequence, renders suspects/defendants vulnerable to wrongful convictions even when they are factually innocent.

As in the last chapter, this chapter is structured into two broad parts. First, the internal causes of miscarriages of justice are outlined through an analysis of the role and nature of police investigations, the role of the prosecution, and the part played by the defence in causing miscarriages of justice without direct intent and without breaching the prevailing procedures of the criminal justice process. Then the key external causes of miscarriages of justice are evaluated through an analysis of successful appeals that highlight the inherent fallibilities of forms of evidence that are deemed to be admissible in criminal trials.

Internal factors

Police investigations

The way in which police investigations can cause wrongful convictions is not limited to the kind of abortions-of-justice cases that were cited in the last chapter. It is not confined to where the police intentionally breached policing guidelines and codes of conduct that are supposed to act as safeguards against them, such as the guidelines that currently govern police investigations in England and Wales as contained in PACE. On the contrary, analyses of recent successful appeals demonstrate how normal and acceptable methods of police investigations render suspects vulnerable to wrongful convictions at the initial and most crucial stage of the criminal justice process when information is being gathered and cases are being constructed. These wrongful convictions are here termed 'miscarriages of justice' to denote that no individual intent is involved in causing the wrongful conviction and no police officers have done anything that can be said to be wrong from the perspective of police procedure and working practice.

Such miscarriages of justice are caused because the role of police investigations in our adversarial system is *not* to find evidence that suspects of crime are innocent. Rather, the police treat the situations that they are called to as potential crime scenes and seek evidence that might incriminate suspects of committing alleged criminal offences. Crucially, then, the police are not to be seen as impartial gatherers of evidence but, rather, as an integral part of a criminal justice system tasked with convicting potential offenders. To this end, the role of police officers is to construct evidence to pass on to the Crown Prosecution Service (CPS) to decide whether a criminal charge should be given and the suspect should be prosecuted. The more incriminating the evidence constructed by the police, the more likely it will be that prosecutors will decide that a charge should be made and a conviction will be obtained, and the more in line the criminal justice system will be with its primary goal of obtaining convictions (see, for instance, McConville *et al.*, 1991: 36–55).

For instance, in the successful appeal of Angela Cannings (see Cannings with Davies, 2006), the police investigation focused on constructing evidence that suggested that she murdered two of her children. It did not consider possible innocent explanations for why they may have died or why children generally die suddenly or in unexplained circumstances, such as Sudden Infant Death Syndrome (SIDS), or 'cot death' research (see, for instance, BUPA, 2010; Sweeney and Law, 2001). For Ken Norman (2001), the police in investigating such cases display what he termed 'lynch-mob syndrome' and 'dirty thinking', and come to see unexplained child deaths as possible murders – and investigate them as such – rather than family tragedies.

In specific terms, three of Angela Canning's children died in unexplained circumstances. The death of her first child, Gemma, in 1989 at the age of 13 weeks old was attributed to SIDS and she was never charged in connection with Gemma's death. The police investigation into the deaths of Angela Cannings' children, Jason and Matthew, who died of unexplained causes at approximately 2 months and 5 months old respectively, did not find any direct evidence that conclusively proved that she had murdered them. Instead, it was directed at a character assassination that tried to incriminate her through an interrogation of the kind of person, mother, wife, woman that she was/is, asking questions about whether she had had a happy childhood, about her relationship with her family, how she and her husband got along, about her ex-boyfriends, how she felt about her dead children, and so on (see Cannings with Davies, 2006: 47). The eventual case for the prosecution that was constructed by the police was based on the circumstantial evidence that she was always alone when her children died and that her general behaviour after they had died suggested that she was guilty. To support this latter hypothesis, a health visitor testified about her 'suspicious' actions when she had resuscitated Jason and reference was made to how she had phoned her husband instead of an ambulance when Matthew had died. The case against Cannings was reinforced by the expert testimony of the now infamous Professor Sir Roy Meadow (discussed further below) who was confident that Jason and Matthew had been smothered by their mother (see Cannings with Davies, 2006: 129–131). In effect, this meant that she was regarded as guilty and was expected to prove that she had not murdered her children, something that was impossible to prove.

Normally, miscarriages of justice are cases in which the wrong person is convicted for a crime that someone else committed. The problem for Cannings, as for all such suspects in such cases, is that she was charged and convicted for a crime, in this case the murder of her children, when no crime may have actually occurred (for a discussion, see Naughton, 2005c: 8–9). As Michael Mansfield (2006: ix–x) put it, such cases are not so much a 'who dunnit' as a 'what dunnit'. Until the cause of SIDS/'cot death' is established, which is the single largest category of infant death for those under 12 months old, there is a need to guard against assumptions that such children are victims of murder.

This was confirmed in the landmark successful appeal judgment that quashed Angela Cannings' convictions by Judge LJ in the following terms:

> We recognise that the occurrence of three sudden and unexpected infant deaths in the same family is very rare, or very rare indeed, and therefore demands an investigation into their causes. Nevertheless the fact that such deaths have occurred does not identify, let alone prescribe, the deliberate infliction of harm as the cause of death. Throughout the process great care must be taken not to allow the rarity of these sad events, standing on their own, to be subsumed into an assumption or virtual assumption that the dead infants were deliberately killed, or consciously or unconsciously to regard the inability of the defendant to produce some convincing explanation for these deaths as providing a measure of support for the Prosecution's case. If on examination of all the evidence every possible known cause has been excluded, the cause remains unknown ... With unexplained infant deaths, however, as this judgment has demonstrated, in many important respects we are still at the frontiers of knowledge. Necessarily, further research is needed, and fortunately, thanks to the dedication of the medical profession, it is continuing. All this suggests that, for the time being, where a full investigation into two or more sudden unexplained infant deaths in the same family is followed ... the prosecution of a parent or parents for murder should not be started, or continued, unless there is additional cogent evidence, extraneous to the expert evidence ... which tends to support the conclusion that the infant, or where there is more than one death, one of the infants, was deliberately harmed. (R v Cannings, paragraphs 177–178)

Firmly grounding Cannings' successful appeal within the presumption of innocence, Judge LJ concluded as follows:

In expressing ourselves in this way we recognise that justice may not be done in a small number of cases where in truth a mother has deliberately killed her baby without leaving any identifiable evidence of the crime. That is an undesirable result, which however avoids a worse one. If murder cannot be proved, the conviction cannot be safe. In a criminal case, it is simply not enough to be able to establish even a high probability of guilt. Unless we are sure of guilt the dreadful possibility always remains that a mother, already brutally scarred by the unexplained death or deaths of her babies, may find herself in prison for life for killing them when she should not be there at all. In our community, and in any civilised community, that is abhorrent. (R v Cannings, paragraph 179)

Despite this, the approach of the police investigation into Angela Cannings is not unusual or peculiar to the phenomenon of unexplained child deaths. It is also apparent in other successful appeal cases too. For instance, Barry George spent seven years in prison for the shooting and murder of television presenter Jill Dando on the doorstep of her Fulham flat in south-west London in April 1999 (see R v Barry George; Boggan, 2001; Hopkins and Morris, 2001). The only alleged physical evidence linking George to the murder was a single particle of firearm discharge residue (FDR) that was alleged to have been found in the inside right-hand pocket of an overcoat found in his flat a year after the murder. This was seen to be compelling proof of his guilt. But the particle matched those found on the victim only in that they were composed of the same elements. As such, an objective investigation should have been alive to the reality that it meant only that the particle in the jacket came from a source of powder that was of the same type as that found in the murder weapon cartridge. Crucially, this does not prove that the particle came from the murder weapon. In fact, it transpired that it could have come from any one of the estimated 230 million gun cartridges that sold in the UK in the year that Jill Dando was murdered (BBC Press Office, 2007). It is also possible that the particle could have come from a blank firing gun, a firework, an army surplus shop that George had visited when he tried to join a gun club, or, most likely given that it was single particle that was found, from contamination in the forensic laboratory (see Lomax, 2003; BBC News, 2007; Laville, 2007). At his appeal in November 2007, the speck of FDR was accepted as having 'no probative value'. On this basis, his conviction was quashed and a retrial was ordered. He was later acquitted at a retrial in August 2008.

What is perhaps more relevant for this discussion is not the inculpatory limits of the forensic evidence against Barry George, but the way that the police embarked on what can only be described as a 'suspect-led policing' operation, focusing entirely on actively manufacturing an incriminating case against him with circumstantial evidence to increase the possibility of obtaining a conviction. Having identified George as a 'loner' and 'misfit' who lived near to the crime scene, he almost inevitably became a potential suspect in the eyes of the police. To establish a motive, they trawled through 800 newspapers that George hoarded at his flat and found eight stories relating to Ms. Dando, which they then presented as evidence of his 'obsession' with her (see Bloxham, 2008). To establish that Barry George was capable of carrying out the shooting, reference was made to him joining the Territorial Army almost 20 years earlier, although he left the following year before completing his basic training. Reference was also made to gun magazines and books on firearms found at his home, also dating from the 1980s (see Lomax, 2003).

Eamonn O'Neill's (2010) analysis seems apposite in explaining the psychological reasons why police officers construct cases in this way. As he argued, we tend to see what we are looking for, what we want to see, and as this relates to police investigations they often work from an approach that he termed 'hypothesis in'. That is, finding evidence to support a predetermined hypothesis of guilt, rather than from the 'facts out', i.e. neutrally assessing the evidence to ascertain what might have occurred (O'Neill, 2010: 6).

This phenomenon is well established in wrongful conviction studies and is commonly termed 'tunnel vision'. In an extensive analysis in the context of the United States, Findlay and Scott (2006: 292) defined tunnel vision as follows:

> Tunnel vision is a natural human tendency that has particularly pernicious effects in the criminal justice system. By tunnel vision, we mean that 'compendium of common heuristics and logical fallacies', to which we are all susceptible, that lead actors in the criminal justice system to 'focus on a suspect, select and filter the evidence that will "build a case" for conviction, while ignoring or suppressing evidence that points away from guilt'. This process leads investigators, prosecutors, judges, and defense lawyers alike to focus on a particular conclusion and then filter all evidence in a case through the lens provided by that conclusion. Through that filter, all information supporting the adopted conclusion is elevated in significance, viewed as

consistent with the other evidence, and deemed relevant and probative. Evidence inconsistent with the chosen theory is easily overlooked or dismissed as irrelevant, incredible, or unreliable. Properly understood, tunnel vision is more often the product of the human condition as well as institutional and cultural pressures, than of maliciousness or indifference.

As this relates to the aforementioned cases, instead of objective fact-finding investigations the police actively trawled for (and found) circumstantial evidence to link Barry George to the murder of Jill Dando, and to depict Angela Cannings as a 'bad mother' to support the hypothesis that she had, indeed, killed their own children. Yet the way in which the police investigated the deaths of Angela Cannings' children and Jill Dando's murder to help to secure the convictions was entirely legitimate. No police officers did anything contrary to normal routine policing: they did not put guns into people's mouths or beat them up for confessions (as in the cases of the Guildford Four and the Birmingham Six); they did not put plastic bags over their heads (as in the case of Keith Twitchell); nor they did not do deals with criminals to obtain incriminating testimonies against suspects (as in the cases of Dudley and Maynard). Nonetheless, such methods are responsible for causing miscarriages of justice as the working hypothesis was to presume guilt at the beginning of the process and the entire investigation focused on constructing a case against the suspects to substantiate (prove) that hypothesis.

Prosecution

To understand how prosecutors can cause miscarriages of justice without breaching their guidelines, a distinction needs to be made between the theory and practise of the presumption of innocence in the context of the adversarial system. In practice, the burden placed on the prosecution by the presumption of innocence seems at odds with the adversarial tension with the defence and the wish to win cases can take precedence over the need to ensure substantive justice in the lay sense (see, for instance, McConville *et al.*, 1991). Indeed, a burden is generally not a good thing. It is defined by the *OED* (2012) as: 'a load, typically a heavy one'; 'a duty or misfortune that causes worry, hardship or distress'. To ease the 'misfortune' on the prosecution to thoroughly prove its case, a legislative framework favourable to facilitate obtaining convictions can be conceived to have been created in response to the supposed obstacles of the presumption of innocence. This is further bolstered by political discourses calling for statutory changes to increase the possibility and number of criminal convictions.

This relates to the dominant criminal justice system discourse on the need to 'rebalance' it from start to finish as, in the words of the then Prime Minister, Tony Blair, 'it's perhaps the biggest miscarriage of justice in today's system when the guilty walk away unpunished' (Blair, 2002). This led to a raft of reforms aimed at reforming what was termed a nineteenth-century criminal justice system that is not fit for twenty-first-century crime problems (for a critical discussion, see Naughton, 2005d). For instance, long-standing safeguards against wrongful convictions were removed by the Criminal Justice Act 2003. These include the introduction of 'hearsay' evidence under ss. 114–124 of the Criminal Justice Act 2003. This applies where a witness testifies that she/he heard a matter stated that she/he believes to be true and the person who is claimed to have made the statement is not present in the court proceedings to give evidence directly. It also includes a widening of the channels in which 'bad character' evidence is admissible in criminal proceedings under ss. 98–101 of the Act, which can include not only the previous convictions of the defendant but also previous misconduct other than misconduct relating to the offence(s) charged.

In this context, it is clear that prosecutors do not need direct evidence, such as fingerprints, DNA, CCTV, eyewitness identification, confessions, and so on, linking defendants with alleged crimes to obtain convictions. Rather, the rules give an upper hand to the prosecution in the adversarial contest, allowing highly circumstantial and tenuous forms of evidence to be legally admissible and sufficient to be put before a jury.

This is supported by Doreen McBarnet's (1981b) study of 105 cases in the Sheriff and district courts of Glasgow which found that the legal procedures which guide the criminal process are essentially structured to produce convictions. To achieve this:

> The concept of 'proof beyond reasonable doubt' is thus redefined from the awesome heights of abstraction into pragmatic minimal standards that can be all too readily obtained. (McBarnet, 1981b: 15)

McBarnet's research further observed that:

> A wide range of prosecution evidence can be legally produced and presented, despite the rhetoric of a system geared overwhelmingly to

safeguards for the accused, precisely because legal structure, legal procedure, legal rulings, *not* legal rhetoric, governs the legitimate practice of criminal justice, and there is quite simply a distinct gap between the substance and the ideology of the law. (1981b: 155, original emphasis)

At the same time, this contextualises why police investigations build cases around circumstantial and inherently unreliable forms of evidence to incriminate suspects and assist the prosecution in obtaining convictions, absent any direct evidence linking them with the crimes alleged.

For Andrew Sanders (2002), this firmly locates the police as playing the dominant role vis-à-vis the CPS as the role of the CPS in reality is merely to review the quality of police cases on the basis of the evidence provided solely by the police. As he argued:

[In reality] … [c]ases being prosecuted are usually shaped to appear prosecutable; the facts to support this are selected, and those that do not are ignored, hidden or undermined. (2002: 158)

Moreover, for Sanders, in the context of an adversarial criminal justice system it is therefore not surprising that the CPS is often seen as a 'police prosecution agency' as it is effectively more of a 'decision *reverser*' rather than a 'decision *maker*' (2002: 158, original emphasis). Highlighting the difficulty that the CPS would have in its attempts to reverse the decisions made by the police, a body that it has a collaborative relationship with, Sanders (2002: 159) observed that this accounts for the development of what he termed 'prosecution momentum', which undermines the independence of the CPS, such that cases which otherwise would not go to court do.

Defence

In theory, the defendant in a criminal trial has a defence team to fight their corner, representing what might be believed to be the greatest safeguard against wrongful convictions. Also, in theory, defence lawyers are depicted as combative, with a dominant discourse flowing from this view that they can be, and are, an impediment to justice as they assist guilty offenders to be acquitted and escape their punishments. Yet the successful appeal case law and academic research suggests that they do not always provide as rigorous a service for their clients as they might. Taylor LCJ, for instance, highlighted the inadequacy of Stephen Miller's defence solicitor in the successful appeal judgment of the Cardiff Three in the following terms:

> [Miller's] solicitor was present to look after his interests. In our view … the solicitor appears to have been gravely at fault for sitting passively through this travesty of an interview.

Indicating that this could be a general problem, John Baldwin's (1992: 1762) analysis which he undertook for the RCCJ of 400 audio- and video-taped police interviews with suspects to determine what defence advisers actually did in police interview rooms found that:

> When one examines the tapes of interviews, one cannot fail to be struck by the general passivity of most legal representatives. They may or may not have given suspects forceful advice before an interview started, but the great majority said little, if anything, in the course of the interview itself. In three quarters of the interviews in which a legal adviser appeared, the role played was nominal or entirely silent. The video tapes show clearly that most advisers confined their involvement to passive note-taking and that active intervention in an interview was rare. Indeed, when a lawyer did intervene, it was as often to facilitate police questioning as to push a client's interests. On occasion it was even possible to see on the video conspiratorial nods being exchanged between lawyers and interviewers as the assistance offered was acknowledged. In a few cases, the legal adviser virtually played the role of a third interviewer, and one strange benefit of having interviews on video is that it reveals whether it is a police officer or a lawyer who is putting questions to a suspect. (see also Bridges and Hodgson (1995: 95), which found the quality of legal advice by non-solicitors was also questionable)

This links with another problem identified in the academic research literature, namely that defence lawyers are inclined to see their clients as guilty and pressure them into pleading guilty. The classic study on plea-bargaining in England and Wales is Baldwin and McConville's (1977) examination of Birmingham Crown Court and the pressures that defendants said that they were subjected to by their defence lawyers to plead guilty even though they claimed that they were innocent, may well have been innocent, and may well have been acquitted at trial. It found that the negative pressure exerted by counsel was a key factor in causing defendants who may be factually innocent to be fatalistic about their chances of an acquittal, which induced them to accept counsel's advice to plead guilty in the hope of obtaining a lower sentence (Baldwin and McConville, 1977: 70; for a wider discussion of the pros and cons of plea bargains, see Scott and Stuntz, 1992; Easterbrook, 1992).

Aogán Mulcahy's (1994) research built on Baldwin and McConville's (1977) research by examining the accounts which legal practitioners use to justify plea negotiations in magistrates' courts. His findings were based on in-depth, semi-structured interviews with 26 legal practitioners, which included seven defence solicitors, seven crown prosecutors, ten court clerks and two magistrates. A main finding was that legal practitioners largely view defendants as both morally culpable and substantively guilty. He found that this view was shared by court clerks whose duties include advising magistrates on points of law and safeguarding the rights of unrepresented defendants. He argued that it would not be possible for such criminal justice officials to negotiate guilty pleas in the way that they do if they did not first construct such negative images of defendants (Mulcahy, 1994: 414–426; see also, Choongh, 1997).

But, it is not only the passivity of defence lawyers and/or a general belief in the moral unworthiness and likelihood of guilt of their clients that accounts for the role that defence lawyers can play in causing miscarriages of justice. It is also linked to the forms of knowledge that are produced in criminal investigations and the limits of such forms of knowledge in terms of its ability in assisting defence lawyers to mount successful defences for their clients. The crucial factor is that evidence presented in a criminal trial is largely a product of the police investigation to prove the suspect, now defendant, guilty of an alleged crime. Knowledge produced by the police investigatory method seeking only to find and present evidence of possible guilt does not lend itself to defence attempts to prove innocence (for a detailed explanation of this thesis, see Green, 2008). It is simply not fit for defence purpose.

Whatever beliefs exist in the ability of the presumption of innocence to safeguard against miscarriages of justice, in reality the defence in the adversarial process has to work within the agenda, the pre-existing narrative, that has been constructed by the evidence collected by the police investigation and presented at trial by the prosecution. This renders the defence at a significant disadvantage. Without the resources to actively investigate cases for positive proof of their client's innocence they can be seen as trying to make the best of a bad lot. This situation is worsened by the recent major cuts to legal aid provision that so many alleged innocent victims of wrongful convictions are reliant upon (Law

Society, 2010). In response, defence lawyers strive to achieve the best outcome for their clients by employing strategies such as advising clients to give 'no comment' interviews to the police, despite the adverse inferences that can be drawn. Overall, defence lawyers often attempt to counter prosecution evidence at trial with little more than unsupported counter-arguments that the evidence presented is not beyond a reasonable doubt. Some defence lawyers even advise clients to plead guilty to receive a reduction in their sentence (McConville and Mirsky, 2005).

Despite this, it is widely believed that the requirement for the prosecution to prove guilt beyond a reasonable doubt sets a high evidential bar, protecting the innocent from being convicted. It is this belief that underpins the theory of the presumption of innocence; it renders suspects of crime passive, while cases are constructed against them; and it justifies minimal resources to the defence. The logic seems to be that the suspect/defendant/defence does not need resources when the burden is entirely on the prosecution to prove the case against the defendant.

External factors

Eyewitness identification

Eyewitness misidentification is the most common cause of wrongful convictions experienced by innocent victims in the United States. It features in over 75 per cent of the convictions which have subsequently been overturned through DNA testing by The Innocence Project, amounting to 300 cases at October 2012. These cases highlight that while eyewitness evidence can be persuasive in obtaining convictions such evidence is unreliable, particularly if it forms the main evidence against an accused. Further, the voluminous psychological research dating back decades (for instance, see Loftus, 1979; Wells and Loftus, 1984; 2003; Gudjonsson, 2005) shows that the human mind is not like a video recorder: we neither remember events exactly as we see them, nor recall them like a tape that has been rewound. On the contrary, witness memory, like any other evidence at a crime scene, must be preserved carefully and retrieved methodically, or it can be contaminated. The cases overturned by The Innocence Project (2012) include those in which:

- A witness who made an identification in a 'show-up' procedure from the back of a police car hundreds of feet away from the suspect in a poorly lit car park in the middle of the night.

- A witness in a rape case who was shown an array of photos where only one photo of the person police suspected was the perpetrator was marked with an 'R'.
- Witnesses who substantially changed their descriptions of alleged offenders, for instance including key information such as height, weight and presence of facial hair only after they learned more about a particular police suspect.
- Witnesses who only made an identification after multiple photo arrays or line-ups and then made hesitant identifications, for instance saying they 'thought' the person 'might be' the perpetrator, but at trial the jury was told the witnesses did not waver in identifying the suspect.

Against this background, it is not surprising that a major focus in the United States is to effect law reforms to guard against wrongful convictions that are caused by mistaken eyewitness identification evidence (see Scheck *et al.*, 2003: 352–354). However, on the face of it the kind of issues that arise in The Innocence Project cases should be largely absent in England and Wales. Indeed, the unreliability of eyewitness identification evidence has long been acknowledged as a cause of wrongful convictions in England and Wales and has had significant impacts on both shaping the criminal justice system and the development of procedures to try to safeguard against them.

The first significant moment was linked with the case of Adolf Beck (see Coates, 2001; also discussed in Chapter 1 of this book), a Norwegian immigrant who was twice wrongly convicted in 1896 and 1904 on mistaken eyewitness identification evidence. Beck was alleged to have swindled scores of women out of their jewellery and money. The crimes had actually been committed by a German with the surname Weiss who went by the name of John Smith and to whom Beck was said to have had an uncanny resemblance. In July 1904, Beck's innocence was accepted and he received free pardons for the offences (see Coates, 2001: 202–206).

The next defining moment in the history of the criminal justice system and eyewitness evidence was the Report of the Departmental Committee on Evidence of Identification in Criminal Cases in 1976. Chaired by Lord Patrick Devlin, the Devlin Report looked into the law and procedure relating to eyewitness identification in the light of the cases of Laszlo Zirag and Luke Dougherty, both of whom were victims of wrongful convictions caused by mistaken eyewitness evidence.

In brief, Virag was convicted in July 1969 of two offences of theft of parking meter coin boxes in Liverpool and for using a firearm to resist arrest for which he was sentenced to three years' imprisonment. He was also convicted of two offences of theft of parking meter coin boxes committed a few weeks later in Bristol and for wounding a police officer with intent to cause grievous bodily harm or resist arrest for which he was sentenced to seven years' imprisonment. The sentences were ordered to run consecutively, making ten years in total (HC Deb, 1974). The convictions were supported by the evidence of eight different eye-witnesses, five police officers and three other witnesses. However, it turned out that Virag was not the perpetrator of the Bristol offences when Roman Ohorodnyckyi, who went by the name of Georges Payen, was found in possession of the gun that had been used in the wounding of the police officer in Bristol and he duly confessed (see Bingham, 2000: 260; Bruce, 1998: 331). Interestingly, it transpired that Virag and Payen were not all that similar in appearance: Virag was 5 ft 10 inches while Payen was almost 6 ft tall; Virag's hair was dark and his eyes brown while Payen's hair was brown and his eyes green; Virag's hairline was described as full, Payen's as receding. In April 1974, when Virag's innocence was known for the Bristol offences, he was immediately released from prison by the Home Secretary and was later given a free pardon (Devlin, 1976: ch. 3; BBC News, 2005a).

As for Dougherty, he was convicted of shoplifting curtains in August 1972 from British Home Stores in Sunderland. He was convicted at Durham Crown Court in February 1973 and given a 15-month prison sentence. The evidence against Dougherty was identifications by two eyewitnesses, an assistant manager and a shop assistant, from police photo albums of known offenders. The police failures in the case of Dougherty were numerous. The photos were black and white so the police failed to see the disparity in the description by the shop workers that the alleged offender had ginger hair when Dougherty's hair was black. The police also failed to notice other differences in the description that the shoplifter was around 55 years old, 5 ft 8 inches tall and wore glasses and the fact that Dougherty was aged 43, was 5 ft 5.5 inches tall and he did not wear glasses. The police also failed to verify his claimed alibi that he was on an outing at the seaside and/or to conduct an identification parade (HL Deb, 1974). He was released on bail in November 1973 after he had served nine months in prison. His conviction was quashed by the CACD in March 1974 in an uncontested appeal. The month before, the prosecution had decided not to challenge the appeal after the evidence from a number of alibi witnesses had been heard (see Devlin, 1976: 193–212; for a critical analysis of the Devlin Report, see Burton and Carlen, 1979: 88–103).

The main finding of the Devlin Committee (1976: 149) was to note that in cases that depend wholly or mainly on eyewitness evidence of identification there is a special risk of wrongful conviction. For that reason, its main recommendation was the introduction of a new statute that required trial judges:

(a) to direct the jury that it is not safe to convict upon eye-witness evidence unless the circumstances of the identification are exceptional or the eye-witness evidence is supported by substantial evidence of another sort;

(b) to indicate to the jury the circumstances, if any, which they might regard as supporting the identification; and

(c) if he is unable to indicate either such circumstances or such evidence, to direct the jury to return a verdict of not guilty. (Devlin, 1976: 149–150)

It was hoped that this would ensure that prosecutions would not be brought on eyewitness evidence alone and that if they are brought that they will fail on the basis that eyewitness identification evidence on its own is insufficiently reliable to find guilt (Devlin, 1976: 149–150).

The Devlin Committee's recommendation for a new statute to protect against wrongful convictions that are caused by mistaken eyewitness evidence did not materialise. However, the following year the CACD used the case of R v Turnbull to incorporate the findings and recommendations of the Devlin Committee into new common law rules to be followed by trial judges in guiding juries in cases which depend wholly or substantially on disputed eyewitness identification evidence. The case concerned Raymond Turnbull and Joseph Camelo who were convicted at the Newcastle-upon-Tyne Crown Court of conspiracy to commit burglary and were each sentenced by Smith J to three years' imprisonment. They appealed against conviction on the ground that the verdict of the jury was based upon the identification of Turnbull by a single detective constable who knew him previously, who was in a moving car looking across a road at night and who caught a glimpse of him as he momentarily turned his head (see R v Turnbull). Although Turnbull and Camelo were unsuccessful in the appeal, the case is the basis for the *Turnbull* direction and/or *Turnbull* warning which now has to be given in such cases. Widgery LCJ outlined the guidelines for judges as follows:

First, whenever the case against an accused depends wholly or substantially on the correctness of one or more identifications of the
accused which the defence alleges to be mistaken, the judge should
warn the jury of the special need for caution before convicting the
accused in reliance on the correctness of the identification or identifications. In addition he should instruct them as to the reason for the
need for such a warning and should make some reference to the possibility that a mistaken witness can be a convincing one and that a
number of such witnesses can all be mistaken. Provided this is done
in clear terms the judge need not use any particular form of words.
Second, the judge should direct the jury to examine closely the circumstances in which the identification by each witness came to be
made. How long did the witness have the accused under observation? At what distance? In what light? Was the observation impeded
in any way, as for example by passing traffic or a press of people? Had
the witness ever seen the accused before? How often? If only occa-
sionally, had he any special reason for remembering the accused?
How long elapsed between the original observation and the subsequent identification to the police? Was there any material discrepancy between the description of the accused given to the police by
the witness when first seen by them and his actual appearance? If in
any case, whether it is being dealt with summarily or on indictment,
the prosecution have reason to believe that there is such a material
discrepancy they should supply the accused or his legal advisers with
particulars of the description the police were first given. In all cases
if the accused asks to be given particulars of such descriptions, the
prosecution should supply them. Finally, he should remind the jury
of any specific weaknesses which had appeared in the identification
evidence. Recognition may be more reliable than identification of a
stranger; but even when the witness is purporting to recognise someone whom he knows, the jury should be reminded that mistakes in
recognition of close relatives and friends are sometimes made. All
these matters go to the quality of the identification evidence. If the
quality is good and remains good at the close of the accused's case
the danger of a mistaken identification is lessened, but the poorer the
quality, the greater the danger. In our judgment when the quality is
good, as for example when the identification is made after a long
period of observation, or in satisfactory conditions by a relative, a
neighbour, a close friend, a workmate and the like, the jury can safely be left to assess the value of the identifying evidence even though
there is no other evidence to support it: provided always, however,

that an adequate warning has been given about the special need for caution. Were the courts to adjudge otherwise, affronts to justice would frequently occur. (R v Turnbull, paragraphs 228–229)

The final landmark for the criminal justice system and eyewitness identification evidence was the introduction of extensive statutory procedures in PACE, Code D (which came into effect on 31 January 2008) on the methods used by police officers to identify people in connection with the investigation of alleged criminal offences and the keeping of accurate and reliable criminal records. Of the 56 pages of detailed guidance, Code D 1.2 makes it clear that the procedures are designed to protect against wrongful convictions by:

- testing the witness' ability to identify the person they saw on a previous occasion; and
- provide safeguards against mistaken identification.

The key safeguards contained in Code D which cover the general procedures to be adhered to in obtaining identifications by eyewitness include the requirement that an identification procedure (either by a video identification, an identification parade or a group identification) *must be held* if the suspect disputes being the person the witness claims to have seen (Code D 3.12). The exception is if it is not deemed to be practicable or it would serve no useful purpose in proving or disproving whether the suspect was involved in committing the offence. The example given in PACE, Code D is when it is not disputed that the suspect is already well known to the witness who claims to have seen them commit the crime. Further requirements are that records are made of the suspect's description as first given by a potential witness *before* the witness takes part in any identification procedures (Code D 3.1); if police staff accompany witnesses to a particular neighbourhood or place to see whether they can identify a person they must take care not to direct the witness' attention to any individual (Code D 3.2b) and they must record, in their pocketbook, the action taken in as much details as they can and as soon as possible (Code D 3.2e); where there is more than one witness, every effort should be made to keep them separate and witnesses should be taken to see whether they can identify a person independently (Code D 3.2c); and witnesses must not be shown photographs, computerised or artist's composite likenesses or similar likenesses or pictures, including 'E-fit' images, if the identity of the suspect is known to the police (Code D 3.3).

Despite the care that appears to have been taken to avoid mistaken eyewitness evidence causing wrongful convictions, both in terms of legislation and police practice, recent successful appeals shows that they have not been eradicated. Indeed, miscarriages of justice continue to be caused precisely because of unintentional breaches of formal procedures that must be complied with, notwithstanding the innocence or guilt of the successful appellants. Such miscarriages of justice can be caused by judges who unintentionally fail to give correct *Turnbull* warnings and police officers who unintentionally fail to comply with the complex labyrinth of procedures that now govern how they are required to obtain evidence from eyewitnesses so that it is accepted as admissible by the courts.

An example of a successful appeal due to a failure of the judge to issue the correct *Turnbull* warning is that of Kenneth Irvin who was convicted of attempted robbery in November 2006 at Blackfriars Crown Court. He was sentenced to a community order of 12 months with an unpaid work requirement of 300 hours and a provision that he pay £400 prosecution costs. The alleged victim, Mr Van Ta Ba, a takeaway delivery man, was followed by two men in the street at night; the taller of the two men grabbed the bag in Van Ta Ba's possession. After a struggle, the bag fell to the ground and the two ran away. In his initial police complaint, Van Ta Ba described the man who had grabbed his bag as 16 years old, about 6 ft 4 inches tall and wearing a black hood. He had also stated that he was unable to give any further details. The police had then taken Van Ta Ba in their car to see if the men could be found. From the car, Van Ta Ba identified Irwin in the street. Subsequent to this, and after Van Ta Ba had seen Irwin in police custody, he provided more details and described the man who attempted to rob him as being 17 to 20 years old, 6 ft tall and clad in a dark hooded coat with toggles. In quashing Irwin's conviction, Pill LJ found that the judge's summing up of the eyewitness identification evidence at trial was insufficient against the strict requirements of *Turnbull*: the judge should have given a specific direction about potential weaknesses in the identification evidence, referring in particular to Van Ta Ba's failure to give further particulars in his first report; the fact that Van Ta Ba had only guessed the offender's age; the absence of any mention of the toggle coat that Irwin was subsequently found to have been wearing; and the inconsistent account about Irwin's height (see R v Irwin).

In a similar case on its facts, Robert North was convicted for the robbery of a pizza delivery rider and sentenced to four years' imprisonment in November 2005. The victim alleged that late one evening he had been prevented from riding off by four men – two black and two white. The two in front, one black and one white, obstructed him, demanded money, struck his helmet, took everything out of his bag and ran away, as did the other two. He called the police and described the alleged white male in front of him as about 20 years old, wearing a grey hooded top. Within an hour, he was being driven around by the police to look for his attackers. At trial, there was some inconsistency between his own memory as to whether he had in the course of that journey seen and recognised his alleged white attacker in the park, which was a rather dark area, or whether he had not at that stage pointed anyone out, which was the police's recollection. In any event, during his journey with the police he added to his description of his alleged white attacker that he was about 5 ft 8 inches tall, of slim build, short fair hair, with light bottoms and a grey top. At the successful appeal, Smith LJ noted that in *Turnbull* the prime example of a 'poor' identification was 'when it depends solely on a fleeting glance or on a longer observation made in difficult conditions'. In the instant case, it was dark, the victim was wearing his motorcycle helmet, he was surrounded by four other men and he was being robbed with some violence, including being struck on the helmet. The incident lasted but a few seconds. In those circumstances, it was ruled that the judge should then withdraw the case from the jury and direct them to acquit as there was no other evidence to support the correctness of the identification (see R v North; also R v Devlin, for another example of a successful appeal on the grounds that the evidence was poor and that the correct *Turnbull* warning should have been given).

A case that illustrates that breaches of PACE, Code D by police officers can lead to convictions being quashed is that of Joseph Quinn, convicted for a number of offences including two robberies at Norwich Crown Court in January 1992. He was sentenced to a total of 12 years in prison. Although there were no doubts of his guilt for one of the robberies, he appealed against his conviction for the other. For that robbery charge, the trial judge had accepted that there had been some breaches of Code D, but declined to exclude the identification evidence. However, Quinn's conviction for that robbery was overturned in March 1994 and his sentence reduced to six years. Taylor LCJ argued in the successful appeal judgment that the trial judge ought to have made a specific reference in his summing up to the breaches of the Code and left it to the jury to consider what their approach to the identifications should be in the light of the proved breaches. The CACD made it clear *per curium* that where a detailed regime is laid down in a Statutory Code it is not for the police to substitute their own procedures and rules: 'The Statutory Code is there to be observed and not to be varied at will' (R v Quinn, p. 481).

A final successful appeal example shows how strictly the failure by judges to give adequate *Turnbull* directions is taken by the CACD, even in cases where it is believed that child sex offenders may escape justice. Barry Stanton was convicted on two counts of indecent assault on two 12-year-old girls in a swimming pool at Worcester Crown Court in October 2003. He was sentenced to two concurrent terms of six months' imprisonment. For Waller LJ, the prosecution had a strong case, which is clear in the following extract from the successful appeal judgment:

> Clearly the prosecution had potentially a strong case with the combination of the girls' opportunity to see the offender, the small number of men in the pool, the distinctive swimming trunks and the presence of a teenage boy ... It was with some degree of hesitation that we allowed this appeal ... Had the judge directed the jury as we have held that he should have done, they would still have had ample evidence upon which to convict had they thought it right to do so. (R v Stanton, paragraphs 9–16)

Despite this, Stanton's convictions were quashed on the basis that the trial judge erred in not properly providing the jury with important aspects of the *Turnbull* warning in his summing up. The girls had effectively identified Stanton twice, first while swimming and then through the swimming pool door with the assistant manager when they had made their complaint. For Waller LJ, the jury should have been given a *Turnbull* warning for both identifications and not only for the first. He noted:

> Identification in circumstances such as these is a two stage process each with its well recognised dangers; were that not so, it is difficult to see why there are such elaborate rules and procedures for Identification Parades and other formal Identifications. In this case ... only an informal identification took place. It follows that any weakness and liability to error in that would require attention in just the same way as would relate to the original observations. (R v Stanton, paragraph 10)

Initially the CPS indicated that it may request a retrial. However, in a letter dated 25 February 2004 it notified the CACD that it would not be seeking a retrial, presumably because Stanton had already served his sentence (see R v Stanton, paragraph 17).

Voluntary confessions

False confession has featured in many high-profile successful appeal cases in England and Wales. In the previous chapters, examples were given of how police officers can be conceived as a key cause of abortions of justice that is internal to the criminal justice system when they use forms of physical force and torture to extract confessions from suspects to bolster the case against them. Cases cited included the Birmingham Six, Bridgewater Four, Robert Brown, Derek Treadaway and Keith Twitchell. However, the research over the last four decades shows that false confessions can also cause miscarriages of justice without any intentional physical coercion from police officers, particularly if the suspect is young or suffers from a psychological or personality disorder that makes them vulnerable to making false confessions. For instance, Brandon and Davies (1973: 49–65) conducted an analysis of Home Office pardons and referrals between 1950 and 1970, as well as material on individual cases of wrongful imprisonment provided by JUSTICE, the all-party law reform organisation. They offered three categories to account for why the innocent may admit to crimes that they did not commit: (1) the 'mentally retarded'; (2) the 'young'; (3) 'people with a psychological predisposition that makes them prone to make false confessions to crimes with which they have no connection'.

JUSTICE (1989: 15–16) then updated Brandon and Davies' (1973) research by drawing from their own case files to also discern three categories of false confessions that can cause unintentional miscarriages of justice as follows: (1) the 'voluntary group' who confess to notorious crimes because they want publicity or have fantasies about committing crime; (2) the 'guilt group' who want to be punished for a crime because they have general feelings of guilt about some aspect of their lives; (3) a range of 'coerced groups' who are essentially suggestible in personality or in a situation which they find intolerable.

In the intervening years, Gisli Gudjonsson's (2005) pioneering research into the measurement and application of interrogative suggestibility, psychological vulnerabilities and false confessions has become the principal source for the psychological reasons why suspects admit to committing crimes that they may not have committed. Perhaps most significantly, Gudjonsson (2005: ch. 18) outlined the leading successful appeal cases over the last two decades on the basis of psychological vulnerability. His analysis started with the successful appeal of Engin Raghip, one of three defendants convicted for the murder of PC Blakelock in the Tottenham Riots of 1985 (Gudjonsson, 2005: 458). He argued that the case was a landmark in disputed confession evidence. It widened the criteria for the admissibility of expert psychological evidence from restricted opinions on mental illness, learning disabilities, personality disorders, and the like, to the inclusion of personality traits (for example suggestibility, compliance, anxiety proneness, poor self-esteem, impulsivity, and so on) that fall outside the normal range but which render confessions unreliable (Gudjonsson, 2005: 458).

More specifically, Raghip was 19 at the time of his arrest. He had learning difficulties and was illiterate. He was interviewed over a period of five days and on ten separate occasions, lasting over 14 hours. There was no solicitor present. For Pearse *et al.* (1998: 3) his case is insightful of the harmful effect of prolonged police interrogation on suggestible individuals. 'Suggestibility' in this context is defined as the tendency of certain individuals to give in to leading questions and interrogative pressure (Pearse *et al.*, 1998: 3). Put simply, it relates to the tendency and extent to which individuals 'go along with' propositions either for gain or to avoid confrontation (see Bond-Kaplan, 1998). The suggestibility tests carried out on Raghip at the request of his defence team found that he had a profound inability to cope with interrogative pressure, which together with other identifiable psychological vulnerabilities persuaded the CACD to quash his conviction (see R v Silcott, Braithwaite and Raghip).

In all, Gudjonsson (2005: 458–513) cited the following 12 further high-profile successful appeal cases that have had a significant impact on the admissibility of psychological expert testimony in cases of disputed confessions. They illustrate the different types of psychological vulnerabilities that can cause individuals to confess to crimes that they did not commit:

1. Jacqueline Fletcher, who confessed to drowning her baby son, had her conviction quashed when the CACD accepted the expert evidence that found her to have 'unidentified borderline intelligence'.
2. Judith Ward's admission to IRA bombings that killed 12 people was accepted as unreliable by the CACD because of her 'personality disorder'.
3. David McKenzie pleaded guilty to the manslaughter through diminished responsibility of 76-year-old Barbara Pinder and 86-

year-old Henrietta Osbourne but his conviction was quashed when it was accepted by the CACD that he had an 'inability to distinguish between fact and fantasy'.

4. Idris Ali, convicted for the murder of 15-year-old Karen Price, had his conviction quashed by the CACD on the grounds that he was a 'pathological liar', although he was subsequently convicted of manslaughter in a retrial.

5. George Long's confession to the murder of 14-year-old Gary Wilson was deemed unreliable by the CACD and his conviction overturned because he had 'clinical depression' at the time of his confession.

6. Patrick Kane, convicted of the murder of two British soldiers by the IRA, was successful in appeal to the CACD after he was diagnosed as having 'anxiety and compliance disorders'.

7. Andrew Evans, who confessed to the murder of 14-year-old Judith Roberts, had his conviction overturned when the CACD accepted new expert testimony that at the time of his confession he was suffering from 'misdiagnosed psychogenic amnesia'.

8. John Roberts, convicted for the murder of Daniel Sands, had his conviction quashed on the basis of fresh expert evidence that he had 'abnormal compliance'.

9. Ashley King, who confessed to the murder of Margaret Greenwood, had his conviction overturned when fresh evidence convinced the CACD that his confession was unreliable because he suffered from 'abnormal suggestibility and compliance'.

10. Darren Hall, one of the Cardiff Newsagent Three, had his conviction overturned for the murder of Philip Saunders despite his confession to the murder on the ground that he had a 'disorder in the absence of psychiatric diagnosis'.

11. Ian Hay Gordon, who confessed to the murder of Patricia Curran, had his conviction quashed by the CACD when his confession was deemed to have been internally pressurised because he did not want it to be known that he was a homosexual, which psychologically transmits to an 'exploitation of his sexuality'.

12. Peter Fell, who confessed to the murders of Ann Lee and Margaret Johnson, had his convictions overturned when the CACD accepted the fresh expert evidence that he had made the confession because he was a depressed attention seeker who had 'poor self-esteem'.

Against this background, it may be surprising that successful appeal cases continue to reveal that miscarriages of justice that are caused by undiagnosed psychological vulnerabilities and a lack of vigilance on the propensity of vulnerable individuals to admit to crimes that they did not commit. Ian Lawless, for instance, was convicted of the murder of Alfred Wilkins at Kingston upon Hull Crown Court in February 2002 and given a life sentence. Three months before he was murdered, Wilkins had stood trial for, but had been acquitted of, the indecent assault of an 8-year-old girl. On 1 February 2001, two intruders broke into his home and attacked him. Then, early on 9 February 2001 petrol was poured through the letterbox of his home and ignited. As a result of the smoke from that fire Wilkins died (see R v Lawless). The evidence against Lawless amounted to various confessions to third parties, including regulars in a pub and a taxi driver. He said that he was the 'lookout' in the attack on Wilkins' home (see BBC News, 2009c). Lawless' conviction was overturned in June 2009, however, when the CACD heard fresh evidence from three reports by Gudjonsson and a report by Mrs Mechthild Jenkins, a consultant and chartered clinical psychologist who had been instructed by the prosecution. Jenkins, who largely concurred with Gudjonsson's assessment, summarised her position on Lawless' confession in the following terms, which persuaded the CACD to quash his conviction:

> The psychological assessment shows that Mr Lawless suffers with a pathological need for attention. His test-taking attitude showed a tendency of over-reporting psychopathology, which appears to be a 'cry for help' … the … assessment results show that Mr Lawless presents with severe psychopathology, including personality disorders. Mr Lawless' psychological difficulties appear to be very likely long-standing … It was concluded that Mr Lawless' alleged admissions could be false admissions as his psychological difficulties and need for attention might render him vulnerable to making false confessions. In view of this it is deemed unsafe to rely on his alleged self-incriminating admissions as sole proof for his involvement in the murder of Mr Wilkins. (R v Lawless, paragraph 32)

Forensic science and expert evidence

The use of forensic science or expert evidence is a growing form of evidence used by the police and the prosecution to gain convictions. This includes evidence such as DNA, fingerprints, fibres, cell site evidence, digital evidence obtained from computers, facial-mapping analysis, ballistics, voice recognition, and so on. It also includes evidence from a range of specialist experts such as pathologists, paediatricians, toxicologists, entomologists, odontologists, and the like. The 'CSI effect' can be defined as:

> [A]n alleged or supposed influence that watching television shows like *CSI: Crime Scene Investigation* have on juror decision-making during the workings of a criminal trial. (Kim *et al.*, 2009: 2; for an argument that the 'CSI effect' exists, see Thomas, 2006: 70–72; for an argument against, see Shelton, 2008: 1–7)

Despite the possible 'CSI effect' and the widespread belief in its reliability, all forms of forensic science evidence and expert witness testimonies are limited. In consequence, forensic science evidence and experts who give evidence in good faith are implicated in causing unintentional miscarriages of justice, as evident in successful appeals. By way of illustration, the remainder of this final section of this chapter looks, first, at successful appeals that illustrate the limitations of forms of forensic science evidence; then, at successful appeals that show some of the limitations of expert witnesses. Relevant research will also be cited to frame the analysis.

Successful appeals and forensic science evidence

Among the vast array of forensic science specialisms, fingerprint and DNA analysis stand out for the reliance placed on them by criminal investigations to reliably indentify criminal suspects. Yet even with these mature forensic science tools, successful appeals, research and 'near misses', defined here as factually innocent suspects who are accused and/or charged with criminal offences that they did not commit but who narrowly escape being convicted, show that great caution is required to avoid causing unintentional miscarriages of justice.

Hailed as the 'gold standard' in crime science for over a century, successful appeals and research have recently revealed the inherent weaknesses in fingerprint analysis. At the heart of this debate in the UK is the *McKie and Asbury* affair, which illustrated the inherent flaws of fingerprint evidence and how it can result in wrongful convictions. In January 1997, 51-year-old Marion Ross was found stabbed to death in her home in Kilmarnock, Scotland. Shirley McKie, a serving police constable at the time who was part of the investigation team was told by fingerprint experts that her thumbprint had been found on a doorframe at the scene of the murder, but she denied ever being inside the house where Marion Ross was murdered. McKie's refusal to accept that the thumbprint was hers was reported as angering her seniors at Strathclyde Police to the extent that she was charged with perjury (see Burrell, 2000).

The allegation that McKie left her fingerprint at the crime scene was subsequently disproved and she was acquitted of perjury at trial when two American experts, David Grieve and Pat Wertheim, testified categorically that the latent print definitely did not belong to her (see O'Neill, 2006). Latent fingerprints are prints which are not clearly visible. They are deposited when sweat and/or grease is transferred from the finger(s) to the object it comes into contact with, leaving an impression of the fingerprint ridges on the object (see Maltoni *et al.*, 2009: 62). The system of fingerprint identification came under further attack when David Asbury, who was convicted of the murder of Marion Ross, had his conviction overturned when expert evidence also testified that the finger mark on a tin found in his flat that was claimed to be the victim's was proved at the appeal to be entirely incorrect (see BBC News, 2002b).

This raises a pertinent question: how many other people like McKie and Asbury were wrongly accused or convicted because of the belief in the infallibility of fingerprint evidence? Dror *et al.* (2006) questioned the objectivity of fingerprint science. The principal finding was that fingerprint experts are subjective and do not always make consistent judgements on whether a print matches a mark at a crime scene when presented with the same evidence twice (see also, Cole, 1999, 2001, 2005; Epstein, 2002). Indeed, critiques of fingerprint evidence post the McKie and Asbury cases question the rigour of the inherently subjective interpretations made by fingerprint experts in their assessments, describing fingerprint expertise as more of an art than a science proper (see, for instance, Michael Mansfield, cited in Ross, 2006).

In March 2008, The Fingerprint Inquiry Scotland was established to look into the steps that were taken to identify and verify the fingerprints associated with the case of Shirley McKie and to make recommendations as to what measures might be introduced to ensure that any such future shortcomings be avoided. Of the 86 recommendations that were contained in its final report in December 2011 the overriding finding was that fingerprint evidence should be recognised as opinion evidence, not fact, and those involved in the criminal justice system need to assess it as such. As such, fingerprint examiners should no longer report their conclusions on identification or exclusion with a claim to 100 per cent certainty or on any other basis that suggests that fingerprint evidence is infallible. Moreover, the report recommended that fingerprint examiners should receive training which emphasises that their findings are based on personal opinion; and that this opinion is influenced by the quality of the materials that are examined, their ability to observe detail in mark and print reliably, the subjective interpretation of observed characteristics, the cogency of explanations for any differences and the subjective view of 'sufficiency' (see Fingerprint Inquiry Scotland, 2011: 740).

Quickly replacing fingerprints as the new 'gold standard' of forensic science identification, DNA testing has opened up the range of forensic material that can be utilised in the identification of criminal suspects. DNA profiles are obtained in forensic analyses by the identification of variations (known as alleles) within specific regions known as 'loci' within the human genome, which are then added to, or checked against a suspect or profiles already on the NDNAD (see Human Genome Project Information, 2009). Unlike fingerprint analysis, which is only applicable when fingerprints are found at a crime scene, or even blood group testing, which can be conducted only on samples containing blood, DNA testing can be conducted on a wider variety of crime scene exhibits – anything that could contain biological material. This enables criminal suspects to be identified from trace amounts of bodily fluids such as blood, semen or saliva, to minute quantities of skin cells and even a single strand of hair. However, like fingerprint evidence, DNA evidence is equally not foolproof. Therefore great caution is required to avoid causing unintentional miscarriages of justice (see Naughton and Tan, 2011; Gill, 2001).

Initially, a DNA profiling system known as Second Generation Multiplex (SGM) was used which measured six different Short Tandem Repeat (STR) loci to yield a DNA profile. This method of DNA profiling was claimed to have a match probability (i.e. the odds of two individuals sharing the same SGM profile) of 1 in many millions (see Goodwin *et al.*, 2007: 99). However, near-misses such as the case of Raymond Easton highlighted the fallibility of SGM. In 1999, Easton, from Swindon, was arrested for a burglary in Bolton, 200 miles from his home, after an SGM profile from DNA recovered from the scene of crime was found to match his (see Jeffries, 2006; Allen, 2006). Despite the fact that Easton had Parkinson's disease and could neither drive nor barely even dress himself, the police and prosecution were convinced of his guilt due to the apparent DNA 'match'. The charges against Easton were dropped, however, when his protestations of innocence, supported by strong alibi evidence, forced more rigorous DNA testing – a 10-point rather than a 6-point test in which the four additional loci did not match Easton's profile, exonerating him entirely of the crime (see Schiffer and Champod, 2008: 43).

Following Eason, the 6-locus SGM profiling system was replaced with a 10-locus profiling system known as SGM+ which is said to have discrimination potential beyond 1 in a billion, thus providing a surer statistical estimate (see Crown Prosecution Service, 2010b; for an argument that this does not mean that SGM+ is necessarily more reliable, see Jamieson, 2007: 22). However, not all DNA profiles recovered from crime scenes and loaded onto the NDNAD are full, SGM+ profiles from single sources. Often DNA samples are partial, degraded or mixed, and/or in very minute quantities requiring special testing techniques (see National DNA Database, 2006), which impacts on the reliability of what the profile actually means.

Low Copy Number (LCN) DNA is a specific form of Low Template analysis, which is a much more sensitive variation of SGM+. In conventional SGM+ analysis, 50–100 cells are required for there to be sufficient DNA to yield a profile. LCN, however, requires only 15–20 cells, allowing profiles to be yielded from miniscule amounts of biological material – such as skin cells or sweat residue from a single fingerprint on a variety of items which an offender may have touched or come into contact with (see Crown Prosecution Service, 2010c; Forensic Science Service, 2005).

The acquittal of Sean Hoey in 2007 revealed the unreliability of LCN DNA. In 2005, Hoey was charged for the car bomb attack allegedly carried out by the Real Irish Republican Army (RIRA) in Omagh, Northern Ireland, in the August of 1998 which killed 29 and injured 220 (BBC News, 1998b). It was claimed that there was an LCN DNA link between him and a number of exhibits recovered from crime scenes (see R v Hoey). At his successful appeal the evidence against Hoey was discredited by defence experts Professors Allan Jamieson and Dan Krane on the grounds that LCN DNA testing could yield distorted results and was highly susceptible to contamination (see Lotter, 2007). Weir J described the way in which exhibits were recorded and stored as 'thoroughly disorganised', with numerous exhibits either unlabelled or mislabelled, coupled with a lack of a uniform system of logging exhibits recovered from the crime scenes (R v Hoey, paragraph 51).

There is also a need for great care in the use of partial DNA profiles, which currently amount to around 50 per cent of all DNA profiles yielded from samples recovered from crime scenes (Crown Prosecution Service, 2010d). Such profiles are obtained from such small quantities and/or so degraded samples of biological material that neither SGM+ nor LCN DNA analyses is able to yield a full DNA profile. This is because they do not have the full ten loci of a complete SGM+ profile (see

Semikhodskii, 2007: 36–37). And although it is yet to be officially acknowledged in the form of acquittals in criminal trials or convictions overturned, partial DNA profiles are widely acknowledged to be questionable in criminal investigations (see House of Lords Constitution Committee, 2008; Woods and Foggo, 2008; Human Genetics Commission, 2008). The case of Raymond Easton discussed above provides a good illustration. Had the DNA profile obtained from the scene of the burglary that was claimed to have been Easton's been a partial profile that contained six or less STR markers (and assuming that LCN DNA testing could not produce a more complete or full profile), it would not have been possible to distinguish Easton's DNA profile from that found at the crime scene and he would in all likelihood have been convicted for a crime that he did not commit.

Another problem is that DNA samples obtained from crime scenes do not always originate from single sources and can contain a mixture of DNA samples belonging to more than one person. Despite the fact that there is no universal consensus on how mixed DNA profiles should be interpreted (see Gill *et al.*, 2006: 90), the National Policing Improvement Agency (NPIA), the body responsible for overseeing the NDNAD, gives the following description of how it processes mixed DNA profiles:

> If two people leave their DNA together at a crime scene, and this DNA is recovered, a mixed DNA profile may be obtained. There are strict rules for placing a person's DNA profile on the NDNAD, when it has been obtained from a mixture of DNA ... If you know the DNA profile of the person who has contributed to a mixed DNA profile, it may be possible for this DNA profile to be taken away from the mixed one, leaving the DNA profile of the other person. This may be possible in cases where both a victim's DNA and that of an assailant are mixed together. An elimination DNA profile from a victim can be sufficient to identify the DNA profile of an assailant. (National Policing Improvement Agency, 2010)

This oversimplifies the complexities involved in the interpretation of mixed DNA profiles. As mentioned above, DNA profiling compares alleles within specific loci. In a DNA sample from a single source, each marker/locus would contain two alleles, one inherited from each parent. A DNA mixture is identified when there are three or more alleles in a locus (see Mortera *et al.*, 2003: 191–192). However, as several individuals may share many alleles, it is difficult to say with absolute certainty just how many contributors there are in a mixed DNA profile (see Buckleton *et al.*, 2007: 20–28).

Allan Jamieson (2008a) illustrated the problem by highlighting that a mixed DNA profile of two individuals with the profiles AB and CD (notwithstanding that more than one person could share the same alleles) results in the mixed profile ABCD which could yield at least six different potential contributors: AB, CD, AC, BD, AD and BC. Jamieson (2008b) elaborated upon this by calculating that across ten loci (as in a standard SGM+ profile), with two alleles per contributor, there are over one million ways to interpret a mixture of two contributors. That is, a mixture of DNA from two people could produce a million possible profiles (Jamieson, 2008b: 1044–1045).

An example of a successful appeal against a conviction based on a mixed DNA profile is the US case of Timothy Durham. In 1993, Durham was convicted of the rape of an 11-year-old girl in Oklahoma and given a 3,000-year prison sentence. Despite 11 alibi witnesses who placed him in a different state at the time that the rape occurred, Durham was found guilty on the basis of the victim's eyewitness identification, a hair found at the crime scene claimed to be similar to his and most significantly a claimed DNA match between Durham and the semen stain recovered from the crime. After serving four years in prison, Durham's conviction was quashed after further analysis found that the laboratory had misinterpreted the DNA results. The victim's alleles, when combined with those of the true perpetrator, produced a mixed DNA profile which was mistaken as a single source profile matching that of Durham's (see Thompson *et al.*, 2003: 2).

A final problem that I will discuss here to highlight the need for caution in the use of DNA evidence to obtain criminal convictions is the problem of 'adventitious transference' or 'secondary transfer' (see Crown Prosecution Service, 2010d). This is where forensic material can be transmitted from a person who may not be associated with a crime, to the victim or crime scene, through ordinary interactions such as breathing, talking, sneezing and shedding skin and hair (see, for instance, Gill and Kirkham, 2004: 1; Lowe *et al.*, 2000). We all leave forensic trails behind us every day and DNA can be transferred just by brushing against another person, which can deposit our skin cells on that person. For instance, A and B can shake hands and A can leave her/his DNA on B's hand who then commits a crime and deposits A's DNA even when A did not commit the crime and/or has never visited the crime scene; or, A shakes hands with C who is later the victim of a crime and A's DNA is found. This second scenario was accepted by the jury in the prosecution against Shane Barnes who was acquitted for the murder of Kate Allen in New South Wales, Australia. Kate Allen's naked body was found in Illawarra, NSW, in February 2002. A black jacket and a white sports bra hid her face and underneath her body was a pair of trousers that had been turned inside out. Forensic testing found Barnes' DNA on Allen's bra but he was eliminated from DNA belonging to one or two unidentified men found on her trousers. The jury accepted Barnes' defence that he had met Kate Allen on the night of her murder and that his DNA must have come into contact with her bra through secondary transfer. Barnes argued that they must have shaken hands when they met which must have transferred a microscopic skin cell from his to Allen's hand, and from there onto her clothes (see O'Dwyer, 2004).

Successful appeals and expert witnesses

Before looking at successful appeal cases in England and Wales in which flawed expert witnesses have contributed to causing unintentional miscarriages of justice it is instructive to look at the role that expert witnesses play in criminal proceedings and the duties that experts have to the court. The rules governing the role of experts in criminal trials in England and Wales have been developed over the last two centuries in case law. It was established in the case of Folker v Chadd that experts, unlike any other witness in a criminal trial, do not need to restrict their evidence to factual matters but are entitled to give opinions to assist in resolving issues concerning matters of knowledge which can only be acquired by special training or experience (see Folker v Chadd). However, in the case of R v Silverlock in 1894 the court accepted a solicitor as a handwriting expert even though he had acquired his expertise as a hobby (see Shaw, 2009: 146). In so doing, the case defined expert evidence as any evidence of fact or opinion that the trial judge accepts as admissible by anyone possessing a degree of expertise beyond that of the ordinary person in the street (see R v Silverlock). This was clarified in the 1975 in R v Turner, which established the role of experts in criminal trials as being 'to assist the court or jury on matters where their ordinary, everyday experience does not enable them to adequately consider the issues in the case'. In clarifying expert knowledge outside of lay knowledge, Lawton LJ in *Turner* noted:

> The fact that an expert witness has impressive scientific qualifications does not by that fact alone make his opinions on matters of human nature and behaviour within the limits of normality any

more helpful than that of the jurors themselves; but there is a danger that they may think it does ... Jurors do not need psychiatrists to tell them how ordinary folk who are not suffering from any mental illness are likely to react to the stresses and strains of life. (at 841)

A further proviso is provided by the south Australian case of R v Bonython, which is applied by the CACD in England and Wales, that requires expert evidence to be 'sufficiently organised or recognised to be accepted as a reliable body of knowledge or experience' (see also, R v Hodges and Another; Ward, 2009). This was further clarified in R v Robb by Bingham LJ in the following terms:

> [T]he courts would not accept the evidence of an astrologer, a soothsayer, a witchdoctor or an amateur psychologist and might hesitate to receive evidence of attributed authorship based on stylometric analysis ... A defendant cannot be fairly asked to meet the evidence of opinion given by a quack, a charlatan or an amateur.

The general guidance on the duties of experts are laid down in the Criminal Procedure Rules, which determine the way a criminal case is managed as it progresses through the criminal courts in England and Wales (see Ministry of Justice, 2012a). More specifically, the duty on expert witnesses is that their opinions must be objective and unbiased. This duty overrides any obligation that experts may have to the prosecution or defence who appoints the expert and from whom the expert receives instructions or by whom they are paid. Experts are also obliged to inform all parties and the court if their opinion changes from that contained in any report provided for the court as evidence or given in a statement to the court (see Criminal Procedure Rules, 2011: 3.32).

Against this background, it is insightful to consider the case of the then highly distinguished expert paediatrician Professor Sir Roy Meadow who contributed to causing a number of unintentional miscarriages of justice by giving flawed opinion evidence in good faith. What became known as 'Meadow's law' completely reverses the presumption of innocence. It theorised that because unexplained child deaths or Sudden Infant Death Syndrome (SIDS) in a single family is a rare phenomenon and difficult to explain by natural causes, that one SIDS death is a tragedy, two is suspicious and three is murder unless there is proof to the contrary (Meadow, 1989; Moss, 2004).

More specifically, Professor Meadow testified at the trial of Sally Clark that the odds against her two children dying naturally was 73 million to 1, a figure derived by squaring the ratio of births to cot death in affluent non-smoking families such as the Clarks were (approximately 8,500:1). To help the jury better understand his point about how rare it was for two children to die of SIDS in the same middle-class family, Meadow posited that:

> [I]t's the chance of backing that long odds outsider at the Grand National, you know; let's say it's a 80 to 1 chance, you back the winner last year, then the next year there's another horse at 80 to 1 and it is still 80 to 1 and you back it again and it wins. Now here we're in a situation that, you know, to get to these odds of 73 million you've got to back that 1 in 80 chance four years running, so yes, you might be very, very lucky because each time it's just been a 1 in 80 chance and you know, you've happened to have won it, but the chance of it happening four years running we all know is extraordinarily unlikely. So it's the same with these deaths. You have to say two unlikely events have happened and together it's very, very, very unlikely. (R v Clark (Sally), paragraph 99)

The jury found his expert opinion persuasive and found Sally Clark guilty of infanticide. At Clark's successful appeal, however, contrary evidence by the Royal Statistical Society and other experts showed that the jury should have focused on the subtle difference between the odds that she was innocent (given the likelihood of two deaths in a family) not the odds for two deaths occurring in a family (given that she was innocent and it was not murder). Meadow's statistics were thus based on the so-called 'prosecutor's fallacy' (see Fenton and Neil, 2000: 180–187). Moreover, Meadow's calculation assumed that cot deaths within a single family were statistically independent factors related to a probability common to the entire affluent-non-smoking population. As such, he had not considered conditions specific to individual families, such as a theorised 'cot death' gene that is claimed to 'switch off' the immune system which might make some mothers/families more vulnerable to cot death and SIDS than others. Indeed, for Sweeney and Law (2001) that cot death/SIDS happen at all makes it likely that such conditions exist, meaning that the probability of subsequent cot deaths of children by the same mother, or within the same family, may thus be increased against the group average.

In July 2005, Meadow was struck off by the General Medical Council (GMC), following an inquiry that found him guilty of serious professional misconduct. He had strayed into areas that were outside of his remit of expertise by giving statistics-based evidence when he was not a statistician. Highlighting the problem of experts who continue to stand by their flawed opinion evidence that causes wrongful convictions, Meadow was remorseless and continued to defend his theory and the evidence that he gave. The GMC Fitness to Practise Panel considering Meadow's case accepted that he had not meant to mislead the jury in the Sally Clark trial, but found that public confidence in experts is vital and that was why he had to be struck off, rather than be given a lesser penalty (BBC News, 2005b; also, Persuad, 2005).

A year later, Meadow won an appeal at the High Court against the GMC decision and was reinstated on the medical register. Collins J explained that his reasoning for his decision was that Meadow had 'acted in good faith' and that expert witnesses should be 'immune' from prosecution or disciplinary action (see Batty, 2006). Moreover for Collins J, 'It may be proper to have criticised him [Meadow] for not disclosing his lack of expertise, but that does not justify a finding of serious professional misconduct' (see The General Medical Council v Professor Sir Roy Meadow; also Rozenberg, 2006).

A final twist to the saga is the report that Meadow voluntary gave up his status as Doctor/Professor in October 2009 after applying to have his name removed from the UK GMC Register amid allegations of further pending complaints against him and at the GMC and further cases awaiting appeals involving challenges to his evidence. For Blakemore Brown (2009), this meant that Meadow would not be subjected to further potential disciplinary proceedings by the GMC and, on the face of it, he retired with his professional reputation vindicated by his reinstatement onto the GMC register.

Another notable example is Dr Michael Heath, the now discredited Home Office forensic pathologist, who left a trail of poor practice in a plethora of successful appeals throughout the 1990s and early 2000s (see for instance, Sekar, 2009). He resigned from the Home Office register after being severely criticised by a disciplinary hearing in 2006. The hearing was due to reconvene on the Monday after Heath resigned from the Home Office register on the previous Friday and it is widely believed that it would have decided to strike him off the register had he not resigned from it first. In all, the Advisory Board for Forensic Pathology upheld 20 disciplinary charges against Heath, ruling that his conduct brought into question his fitness to practise (see BBC News, 2006d). For instance, the Advisory Board found that Heath was inept in the post-mortem examination of Jacqueline Tindsley that had caused her partner, Steven Puaca to be convicted of her murder in November 2002 at

Ipswich Crown Court and given a life sentence. At trial, the court heard that Tindsley, who had been found dead in bed one morning, had abused both prescription drugs and alcohol, and the post-mortem toxicological evidence showed that she had ingested alcohol, amitriptyline, dothiepin, dilhydrocodeine, codeine and probably diazepam. Puaca's version, and the defence case, was that he woke to find Tindsley dead beside him in the bed who had most likely died from a drug overdose. The prosecution case, based on Heath's theory, was Puaca had smothered the alleged victim while she slept by pressing her face into the bed-clothes so that she could not breathe. Heath's post-mortem report concluded (without having had access to the report of the forensic toxicologist, GP or other medical records) that death had been caused by asphyxia due to upper airway obstruction, indicating that Tindsley had been murdered by smothering. Heath gave no reasons to support his theory and pointed to no other possible cause. However, during his cross-examination at trial he did accept that the findings were consistent also with the cause of death being an overdose of drugs. The defence experts at trial also criticised a number of features of Heath's report and conclusions. This included his failure in reaching his conclusions to allude to the significance of the toxicological findings, his failure to refer to the absence of findings which would have provided support for his theory (including petechiae in the face and eyelids), and his failure to draw attention to the significance of the absence of any pathological indication that there had been a violent struggle. Puaca had his conviction overturned in November 2005. The CACD heard evidence from five further pathologists who did not support the contention that Tindsley had been suffocated and who strongly challenged Heath's analysis and conclusions (see R v Puaca). Three years later before a GMC hearing, and unlike Meadow, Heath admitted that his conduct in previous successful appeal cases was 'arrogant' and that he became his 'own judge and jury': 'At no stage did I seek help. I just carried on going in an arrogant way and that was wrong. It was not in the interests of justice and I can see that now. It has taken me some time to get there' (cited BBC News, 2009d).

The likely scale of the problem and reform attempts

No empirical evidence exists of the likely scale of the problem of flawed forensic science and expert witnesses and unintentional miscarriages of justice in England and Wales. However, we know that of the first 250 DNA exonerations in the United States approximately half of the wrongful convictions were caused by unvalidated or improperly used forensic science (Neufeld and Scheck, 2010). We also know from Garrett and Neufeld's (2009) study of 137 DNA exonerations in the United States that the problem is widespread. It showed that 82 factually innocent victims of wrongful convictions, or 60 per cent, were convicted because forensic science experts gave evidence that misstated empirical data or was not supported by empirical data. The 82 cases included invalid testimony by 72 forensic analysts called by the prosecution and employed by 52 laboratories, practices or hospitals from 25 states (see also Hampikian *et al.*, 2011; Giannelli, 2008).

In response to the growing awareness of the limitations of forms of forensic science evidence that are implicated in successful appeals, the United States Congress authorised the National Academy of Sciences (NAS) to undertake the most in-depth and extensive study anywhere in the world to date to investigate, assess and make recommendations upon the current state of the reliability of forensic science evidence (see National Academy of Sciences, 2009). The issues covered by NAS were comprehensive, including:

(a)   the fundamentals of the scientific method as applied to forensic practice – hypothesis generation and testing, falsifiability and replication, and peer review of scientific publications;

(b)   the assessment of forensic methods and technologies – the collection and analysis of forensic data; accuracy and error rates of forensic analyses; sources of potential bias and human error in interpretation by forensic experts; and proficiency testing of forensic experts;

(c)   infrastructure and needs for basic research and technology assessment in forensic science;

(d)   current training and education in forensic science;

(e)   the structure and operation of forensic science laboratories;

(f)   the structure and operation of the coroner and medical examiner systems;

(g)   budget, future needs, and priorities of the forensic science community and the coroner and medical examiner systems; and

(h)   the accreditation, certification, and licensing of forensic science operations, medical death investigation systems, and scientists. (National Academy of sciences, 2009: 3).

In the firing line were a whole array of crime science tools that are routinely utilised to assist in criminal prosecutions and obtain convictions, such a hair microscopy, handwriting analysis, bite-mark comparisons, fingerprint analysis, firearm testing and tool-mark analysis. Such forms of evidence are not based on firm scientific foundations but, rather, emerged in a pragmatic attempt to utilise emerging forms of science in the quest to bring criminals to justice. However, many forensic science techniques have not been subjected to rigorous experimental scrutiny, and there are no standards or oversight in the United States or elsewhere to ensure that validated, reliable forensic methods are used consistently (see Neufeld and Scheck 2010; Geddes, 2009). For Paul Giannelli (2008: 1), the paradox is that the most scientifically sound procedure – DNA analysis – is the most extensively regulated in the United States, while many forensic techniques with questionable scientific pedigrees go completely unregulated. In line with this, the main finding of the NAS Report was:

> Often in criminal prosecutions … forensic evidence is offered to support conclusions about 'individualization' (sometimes referred to as 'matching' a specimen to a particular individual or other source) or about classification of the source of the specimen into one of several categories. With the exception of nuclear DNA analysis, however, no forensic method has been rigorously shown to have the capacity to consistently, and with a high degree of certainty, demonstrate a connection between evidence and a specific individual or source … The simple reality is that the interpretation of forensic evidence is not always based on scientific studies to determine its validity. This is a serious problem. Although research has been done in some disciplines, there is a notable dearth of peer-reviewed, published studies establishing the scientific bases and validity of many forensic methods. (National Academy of Science, 2009: 7–8)

Although comparable research with that undertaken by the NAS has not been conducted in the jurisdiction of England and Wales, Wheate and Jamieson (2009: 23) observed its applicability to the use of forensic science evidence in criminal trials in England and Wales:

> The shared legal traditions of the United Kingdom and the United States of America provide an opportunity to compare the progress of forensic science as a tool used by the courts of law in both jurisdictions. The problems identified by the National Academy of Science, including the absence of peer-reviewed research, unsatisfactory validation of methods, techniques and interpretation, poor demonstration of reliability and accuracy, disparate accreditation

and certification standards, inconsistent reporting practices, the relationship between laboratories and police/prosecution services, potential bias and sources of human error, and inconsistent quality control are equally as pertinent in the United Kingdom. It is necessary to first address these issues, which go to the root of the scientific validity of forensic science, before the law can be entirely confident that expert scientific evidence is sound.

But this is not a novel problem that has recently emerged in our jurisdiction as flawed forensic science evidence is a long established feature of successful appeals that have prompted three governmental reviews over the last 20 years. In response to the challenge of successful appeals in abortion-of-justice cases such as the Birmingham Six, Guildford Four and Judith Ward, the RCCJ (see Royal Commission on Criminal Justice, 1993: ch. 9) and the House of Lords Select Committee on Science and Technology (see House of Lords, 1993) ran parallel inquiries that reported in 1993. Then, in response to the unintentional miscarriage-of-justice cases of Sally Clark and Angela Cannings the House of Commons Select Committee on Science and Technology inquiry reported in 2005 (see House of Commons, 2005). However, the problem with these three governmental reviews was that they shared a general failure to ask fundamental questions about the validity and/or reliability of forensic science evidence of the kind that were asked by the NAS inquiry. Instead, all three reports saw the wrongful convictions that were caused by flawed forensic science (intentional or unintentional) as not likely to be a significant problem in terms of numbers without any empirical evidence, concluding that improvements by various measures is all that is required to elevate the problem. The measures recommended included such things as better liaison between prosecution and defence, and better training for expert witnesses, lawyers and judges so that forensic science issues are better presented to juries.

More recently, the Law Commission responded to a call for reform from the House of Commons Science and Technology Committee by undertaking its own consultation to 'address the problems associated with the admissibility and understanding of expert evidence in criminal proceedings' (see Law Commission, 2009: 1). The impetus was continuing concerns that expert opinion evidence was being admitted in criminal proceedings too readily and with insufficient scrutiny, as shown in still further successful appeal cases.

However, as noted by Wheate and Jamieson (2009: 2), this approach differed from that of the NAS inquiry in that while the NAS asked fundamental questions of 'what is good science?' and 'how should it be applied in courts of law?', the Law Commission was focused more on the sole question of the legal admissibility of expert evidence. As such, Wheate and Jamieson (2009: 2) queried whether the failure of the Law Commission's 2009 consultation to focus on the underpinning reliability of forms of forensic science ultimately weakens any conclusions that it might draw about admissibility.

Despite this, the Report of the Law Commission's 2009 consultation robustly argued that the previous wrongful conviction cases involving unreliable expert opinion evidence adduced by the prosecution would almost certainly not have occurred if its recommendations had been in force at the time of those proceedings (see Law Commission, 2011: 1, 124–136). In particular, for the Law Commission (2011: 3) a statute is required that sets a new admissibility test for opinion evidence and replaces the existing common law approach which is, in its view, too *laissez-faire*, admitting such evidence without sufficient regard to whether or not it is sufficiently reliable to be considered by a jury. The arbiter of the proposed new statutory admissibility test for the Law Commission (2011: 137) would be trial judges who would be given 'a single list of generic factors to help them apply the reliability test' and who 'should be directed to take into consideration the factors which are relevant to the expert opinion evidence under consideration and any other factors he or she considers to be relevant'.

At the time of writing (July 2012), the Law Commission's (2011) recommendations have yet to be enshrined in statute. However, an obvious problem with the Law Commission's (2011) recommendations is that if they were to be implemented the problem of unintentional miscarriages of justice is likely to still remain as trial judges will still be left with the crucial task of determining the reliability and admissibility of the proposed evidence from a wide range of forensic science disciplines. Put simply, this is a task that all previous inquiries have shown they are not qualified to successfully undertake as the trial judges themselves do not possess the necessary expertise (see, for instance, Wilson, 2010).

Conclusion

This chapter has shown that suspects of crime and defendants in criminal trials are not only vulnerable to intentional abortions of justice as discussed in the last chapter but, also, to unintentional miscarriages of justice where no wrongdoing or breaches of due process occur. This is because the presumption of innocence and the burden of proof on the prosecution to prove its case beyond a reasonable doubt act in reality against the interests of suspects/defendants at every stage of the criminal justice process. The 'presumption', in effect, renders suspects of crime passive, which simultaneously justifies minimal resources to the defence, while the 'burden' places pressure on, and directs the bulk of the resources to, the police and prosecution to chip away at the presumed innocent status and construct cases from only incriminating evidence with a high chance of obtaining a conviction. As a result, the defence side of the adversarial equation, widely thought to be the key safeguard against wrongful convictions, is largely ineffectual as it is resource poor and reliant on police and prosecution evidence that is not suitable for defending against cases constructed from such evidence. Political discourses on the need to be 'tough on crime' assist further in overcoming the apparent resistance of the presumption of innocence by facilitating the creation of legislation that removes safeguards against wrongful convictions and renders admissible inherently unreliable forms of evidence so that criminal convictions are easier to obtain.

In this sense, another way of thinking about what have been defined here as unintentional miscarriages of justice is to widen the conceptualisation of abortions of justice and define them, instead, as 'systemic abortions of justice'. Indeed, the wrongful convictions discussed in this chapter are much more insidious as they do not require individual intent. Overall, there needs to be an ever present vigilance at the pretrial and trial stages on voluntary false confessions that can be made by vulnerable and suggestible suspects and on eyewitness and expert evidence given in good faith. Such ever present features of the criminal justice system that cause unintentional miscarriages of justice are more difficult to spot than abortions of justice that derive from intentional breaches of due process and for that reasons they are less likely to be overturned when they occur.

PART II

The Limits of the Criminal Justice System in Dealing with Claims of Innocence

5

The Parole Board

Introduction

The Parole Board for England and Wales was established in 1968 under the Criminal Justice Act 1967. It became an independent Executive Non-Departmental Public Body on 1 July 1996 under the Criminal Justice and Public Order Act 1994. It is remitted to work in 'partnership' with other agencies of the post-conviction system, namely prison and probation services, with the aim of protecting the public by conducting risk assessments on prisoners who are serving determinate sentences of four years or over and on all indeterminate sentenced prisoners. The Parole Board plays a vital role in the wrongful conviction problematic as it, generally, makes the decisions about whether such prisoners can be progressed through the prison system and be possibly released safely back into society (although following the judgment in the judicial review case of R (on the application of Guittard) v Secretary of State for Justice, the Secretary of State now has the authority in exceptional circumstances to progress some prisoners to open conditions without a reference to the Parole Board). I say 'possibly released' because there is no guarantee that prisoners who do not comply with the Parole Board's risk assessment process will ever be released (see Parole Board, 2011a, b).

To aid the Parole Board with its decision-making function, the prisoners that it decides upon are required to comply with tailor-made sentence plans, known as the Offender Assessment System (OASys) (see National Probation Service, 2003). These are produced by prison and probation staff based on the 'index offence', the offence for which the prisoner was convicted. OASys sentence plans stipulate the accredited offending behaviour programmes (OBPs) that must generally be undertaken for the prisoner to make progress through the prison system towards release. Successfully completed OBPs provide the main evidence to the Parole Board that the prisoner has reduced his or her risk of reoffending (see, for example, Hood and Shute, 2000a, b).

The Ministry of Justice website lists a current suite of 47 accredited OBPs that prisoners are required to take to 'examine the circumstances surrounding how they came to prison, to encourage them to learn from their mistakes and to prevent the chances of them re-offending' (Ministry of Justice, 2012b). One of the most frequently delivered OBPs over the last decade is 'Enhanced Thinking Skills' (ETS), a general programme which claims to address thinking and behaviour associated with offending. ETS includes such things as 'impulse control, flexible thinking, social perspective taking, values/moral reasoning, reasoning, and inter-personal problem solving' (Ministry of Justice, 2012b). In addition, prisoners who were convicted of a crime of a sexual nature, for instance, are required to undertake specific OBPs such as the range of Sex Offender Treatment Programmes (SOTP), which vary according to the deemed level of risk and the needs of the offender.

These programmes have come to dominate regimes within prisons in England and Wales since the mid-1990s. They are almost universally based on the work of cognitive psychologists in the correctional service of Canada. They work from the premise that as offenders 'think' differently to law-abiding citizens, once their 'cognitive distortions' are corrected then they can be released with a reduced risk of reoffending (Wilson, 2001). This thinking has been entirely embraced by the Parole Board and underpins its mode of risk assessment. It places prisoners maintaining innocence in a catch-22 situation that is commonly termed the 'parole deal' (see Hill, 2001): they must, generally, admit their guilt for criminal offences that they say they did not commit and complete the specified accredited OBPs listed on their OASys sentence plans to demonstrate a reduced risk of re-offending in order to make progress through the prison system and/or achieve release on parole (see also Woffinden, 2000; Samuels 2003; Naughton, 2004a, 2005a, c, 2006b, 2009d).

The parole deal first entered public consciousness when Stephen Downing successfully appealed against his conviction in January 2002 for the murder of Wendy Sewell (see R v Downing; Hale, 2002). Downing had served 27 years in prison maintaining his innocence until he had his conviction overturned. At the time, it was widely reported that if he had acknowledged guilt, confronted his offending behaviour and thus demonstrated a reduced risk of reoffending, he would more than likely have served around 12 years. It was also reported that during his imprisonment he was deprived of better jobs, training opportunities and parole consideration to put pressure on him to admit his guilt on the basis that he was – in the terminology of the Home Office – IDOM, 'in denial of murder' (Hill, 2002a). The possibility that he may have been innocent and therefore had no offending behaviour to confront and presented no risk of reoffending was not even considered by the Parole Board.

The successful appeal of Robert Brown (see R v Brown; Hopkins, 2002; Hill, 2002b) quickly followed the case of Downing. Brown had spent 25 years in prison maintaining his innocence, almost double the estimated time that he too might have served in prison had he acknowledged his guilt and complied with his sentence plan. His successful appeal raised further concerns that such cases were just the 'tip of the iceberg' of prisoners who may be innocent.

The parole deal, then, highlights a classic form of coercion by the criminal justice system, which is akin to plea-bargaining (see Baldwin and McConville, 1977, 1979; Henham, 1999: 515–524). Prisoners maintaining innocence are forced to confront their supposed offending behaviour (McCarthy, 2005b) or risk not being recommended for progression or release by the Parole Board at all (see Padfield, 2007). It is an inducement to prisoners maintaining innocence to accept that they are guilty and act accordingly. The other option for prisoners maintaining innocence is to remain in prison protesting their innocence, sometimes over a decade past tariff such as Downing and Brown, with the faint hope of overturning the conviction in the appeal courts.

For Peter Hill (2001), significantly both plea-bargaining and the parole deal offer the same essential 'deal' in an attempt to obtain judicial finality in cases: 'We say you are guilty. Admit it and you get something in return.' In a similar vein, David Wilson (2001), conceived the situation as one that political philosophers would describe as a 'throffer' – the combination of an offer or promise of a reward if a course of action is pursued, with a threat or penalty if this course of action is refused (see also Rhodes, 2000: 40–64, for a theoretical discussion of 'throffers' and 'neutral threats'). This unfolds with the prisoner being offered a huge range of incentives including more out-of-cell time, more visits and a speedy progress through the system if they comply with their sentence plans and undertake the required OBPs. This is made to appear as an entirely rational and subjective choice, especially as it will be the basis for ensuring early release through parole. At the same time, if the prisoner does not complete the accredited OBPs to the satisfaction of the Parole Board and accept guilt for criminal offences that they may not have committed, the threat of continued and indefinite imprisonment remains, as the prisoner may be deemed too much of a risk for release at all (Berlins 2002; Hill 2002a, 2002b; Woffinden 2000, 2001).

Against this background, the remainder of this chapter is presented in three broad parts. First, it details the extent of the parole deal by presenting the findings of survey research on the key obstacles to progression and release that confronts prisoners maintaining innocence who require a recommendation from the Parole Board. Then it considers the Parole Board's response to the claim of the parole deal, detailing the case law that it cites to justify its continuation with its current method of risk assessment. Finally, it considers a possible way forward that moves beyond a mere psychologically oriented perspective on why prisoners maintain innocence with the application of a socio-legal perspective. More specifically, this perspective engages with claims of innocence by prisoners maintaining innocence to reveal a variety of reasons why prisoners say they are innocent when they are not which cannot be attributed to psychological denial. It also establishes that some prisoners maintaining innocence may in fact be innocent; a possibility that the Parole Board has not acknowledged or made accommodation for in its assessments and decisions.

The key obstacles to progression and release for indeterminate prisoners maintaining innocence

A survey on the key obstacles to progression and release for indeterminate sentenced prisoners maintaining innocence was conducted in the summer of 2005 (see Bromley, 2009). The 82 respondents were asked uncomplicated questions pertaining to the alleged crime or index offence that they were convicted of; the tariff; sentence planning requirements and offending behaviour programmes; appeal history; prison category; information on files and reports; parole history; and crucially the reasons for non-progression and/or release as the prisoner maintaining innocence saw them (for an abridged version of the findings and recommendations see, Naughton, 2005a). The main findings of the survey are as follows.

Refusal to undertake offence-related courses

Perhaps unsurprisingly, the most significant finding of the survey was a claim that a refusal on the part of indeterminate sentenced prisoners maintaining innocence to undertake offence-related courses may result in an almost insurmountable barrier to progression and release. Since certain offence-related courses require an explicit or implicit admission of guilt, prisoners maintaining innocence feel they would have to lie about their involvement in the offence for which they were convicted, and so cannot participate in such courses. For instance, SOTP requires an admission of guilt before it can be taken. The programme itself requires a full and frank account of the crime and the reasons for it, which prisoners maintaining innocence reported they are simply unable to do. As a consequence, prisoners maintaining innocence required to make such admissions said that they are often denied higher status and the privileges that accompany it, remain longer in higher security categories, and are not released on parole or are kept in prison beyond their tariff date. This situation was claimed to be experienced by 80 per cent of the respondents. It was claimed to come from all quarters of the penal system, probation, prison, psychology and parole staff and even by appeal lawyers acting on their behalf. It is exemplified in the following quotation from a Category A prisoner convicted in 1996 for murder, which is typical of many responses that the survey received from prisoners who claimed that they were stuck in the same frustrating scenario:

> Each and every Cat A Board [since I was convicted] has said that I must remain Cat A because I haven't addressed my offending behaviour. (Respondent 49)

In an almost identical response, Respondent 61, convicted of murder in 1991, stated:

> I have not taken any offence related courses. I have been told by the prison officers that I will never be released as long as I persist in my innocence and will not progress.

This issue was further supported by Respondent 64 to the survey who was convicted of murder in 1995, as follows:

> Sentence Planning Reports are always the same – until I address my offending behaviour I must remain in a Dispersal Prison. I have maintained my innocence since the day I was arrested. I did not commit this crime. I have done no offence related courses

because I have committed no offence, so I am stuck, no progressive move.

Respondent 37, convicted of murder and arson in 2002, asserted:

> If I had a £1 for every time I've been told by Prison Officers that unless I do courses and address my offending behaviour I will never be released, I would be a lot richer than the Chelsea owner. It is quite clear to me that until I … do my courses … and admit to a crime that I did not commit, I will never progress towards my release.

A final example of the catch-22 that prisoners maintaining innocence can experience is the response by Respondent 69, convicted of murder in 1997, who claimed that she/he had been caught up in high-security prisons for the last 15 years:

> Staff at two different High Security prisons have stated that I will not progress until I complete offence related courses. I am told I must face up to the fact that if I want to progress I must do such courses that are recommended to me.

Files and reports

It was claimed by survey respondents that files and reports were just not accurate and that they can repeat, and therefore reinforce, misinformation that can damage the chances of prisoners maintaining innocence making progression or being released. In the words of Respondent 49, convicted of murder in 1996:

> Most of the reports are ghost written and written from other reports that are themselves ghost written and in the event that you are actually interviewed, you find that you have been grossly misquoted and anything you say is gleefully twisted to what they say you said, with no chance whatsoever of having it put right.

Adding further weight to this matter, Respondent 68 convicted of murder in 1991, claimed that:

> When my last OASys was done … I found it contained 45 errors about me and I am still in the process of getting this sorted out without much luck.

Relating the issue back to appellants, Respondent 4, convicted of murder in 1998, said:

> I refuse to go on any courses and because I refuse to accept the conviction there will never be an unbiased report about me. They are trying to bury me under an avalanche of lies.

As this relates specifically to the Parole Board, Respondent 70, convicted of murder in 1992, claimed:

> Being a model prisoner is meaningless ... [the] Parole Board do not pay any attention to positive reports of my behaviour. Instead they focus on the negative reports which are full of errors, misinformation and lies. At my last hearing, a false report by a psychologist was the only thing that I was refused on.

Appellants

Prisoners maintaining innocence appealing against their convictions or who have applied to the Criminal Cases Review Commission (CCRC) for a review of their conviction reported that they either decided themselves or were advised by their lawyers not to participate in any course when participation requires or implies an admission of guilt. The reasoning was that such admissions could damage their chances of a referral back to the appeal courts by the CCRC and, ultimately, their chances of overturning their convictions. For instance, Respondent 10, convicted of murder in 2004, claimed that:

> Non-progression and non-release at point of tariff unless you 'confess' is used as leverage to get appellants to drop their cases.

Adding a structural dimension to the matter, Respondent 32, convicted of rape in 2002, said that certain prisons are:

> Dumping ground[s] for Appellants and as such it offers nothing for us. Rather the system of psychological bullying is designed to lure or force an Appellant into compliance with coursework by deprivation.

Respondent 46, convicted of murder in 1997, summed up the general problem as follows:

> I have been a Cat A prisoner since my conviction because I will not undertake any offence related courses. I am an appellant fighting my case because I am innocent and cannot make any progression.

Respondent 50, convicted of rape and murder in 2001, explained this issue in further detail:

> My sentence plan constantly includes courses that I cannot do because I am an Appellant. As a 'in denial' innocent person you are deemed to be deliberately refusing to comply with the prison regime and as such they set you courses that they know you will not be able to attend. Every time you attend a Sentence Planning it is evident that you will not be able to comply therefore placing you at odds with the system. Thus no movement except backwards.

As this relates, specifically, to the Parole Board, Respondent 74, convicted of rape in 1999, claimed:

> I had an Oral Hearing in Feb 2005 and was informed that I was not being released as I was still appealing against my conviction.

Pressure to undertake offence-related courses

It was reported in the survey that prisoners maintaining innocence are placed under pressure to admit to crimes which they say they have not committed. This pressure can be personal, so that they may rejoin their families, for example, as in the following quote from a category A prisoner convicted of murder in 2004:

> I am fully aware that by not giving in to this pressure I may end my days in here and never be with my twin baby boys as they grow up. (Respondent 10)

Alternatively, prisoners maintaining innocence claimed that they experience systemic pressure from prison officers and the psychologists who deliver the offence related courses who regard them as ineligible to participate in courses because they are 'in denial':

> I have been informed that I will not get out if I do not do courses as I am in denial, but told that I must admit guilt in order to qualify for a place on the courses. (Respondent 29, convicted of murder in 1993)

Even prison governors were claimed to apply pressure to prisoners maintaining innocence to admit their guilt as in the following quote from a Category B prisoner: convicted of murder in 1988:

> I will not undertake any index related courses. In 1993, I was shown a file by a former governor who was leaving the prison service. In it was a directive from the HO [Home Office] which advised that I should be 'pressured' into making a confession. Most of the problems I have had from the prison service and the system as a whole has been psychological in terms of torture and intimidation tactics and the violation of my basic rights. (Respondent 63)

Incentives and Earned Privileges Scheme

The Prison Service operates a scheme of Incentives and Earned Privileges (IEPS). This means that prisoners have the opportunity to get extra privileges through good behaviour, but lose them if they misbehave. The regime is based on a system which places a prisoner on one of three levels: basic, standard or enhanced. Most prisons operate a system which starts prisoners on either the basic or standard level. The privileges that can be earned affect a prisoner's daily life in prison (for details of the scheme, see Ministry of Justice, 2011b). Another key finding of the research was that prisoners maintaining their innocence said that they are often denied 'enhanced' status and the concomitant privileges solely because they would not admit their guilt.

Mark Barnsley (2000), himself a former prisoner who maintained his innocence throughout the whole of his eight years in prison for grievous bodily harm (GBH), described the disparity between enhanced and basic conditions as follows:

> A prisoner on 'Basic' will be held in virtual (or even actual) Segregation Unit conditions, even though he or she may not have committed any disciplinary offence. They will get no 'privileges', one or maybe two half-hour visits per month (possibly behind glass), and only £2.50 per week to spend at most (a 12g packet of tobacco is more than £2). By contrast, a prisoner [on 'Enhanced'] ... status, will have a TV, maybe cooking facilities, four or more visits per month of up to two and a half hours duration, £15 per week 'private cash' plus 'enhanced wages' and a range of other 'privileges'.

But the bar or removal of enhanced status from prisoners maintaining innocence is not merely about quality of life in prison. In the absence of anything else to go on, which is often the case in reviewing prisoners maintaining innocence, the Parole Board have come to view enhanced status as an indicator of general good behaviour and basic standard as an indicator of bad behaviour (Wilson, cited in Woffinden, 2001), thus reducing still further the chances of progression and/or release for prisoners maintaining their innocence. Respondent 12, convicted of murder in 2001, reported how she/he had enhanced status removed because of her/his innocence stance:

> I have steadfastly maintained my innocence and as such have refused to partake in any offending behaviour work. Because of this ... I was reduced from enhanced status to standard and subject to loss of privileges. I have recently been given a set of written objectives to complete – one of which was 'to give a full and honest account of the index offence'. I was further warned that if I do not comply with my Sentence Plan, a 'regressive move will be sought' I have this in writing.

Respondent 32, convicted of rape in 2002, supported this:

> I have had my enhanced status withdrawn and all privileges that go with it taken away because non-compliance with sentence plan means no progress.

Linking the general problems faced by prisoners maintaining innocence who want to undertake risk assessment programmes with the specific problems of appellants and the denial of enhanced status, Respondent 58, convicted of rape in 2002, claimed:

> The CCRC have ... referred my case back to the Court of Appeal. In the meantime, I have completed a range of courses so that I can progress to Cat D. I have asked to do the SOTP course but have been told that I cannot do the course because I am waiting for an appeal in the Court of Appeal. However, in April 2005 I was informed that because I had not taken part in the SOTP course that my enhanced status was being withdrawn.

Security category

Sometimes, no matter what courses have been completed, prisoners maintaining innocence can still face difficulties in progressing due to being kept in a higher-security category than equivalent prisoners who admit their guilt:

> I have taken a range of courses ... but because I am a Cat A prisoner the Parole Board has not been able to grant 'open conditions' or recommend release. (Respondent 73, convicted of false imprisonment, indecent assault and actual bodily harm in 1997)

Not all prisons provide courses to demonstrate lack of risk

Given the importance of index offence related OBPs in the Parole Board decision making process, a surprising finding of the Survey was that not all prisons provide the opportunity for prisoners to undertake the accredited OBPs that may be listed on their sentence plans. Moreover, no prisons at all in England and Wales provide the opportunity to undertake all of the programmes in a single institution. This has significant impacts on the ability of prisoners maintaining their innocence to demonstrate that they do not present a risk to public safety, especially where a particular programme has been identified as a requirement on the sentence plan. In consequence, a bottleneck of prisoners maintaining innocence can be created with prisoners stuck in certain establishments unable to make progress towards release. For instance, Respondent 52, convicted of murder in 2000, claimed:

> As I am in Cat B establishment, I cannot undertake any courses to show my lack of risk.

Similarly, Respondent 72, convicted of rape in 2002, said:

> As I am making an appeal I have been advised by my legal representative not to do the SOTP. I have undertaken the ETS course and want to do other courses to show that I am not a risk – e.g. anger management, social life skills and so on – but they are not available at the Cat C prison I am in. I have asked for a transfer so that I can do the other courses but have been told that I cannot be transferred until I complete the SOTP.

The Parole Board's response

In response to claims that prisoners maintaining innocence are faced with the catch-22 of the parole deal, the Parole Board argued that such claims are 'untrue', and that it is a 'myth' to say that prisoners maintaining innocence must admit and express remorse for the crimes that they have been convicted of in order to get parole (see McCarthy, 2005b, 2006). In support of its argument, the Parole Board stressed that legal precedent in judicial reviews against the Parole Board has established that it would be unlawful for it to refuse parole solely on the grounds of denial of guilt or anything that flows from that (such as not being able to take part in offending behaviour programmes which focus on the crime committed) (see Parole Board, 2004; R v Secretary of State for Home Department, *ex parte* Hepworth, Fenton-Palmer and Baldonzy and R v Parole Board, *ex parte* Winfield).

On the other hand, however, the Parole Board asserted that although it is required not to discriminate against prisoners maintaining innocence, it is also legally bound to assume the correctness of any conviction and take account not only of the offence, and the circumstances in which it was committed, but the circumstances and behaviour of the individual prisoner before and during the sentence (Parole Board, 2004; R v Secretary for the Home Department and the Parole Board, *ex parte* Owen John Oyston).

> [We] are a[n] organisation created by law, and operating under the law. The law says the [Parole] Board must treat all prisoners as guilty … What the courts have said repeatedly, is that the Board must ignore any representations by the prisoner that he is innocent. The Board must assume he is guilty. (McCarthy, 2005a: 1–2; Thornton, 2008: 1)

The rationale for the working practices of the Parole Board as it tries to find a way to not discriminate against prisoners who say that they are innocent and refuse to undertake specified offending behaviour programmes – while simultaneously working on the basis that they are guilty – was underlined as follows:

> It is important to understand that the Board is not entitled to 'go behind' the conviction. That means we cannot overrule the decision of a judge or jury. That is the job of the appeal courts and the Criminal Cases Review Commission. The Board's remit extends only to the assessment of risk, and the bottom line is always the safety of the public. (Parole Board, 2004)

From such a perspective, the Parole Board continues to regard all prisoners maintaining innocence as 'deniers' who are guilty of the crimes for which they were convicted. This takes no account of the fact that criminal investigations are imperfect; that criminal trials can convict the innocent; that the criminal appeals system and the CCRC cannot guarantee to overturn the wrongful convictions given to the innocent (discussed in the next two chapters). Overall, then, the Parole Board sidesteps entirely the reality that some prisoners maintaining innocence languishing in prison are in fact innocent and may never have their convictions overturned (see Naughton, 2005c, 2009d).

However, the Parole Board maintains that it still believes that it satisfies its statutory remit not to discriminate against prisoners maintaining innocence who will not comply with their sentence plans. It argues that it does not base its decisions not to recommend progression or release on the ground that a prisoner maintaining innocence will not acknowledge their guilt and undertake offence-related work. Rather, it claims that it is generally unable to recommend progression or release to prisoners maintaining innocence who refuse to undertake offence-related work because it does not have the necessary evidence to show that the prisoner maintaining innocence has reduced his/her risk of reoffending (McCarthy, 2005a: 9). This logic, to my mind at least, does not dispel the parole deal, it proves it.

In defence of the Parole Board it must be acknowledged that risk assessment of prisoners is a complex and difficult task with many real responsibilities and pressures. The Parole Board deals with prisoners convicted of the most serious of crimes and if it gets it wrong it risks releasing dangerous individuals back into society with the potential to commit further crimes. The Board would then face a backlash of criticism in the media that would almost inevitably follow. The official data for 2010/11 shows that 41 parolees or 6.3 per cent of offenders released from prison on a life licence and under active supervision in the community were sent back to jail for breaching their parole conditions during the year following an allegation of a further offence (Parole Board, 2011c). Among those recalled to custody in the period was Jon Venables who was convicted along with Robert Thompson in 1993 when they were both 10 years old for the murder of 2-year-old James Bulger. Another notable parolee who was recalled in 2010/11 was Learco Chindamo who was convicted when he was 15 years old of murdering headmaster Philip Lawrence in 1995. Venables was jailed in 2010 for downloading indecent images of children; Chindamo was cleared of robbery in 2011 but was ordered to remain in custody while his case was reviewed. Both cases prompted media criticism of the Parole Board's decision to recommend that they be released (see BBC News, 2012). In another high-profile case that was widely reported in the media Mark Shirley raped a 40-year-old woman at knifepoint in Bristol in 2009 while he was on parole. Shirley was convicted of murdering 67-year-old Mary Wainwright when he was 16 years old and given a life sentence at Cardiff Crown Court in 1987. He was released on parole after 16 years in 2003, but was later recalled to prison for excessive drinking. He was released again in August 2008. Seven months after his second release from prison Shirley raped the 40-year-old woman in Bristol (see Savill, 2009).

In this context, it is, perhaps, understandable that the Parole Board would exercise caution in its risk assessment processes and in its recommendations and decisions on who to progress and release. The criticism that it receives when parolees reoffend will, arguably, serve to reinforce an even more cautious stance on subsequent cases. This is likely to further impact detrimentally on the likelihood of prisoners maintaining innocence who fail to comply with the Parole Board's system of risk assessment being progressed and/or released.

On the other hand, the Parole Board's lack of active engagement with the problem of prisoners maintaining innocence following the equally negative criticism that it received when the cases of Downing and Brown were overturned on appeal seems profoundly problematic in organisational terms. Put simply, such cases challenge the continuation of the Parole Board's principal method of risk assessment and an organisational rethink on its continued reliance might have been expected. This is precisely what was called for by Judge Anthony Thornton, a Judicial Member of the Parole Board, who argued in response to the parole deal that 'there is a need for the risk assessment process to take greater account of all forms of innocence assertion' (Thornton, 2008: 2). More specifically, Thornton (2008: 2) recommended a wide range of initiatives that address the findings of the survey cited above on how the Parole Board could identify and assist prisoners maintaining innocence who may be innocent as follows:

> [T]he nature and extent of, and reasons for, any assertion of a prisoner's innocence should be explored and challenged in much greater detail than at present using archived material that may not be readily available in prison files or the parole dossier. Suitable sexual and violent risk reduction work should be devised for those maintaining innocence. Furthermore, one to one motivational work should be more readily available for such prisoners, particularly when their stance is holding back their sentence progression. Psychologists and

other assessors and report writers need further training in how to assess the risk of innocence-maintainers. This training should include an analysis of the different types of denial and of the varied reasons for adopting that stance. Additionally, reports and assessments, including the OASys form, should be adapted to allow for details to be provided about the maintenance of innocence and the reasons for that position ... A ... [Parole Board] ... working group could investigate ... the current risk reduction and risk assessment processes.

Thornton's (2008) recommendations were not acted upon and a working group was not established to even explore how prisoners maintaining innocence might be dealt with differently. Indeed, at a conference in 2011 the Head of Casework at the Parole Board continued to simply describe prisoners maintaining innocence as 'deniers'. Moreover, he confirmed that the parole deal still confronts such prisoners in making it clear that the main, if not only, route to progression and release is the successful completion of accredited OBPs that are listed on prisoners' OASys:

> Are deniers at a disadvantage? Of course they are ... Prisoners who deny their offences cause us problems as their risk assessment reports are often full of gaps. Frequently, the assessment reports conclude that they have no risk of reoffending, or breach of licence, but *cannot recommend release* as they have not undertaken offending behaviour courses. (Terry McCarthy, cited in Tan, 2011: 10, my emphasis)

A possible way forward

As indicated above, underpinning the Parole Board's stance on potential parolees, whether they are prisoners who admit their guilt or prisoners who maintain innocence, is a resolute commitment to a purely psychological understanding of crime causation and the reduction of the risk of reoffending: criminals think differently to law-abiding citizens and if their thinking can be changed then their risk of reoffending will be reduced. This perspective might also account for the Parole Board's persistence in psychologising the prisoner maintaining innocence as problematic, despite evidence in the form of successful appeals that might logically be thought to disturb a blind adherence to such a perspective. It is as though the perspective adopted by the Parole Board does not allow the possibility of a more nuanced analysis that delves deeper into the reasons for an innocence stance by prisoners or to even contemplate that prisoners maintaining innocence may be innocent. Instead, all prisoners maintaining innocence are viewed as suffering some form of psychological denial syndrome that needs to be broken down so that they can admit their guilt, show their remorse and present less of a risk to society. In this light, it is perhaps not surprising that the reach of the parole deal is so extensive in all aspects of the prison, probation and parole systems implicated in the foregoing survey. In addition, it presents potential obstacles to the progression and release of prisoners who say that they are innocent.

Against this background, rather than argue against the possibility that prisoners who maintain innocence do so because they are in psychological denial, this section seeks to extend the conceptual framework of possible reasons for claims of innocence by prisoners from a socio-legal perspective. More specifically, a 'Typology of Claims of Innocence' will be presented that derives from an analysis of the letters and completed questionnaires from prisoners maintaining innocence to the Innocence Network UK (INUK) (see also, Naughton, 2008a, 2009d). In an attempt to decide eligible cases for further investigation by a member innocence project it became immediately apparent that there is a great deal of confusion on both sides of the prisoner-maintaining-innocence conundrum. Put simply, not all prisoners maintaining innocence are in fact innocent. Moreover, those prisoners who maintain innocence when they are not may not always be doing so for deceitful reasons or because they suffer from psychological denial. As such, it is too crude to simply label all prisoners maintaining innocence as 'deniers' as there are important distinctions to be made between claims of innocence that can help to provide a better understanding of the problem and how it might be addressed. So far, at least five broad categories of prisoners maintaining innocence have been identified. They do so:

1. Because they want to keep alive their chances of a successful appeal.
2. Because they are ignorant of or misunderstand criminal law.
3. Because they disagree with the correctness of criminal law.
4. Because they want to protect their family and/or friends.
5. Because they are in fact innocent.

For reasons of confidentiality, no actual applicants to INUK will be identified in the following analysis. Cases in the public domain which fit with the typology, however, will be cited for illustrative purposes.

Because they want to keep alive their chances of a successful appeal

INUK has received applications for casework assistance from numerous applicants claiming 'technical' innocence in order to keep open the possibility of overturning their convictions on appeal. The following quotation from a letter to INUK illustrates this category of claims of innocence by applicants who are not factually innocent:

> My challenge to the conviction rest[s] on technical, rather than 'actual' innocence. The appeal hearing I was allowed rested on improper behaviour by a jury member, but it was judged that the behaviour did not compromise the jury and my conviction was upheld.

Such attempts to overturn convictions by factually guilty offenders are inevitably linked to notions of due process and the presumption of innocence that underpins criminal trials and the requirement that the prosecution must prove with evidence that the defendant is guilty of the alleged offence beyond a reasonable doubt. As such, a possible strategy exists whereby guilty offenders often try to escape conviction by pleading not guilty at trial, apply to have an appeal when convicted and then apply to the CCRC. They even apply to other organisations such as INUK in the hope of finding some loophole or breach of process through which they can have their convictions overturned. The cases of Nicholas Mullen and Michael Weir were given as examples of successful appellants who were believed to be factually guilty by the CACD in Chapter 2.

Because they are ignorant of or misunderstand criminal law

There are a range of possible scenarios that emerge from an analysis of the applications to INUK whereby ignorance or misunderstandings of criminal law can result in prisoners maintaining innocence when they are not factually innocent. This can include prisoners who maintain innocence because they were intoxicated at the time of the offence. Such prisoners can believe that this somehow excuses criminal culpability on the assumed grounds that they cannot be responsible or legally blameworthy for a crime that they have no memory of committing. The short answer to such claims of innocence is that such prisoners are not innocent, but, in certain circumstances, such as if the intoxication was involuntary, there may well be grounds for a legal defence (see for example, R v (Nigel John) Richardson; DPP v Majewski; R v

Fotheringham; R v Kingston). If grounds for a defence cannot be found, they are factually and legally guilty, as voluntary intoxication is not a valid defence.

Prisoners maintaining innocence can also be ignorant of or misunderstand the law on sexual offences (discussed further in the next section under the heading of disagreements with criminal law). An applicant to INUK, for example, claimed that because he had video evidence of himself and his ex-partner having consensual sex that he could not possibly be guilty of an alleged rape for which he was subsequently convicted. He believed that because his ex-partner had consented in the past that he had an ongoing, even permanent consent to sex with her. The remainder of this section covers the two most common claims of innocence in applications to INUK in terms of how they relate to ignorance or misunderstandings of criminal law: convictions for joint enterprise crimes; and claims of self-defence to murder convictions.

Joint enterprise

An applicant to INUK convicted of joint enterprise murder and given a life sentence claimed that he took no part in the actual killing and should have been convicted of manslaughter instead. His version of events was that he and his co-defendant were out buying drugs when his co-defendant attacked and murdered the victim. He claimed that he played no part at all in the killing:

> I'm not denying I was their [*sic*], all I'm saying is that it was never murder, manslaughter at the most on my CO-D's [co-defendant's] doing, so how can I be done for murder when I never touched the man? I'm innocent of murder.

Such claims of innocence raise the tension between lay and legal notions of guilt:

- From a lay perspective, the prisoner maintaining innocence in such a case might think that they cannot be guilty of murder as they did not actually kill the victim.
- From a legal perspective, however, they are guilty according to criminal law, which dictates that those engaged on joint enterprise crimes share culpability if the outcome was foreseeable.

In simple terms, joint enterprise crimes are based on public policy and arise when two or more persons embark on a common purpose to commit a crime. If that crime is committed by one of the persons, then the other person(s) are also guilty by association: each of the participants in the joint enterprise acts as a primary offender and is equally liable, regardless of their degree of involvement (see Brown and Isaacs v The state, paragraphs 7–14). Joint enterprise becomes more complex when additional offences are committed by one of the parties in the committal of the agreed common purpose offence, for instance, and staying with the same example, if X and Y agree to buy illegal drugs and Y then murders the drug dealer independently. According to joint enterprise, for X to be guilty of the murder of the drug dealer he need not specifically assist or encourage Y to commit the murder to be criminally liable. Rather, X becomes a party to the additional offence, in this case murder, if it could have been foreseen that it was a possible consequence of proceeding with the original plan to commit the first crime, i.e. buy the drugs, even though he may not have intended or even been directly involved in the commission of that further, or 'collateral', offence (murder) that was committed by Y (see Simester *et al.*, 2010: 233–244; Krebs, 2010).

In R v Hyde, the CACD ruled that a secondary offender is equally liable if they subjectively realised or contemplated that during the course of the joint enterprise it is possible that the person who commits an additional offence might commit it. Only if the greater offence or force used was entirely unforeseen, and therefore something 'fundamentally different' or a complete departure from the initial enterprise will the participant escape liability (see also, Chan Wing Siu v The Queen).

This raises the crucial issue of whether X in the foregoing example had foresight of the additional crime of murder that was committed by Y. The 'foresight' requirement of joint enterprise in the present example can be explained as follows: X must actually foresee the potential that Y might go on to commit the additional crime (murder). Davies v DPP concerned a fight between two groups of youths. During the fight, one of the group, Davies, produced a knife and stabbed one of the other youths to death and was convicted of murder. However, a joint enterprise partner in the fight, Lawson, was acquitted of being a party to the murder because there was no evidence that he actually knew that Davies had a knife. Therefore, Lawson could not have foreseen that a death could have occurred from a stabbing. Yet, had the victim died of injuries obtained in the fight, from punches or kicks to the head, for instance, then Lawson could have been found guilty as a collaborator, because such a death could have been a foreseeable consequence of the fight to which Lawson willingly participated (see also R v English).

Alternatively, in the failed appeal case in the House of Lords of R v Powell (see R v Powell), which has close parallels with the aforementioned INUK applicant, the purpose of the agreed joint enterprise between the appellants Powell and Daniels and another was to purchase drugs from a drug dealer. The three men went to the house of the drug dealer to buy the drugs, but when he came to the door he was shot by the third man. At trial, the Crown was not able to prove which of the three men fired the gun which killed the drug dealer. But it was the Crown case that if the third man fired the gun, the two appellants were equally guilty of murder because they knew that the third man was armed with a gun and knew also, i.e. had foresight, that he might use it to kill or cause grievous bodily harm to the murder victim (see also R v Rahman).

Self-defence

There is a lot of confusion in the applications to INUK on the issue of self-defence. Indeed, a distinction needs to be made between lay understandings of self-defence and how the legal system defines self-defence. For instance, an applicant to INUK who exemplifies the problem was convicted of murder and serving a life sentence. The applicant admitted to killing his ex-partner's ex-partner. However, he claimed that it was not murder but, rather, self-defence and that he was innocent. His initial letter stated:

> Their was a knock at the door it turned out to be her ex boyfriend who then kicked in the door and run across the room and punched me in the head. I picked up one of the two knifes that I had took to sell to someone who lived in a flat opposite her, and their was a violent struggle in which he received 13–14 wound's [and] he later died … I am innocent and [that is] why me and my family can not accept that I am being classed as a murderer.

Criminal law understands that a person may use such force as is reasonable in the circumstances for the purposes of:

- self-defence;
- defence of another;
- defence of property;
- prevention of crime; and/or
- lawful arrest.

The basic principles of the law of self-defence are set out in R v Palmer in the following terms:

> It is both good law and good sense that a man who is attacked may defend himself. It is both good law and good sense that he may do, but only do, what is reasonably necessary.

In simple terms, then, self-defence is a response to a real or potential criminal act of violence where the principal reason for the use of force is protection. In this sense, the applicant to INUK may appear to have acted in self-defence as he claims that he was punched first before he retaliated and killed his attacker. However, s. 3(1) of the Criminal Law Act 1967 requires that those acting in self-defence must use only reasonable force as is deemed necessary in the circumstances:

> A person may use such force as is reasonable in the circumstances in the prevention of crime, or in effecting or assisting in the lawful arrest of offenders or suspected offenders or of persons unlawfully at large.

The Criminal Justice and Immigration Act 2008, s. 76(6) states further that:

> The degree of force used by D [the defendant] is not to be regarded as having been reasonable in the circumstances as D believed them to be if it was disproportionate in those circumstances.

In assessing the reasonableness and proportionality of the force used, prosecutors ask two questions, both of which the applicant to INUK cited above would fail:

1. was the use of force justified in the circumstances, that is, was there a need for any force at all?; and,
2. was the force used excessive in the circumstances?

The test of whether the force used in claims of self-defence has both subjective and objective elements. R v Williams indicated that the reasonableness of the force used will be assessed on the basis of the facts of the situation as the accused 'honestly believed them to be'. However, the question for the jury is whether, on the basis of the facts as the defendant claims that they believed them to be, a 'reasonable person would regard the force used as reasonable or excessive' (Crown Prosecution Service, 2011).

To assist with the question of reasonable force further, Reed v Wastie instructs judges to advise juries that 'reasonableness' and 'proportionality' should be understood in a broad and liberal sense. This was expressed in R v Palmer in the following terms:

> If there has been an attack so that defence is reasonably necessary it will be recognised that a person defending himself cannot weigh to a nicety the exact measure of his necessary defensive action. If a jury thought that in a moment of unexpected anguish a person attacked had only done what he honestly and instinctively thought was necessary, that would be the most potent evidence that only reasonable defensive action had been taken.

Or, as s. 76(7a) of the Criminal Justice and Immigration Act 2008 puts it:

> [A] person acting for a legitimate purpose may not be able to weigh to a nicety the exact measure of any action.

Even in this wide, and some might say rather generous context, it is hardly surprising that the applicant to INUK who responded to a punch in the face with 13–14 stab wounds that left his attacker dead failed in his claim that he acted in self-defence.

Because they disagree with the correctness of criminal law

Another possible category of prisoners maintaining innocence is when they do not think that their behaviour is or should be criminal. This category is distinct from prisoners maintaining innocence who are ignorant of or misunderstand criminal law, as the prisoners in this category know full well that their behaviour or activity is criminal; they just do not agree that it should be. This category includes those that believe as a matter of conscience their behaviour is morally right, such as political prisoners, animal rights and anti-war activists.

A popular reason for disagreements with criminal law relates to sexual offences where prisoners maintaining innocence do not deny that they committed the sexual offence but, rather, claim that the sexual act was consensual and that they should not have been convicted. A notable example of this phenomenon is the case of Jonathan King. King was convicted in November 2001 on one charge of buggery, one of attempted buggery and four indecent assaults, committed against five boys, each aged 14–16 at the time in the 1980s (Ronson, 2001; Chalmers, 2012). As he was released from HMP Maidstone, Kent, however, he announced:

> I'm totally, absolutely 100 per cent innocent. (cited in Jinman, 2005)

But later that day in a radio interview the nature of King's 'innocence' and the extent to which he disagrees with the validity of his conviction became apparent when he admitted that:

> The law was in place, and I knew I was breaking it, and I did, knowingly and conscientiously. However, I am not guilty of the convictions against me. (cited in Jinman, 2005)

Even though two of his victims allegedly attempted suicide, King refused to acknowledge that there were any victims of his crimes because, in his words, everyone involved was 'of an age and mental maturity' to 'make their own decisions' (cited in Jinman, 2005; see also, Chalmers, 2012). Most crucially, King believed that he was innocent on the grounds that:

> I am not guilty of ever going with anyone who didn't want to go with me. (cited in Jinman, 2005)

As Chalmers (2012) noted, on this basis King 'could legitimise intimacy with a five-year-old'. At the root of King's claim of innocence seems to be a disagreement with the law at the time of his offences, which stated that males must be over 21 to be able to consent to sex with another male (see Sexual Offences Act 1967). In 1994 the age of consent between males was lowered to 18 in England and Wales. And, in 2001, just before King's trial, the age of sexual consent between males was brought into line with the age of sexual consent for females, i.e. 16 (see, for instance, Chalmers, 2012). Even on the law today, then, King is legally guilty.

Because they want to protect their family and/or friends

The phenomenon where family members, lovers and/or friends make false confessions for crimes that they did not commit to protect others from criminal sanctions is well documented (see, for instance, Cassell, 1998: 512, 518–520; Gudjonsson and Sigurdsson, 1994: 23).

The problem with finding evidence to support the opposite of this occurrence is that it relies on the prisoner admitting that their claim of innocence was based on an attempt to protect their family, loved ones and/or friends. No such examples exist from the INUK letters and completed questionnaires. Yet the following example derives from a letter from a prisoner who previously maintained his innocence but later admitted his guilt. This was in response to the INUK 'Guidance for New Applicants', which spells out the eligibility criteria for casework assistance, crucially detailing the various reasons why prisoners maintain that they are innocent when they are not factually innocent and the impact of this upon victims of crime:

> Please accept my apologies, as I have no excuse, but I am not innocent. I have been running away from taking personal and social responsibility and in the process making true victims suffer unnecessarily. As in my own case, my victim, if she is aware of my contesting the verdict, could be suffering unnecessary trauma. I need to once and for all accept the help that is on offer and work towards potential release in the future.

In addition to this, a specific example does exist that illustrates the reality of this category that was cited by a senior representative from the Parole Board in discussions at a Chatham House Rules meeting at Vaughn House, London (24 May 2004) between representatives from various organisations that support alleged victims of wrongful imprisonment and agencies of the post-conviction system. It was further claimed by the Parole Board representative that this case had been featured on a BBC *Panorama* programme. The case was said to concern a career burglar who had dutifully promised his mother after his last conviction and period of imprisonment that he would 'go straight'. When he was subsequently caught and convicted of yet another burglary, it was claimed that he initially denied the offence, claiming that he had been wrongly convicted by the police and that he was in fact innocent. During the first ten years of his sentence he was said to have steadfastly maintained innocence, did not comply with his sentence plan, undertook no offending behaviour programmes and made no progression towards release. However, when his mother died, the Parole Board representative said that he admitted that he had committed the offence, claiming that had lied to protect his mother's feelings and her trust in him.

Because they are in fact innocent

The following quotation is an example from the completed question-naire of an applicant to INUK who was deemed eligible for further investigation by a member of the innocence project on the basis that his claim of innocence did not readily fit into the foregoing categories of non-factual innocence and he *might*, therefore, be factually innocent:

> I took no part whatsoever in the attack and have never gone into [the] … (scene of attack) … I did not know the deceased or any of his associates, and had no motive for attacking him. At the time of the attack (around 2.40 am) I was in my home with my parents and girl-friend. I took part in 5 identification parades and was not picked out in any of them. There was no forensic evidence linking me to the attack … The witness who says '4 boys' parking up a car stated that they were between 16–18 years of age 5'6' to 5'8' in height and of slight build. I am 6'2' and of an athletic build … I was also 23 at the time of the attack not 16–18.

As the previous chapters of this book have highlighted, it is possible that some prisoners maintaining innocence in England and Wales are in fact innocent, as in the successful appeal cases of Sean Hodgson, the Cardiff Three and Stefan Kiszko, for instance. As the previous chapters have also shown, factually innocent individuals are vulnerable to abortions of justice and miscarriages of justice in a criminal justice system in which the following can occur: errors; police malpractice and misconduct; prosecution non-disclosure; poor defence; incorrect forensic expert evidence; malicious allegations. As such, it is likely, some might say certain, that *some* prisoners maintaining innocence *are* factually innocent, but will never have their convictions overturned.

Conclusion

The Parole Board seems impervious to claims of innocence by prisoners maintaining innocence even in the face of successful appeals and research that give evidence to the parole deal due to a vision of the phenomenon based entirely on cognitive psychology. This is contrary to the word 'parole', which derives from the French for 'word' and was originally associated with the release of prisoners based on their giving their word of honour that they would not reoffend. Against this idea, it seems that the introduction of cognitive psychology assessments as the principal means of determining risk has disconnected the original meaning of parole to a situation where prisoners maintaining innocence claim that they have to say words that they do not believe if they want to be considered for release.

Cases such as Downing and Brown testify to the problematic nature of basing risk assessments purely on a cognitive psychology model. Each spent roughly double the term of imprisonment that they would have served if they had admitted to their index offences and complied with their sentence plans. It is likely that they would still be in prison today had their convictions not been overturned on appeal. Such cases and the negative publicity that the Parole Board endured following the successful appeals had no impact at all on how the Board assesses prisoners maintaining innocence; prisoners who may be innocent and who may die in prison. This sentiment is echoed in the quotation below – from the survey cited above – which is from a life-sentenced prisoner convicted of murder in 1981 and currently almost 20 years over tariff:

> Currently doing no courses and not being blackmailed any longer to drop my appeal case. I have made an application to the CCRC and if I do not walk out a free man then I will die free in prison. (Respondent 11)

A further challenge to the Parole Board's continued intransigence on the problem of prisoners maintaining innocence are two recent initiatives that have been introduced by the National Offender Management Service (NOMS), an executive agency of the Ministry of Justice that brought together prison and probation services when the Ministry of Justice was established in 2007. They have disconnected prison and probation services from the Parole Board in terms of how prisoners maintaining innocence are now to be viewed and to be dealt with. Managing Indeterminate Sentences and Risk (MISaR) is a training programme that is delivered to some 30,000 prison and probation staff who deal with indeterminate-sentenced prisoners. Prison Service Order (PSO) 4700 sets out policy and guidance for the management of prisoners serving an indeterminate sentence, both during custody and after release on licence. Both incorporate the core rationale of the INUK 'Typology of Claims of Innocence' cited above (see Naughton, 2009d). In so doing, and for the first time in British legal history, there is now an official acknowledgement by NOMS, and therefore the prison and probation services, of the need to distinguish between factual innocence and legal guilt; and embrace the reality that, although all prisoners are legally guilty, some prisoners maintaining innocence are likely to be in fact innocent (see Naughton, 2008a). In practical terms, prison and probation staff are now instructed to recognise the many and varied reasons why a prisoner may maintain their innocence, including the possibility that they are factually innocent. They are, then, mandated to no longer simply dismiss prisoners maintaining innocence as 'deniers' but, rather, to conduct an interview with the prisoner to establish the basis upon which they hold their views (see Ministry of Justice, 2011a: 4.14.1–4.14.5).

The main consequence of MISaR and PSO 4700 is that they effectively challenge the Parole Board stance on prisoners maintaining innocence; as it is statutory remitted to work in 'partnership' with prison and probation services. While the Parole Board continues to see all prisoners as guilty 'deniers', prison and probation, at least in theory and policy, must now acknowledge the possibility of factually innocent prisoners; and they are formally required to explore head-on the problem of prisoners claiming to be innocent.

However, the potential improvement that this change of NOMS policy in relation to prison and probation practice *could* have on prisoners maintaining innocence serving indeterminate sentences is compromised. For, it is the Parole Board that makes the final decision as to whether such prisoners should be progressed and/or released. The continuing reality is that the parole deal remains the order of the day. And unless and until the Parole Board adopts different methods of assessment to inform its decisions on progression and release, then prisoners maintaining innocence will continue to face longer sentences than prisoners who admit their guilt. The former may thus never be released at all.

6
The Court of Appeal (Criminal Division)

Introduction

A lay perspective on the criminal justice system was described in Chapter 2 as seeing its principal aim as convicting the factually guilty and acquitting the factually innocent in criminal trials. It was shown that this view is reflected in public and political discourses on the criminal justice system. In keeping with this, a lay perspective on the criminal appeals system can be conceived as an attempt to correct any apparent errors that may emerge at the trial stage of the criminal justice process (see, for instance, Pattenden, 1996: 58). Indeed, as no human system can be infallible, the lay perspective on the criminal appeals system might be forgiven for thinking that it exists to overturn convictions given to the people who are, in fact, innocent of the crimes for which they were convicted (see Naughton, 2009b: 17).

Contrary to this, however, although factually innocent people can be and are victims of abortions of justice and miscarriages of justice (as discussed at length in Chapters 2–5), and although factually innocent prisoners can and do remain trapped in prison unless they have their conviction overturned on appeal (as discussed in the last chapter), the criminal appeals system does not function in a way that corresponds with a lay perspective. It does not seek to determine whether appellants are factually innocent or factually guilty. Moreover, and perhaps most significantly, evidence of factual innocence is not even a guarantee that an individual convicted of a criminal offence will be granted an appeal against that conviction, let alone have their conviction overturned. Instead, a labyrinth of strict legal rules and procedures govern criminal appeals that are more concerned with notions of due process and the 'fairness' of the trial process, where 'fairness' is understood in terms of adherence to the due processes of the criminal justice system rather than the fairness of the outcome in terms of convicting the guilty and acquitting the innocent.

In specific terms, the two main routes of appeal against criminal convictions in England and Wales are appeals to the Crown Court for convictions given in magistrates' courts and appeals to the Court of Appeal (Criminal Division) (CACD) for convictions given in the Crown Court (for a general discussion, see Morrish and McLean, 1971; McLean, 1980). However, the rules that govern these appeals against criminal convictions differ sharply. There are increased appeal rights afforded to those convicted in magistrates' courts for relatively less serious criminal offences which tend to receive non-custodial sentences than those convicted in the Crown Court for more serious indictable offences and which receive longer custodial sentences (see, for instance, Auld, 2001; Spencer, 2006; 677–679).

As stipulated by s. 79(3) of the Senior Courts Act 1981, appeals to the Crown Court against convictions given in magistrates' courts provide alleged victims of wrongful convictions the opportunity to have a full rehearing of their case, although such appeals are not before a jury but before a Crown Court judge and two magistrates. However, and contra the lay perspective, such rehearings follow the general rules of criminal trials in the Crown Court in that they do not seek to determine if appellants are factually innocent or guilty but, rather, whether they are 'guilty' or 'not guilty' of the offence(s) that they are accused of on the evidence presented at court (for a critical discussion, see Naughton, 2005b). In terms of decision making, the Crown Court has powers under s. 48 of the Senior Courts Act 1981 to uphold or quash a conviction or sentence and it may remit the case back to the magistrates' court where the conviction was given for a further rehearing. It is also crucial to note, however, that appellants to the Crown Court risk greater sentences under s. 48(4) of the Senior Courts Act 1981, which, arguably, may act as a disincentive against making an appeal. The Crown Court sitting as an appeal court has the power to increase or lower the severity of the sentence imposed by magistrates' courts, even if the appellant is only appealing against his/her conviction. Further, as an appeal to the Crown Court is by way of a full rehearing, if the appellant was convicted of one offence and found not guilty by a magistrates' court for other charges, the Crown Court has the power to convict the appellant of the charges that they had previously been acquitted of. This can be said to add an additional dimension of risk to the process of making an appeal to the Crown Court and presents a further potential deterrent to making an appeal against a conviction given in a magistrates' court. Finally, if alleged victims of wrongful convictions in magistrates' courts fail to obtain an acquittal in an appeal to the Crown Court, the original conviction will be upheld, but the appellant has further appeal rights to the CACD.

Despite the extensive appeal rights provided to those convicted in magistrates' courts, there is not even an automatic right to an appeal against criminal convictions given in the Crown Court. Instead, under s.1 of the Criminal Appeal Act 1995 alleged victims of wrongful convictions convicted in the Crown Court are permitted only to ask for an appeal (known as a request for leave to appeal) to the CACD, and this usually has to be done within 28 days from the date of the conviction. Appeals to the CACD against criminal convictions given in the Crown Court also have other stipulations that detract from the lay understanding. For instance, the requirement that any evidence to be considered by the CACD is, except in exceptional circumstances, fresh evidence that was not or could not have been made available at the time of the original trial. This also applies to appellants to the CACD against convictions originally given in a magistrates' court that fail in an appeal to the Crown Court (Criminal Appeal Act 1968, s. 23(2)). This means that alleged victims of wrongful convictions who may have evidence of factual innocence that was or could have been made available at the time of the original trial may not have that evidence accepted as grounds of appeal by the CACD.

Yet, it was not always the case that the criminal appeals system was so apparently unconcerned about the question of the likely factual innocence or guilt of appellants, as a historical analysis of the system of criminal appeals reveals. To be sure, the introduction of the appeals system against alleged wrongful convictions was entirely in sync with a lay concern to assist factually innocent victims of wrongful convictions. It was expressly established so they could have their convictions overturned if and when they occurred. However, over the years there has been a dramatic shift from an express concern with overturning the convictions of appellants who may be factually innocent to a system that is narrowly focused on overturning convictions that are deemed to be legally 'unsafe', defined as those cases that can show some breach of due process at the pre-trial or trial stage, or where there is fresh evidence that was not available at the time of the original trial.

Against this background, as disputed convictions given in magistrates' courts can ultimately be appealed in the CACD if they fail on appeal to the Crown Court, there will be no further discussion of such convictions or appeals in this chapter. Instead, the focus is on the workings of the CACD and how it relates, or more crucially does not relate, to notions of factual innocence. From this perspective, this chapter traces the origins of appeals to the CACD against serious criminal offences given in the Crown Court. It shows that the current preference for the procedural propriety of the criminal justice process is far removed from the concern for potentially factually innocent victims of wrongful convictions that lay at the heart of the introduction of the criminal appeal system just over a century ago. In three parts, the chapter first traces the statutes that have governed the functioning of the system of appeals against criminal convictions in England and Wales from the Criminal Appeal Act 1907 through the various statutory amendments that were introduced over the intervening century to provide the system of appeals in the CACD today. Second, it unpacks the CACD's notions on what would constitute an unsafe conviction, showing that it represents a misleading image of the CACD as concerned with factual innocence. In reality, the criminal appeal system is, majorly, at odds with a lay perspective. Finally, it considers a discernible due process perspective in the literature to highlight an example of legal scholarship that appears to have lost sight of the original intention that the appeals system should provide relief to factually innocent victims of wrongful conviction. Instead, the due process perspective sees the legitimate focus of the appeals system on the correction of points of law and incorrect legal rulings. Yet the due process perspective fails to comment on the reality that this approach can benefit factually guilty offenders in overturning their convictions and not even see factually innocent victims of wrongful convictions as having eligible grounds of appeal.

The history of the law on criminal appeals – from innocence to safety

Before there was a formal criminal appeal system, alleged victims of wrongful conviction, or their families if the alleged victim had been executed, would petition the Home Secretary for a free pardon under the Royal Prerogative of Mercy. Free pardons were, and still are, given when the Home Secretary is satisfied that the individual is innocent of the offence for which they were convicted, signifying that the conviction is to be disregarded and the person concerned freed of the consequences (see Home Office, 2012). This form of 'appeal' was, however, highly limited in that petitions stood little chance of reaching the Home Secretary unless an influential person took up the cause. An example by Pattenden is the case of George Edalji who was successful in a petition for a free pardon against a conviction for cattle, sheep and horse-maiming because his case was championed by author Sir Arthur Conan Doyle, the creator of the fictional sleuth Sherlock Holmes (see Pattenden, 1996: 30). It also meant that the large number of pardons and posthumous pardons throughout the nineteenth century largely went unnoticed and certainly caused little disruption to the day-to-day workings of, and belief in the justness of, the criminal justice system. However, the longstanding campaign for the establishment of an appeal system for mistaken criminal convictions, which included more than 30 failed parliamentary bills from the middle of the 1800s (see Pattenden, 1996: 5–27), reached its zenith with the publicity that was generated by the case of Adolf Beck and the public crisis of confidence in the criminal justice system that it caused (see Naughton, 2007: 80–82; Woffinden, 1987: 321). As discussed in Chapters 1 and 4, Beck was twice wrongly convicted on mistaken eyewitness identification evidence and it was the committee of inquiry into the case that recommended the setting up of the Court of Criminal Appeal when it found him to be completely innocent of the offences:

> There is no shadow of foundation for any of the charges made against Mr Beck, or any reason for supposing that he had any connection whatever with them. (cited in Irving, 1921: 2–3)

The scope of the Court of Criminal Appeal that was established by the Criminal Appeal Act 1907 was extensive and could, subject to certain conditions, receive appeals on any ground of law or fact alone or a question of mixed fact and law (s. 3 of the Act). Of most relevance to this discussion of the criminal appeals system and factual innocence, pursuant to s.4 (1), the Court of Criminal Appeal could allow appeals against conviction (this analysis is not concerned with the powers of the Court of Criminal Appeal in sentence appeals) in three broad circumstances:

1. If the 'verdict of the jury should be set aside on the ground that it is unreasonable or cannot be supported having regard to the evidence'.
2. If there had been a 'wrong decision of any question of law'.
3. If 'on any ground there was a miscarriage of justice'.

The Criminal Appeal Act 1907 s. 4(1) also contained a significant proviso, that the Court of Criminal Appeal may, notwithstanding that they were of the opinion that the point raised in the appeal might be decided in favour of the appellant, 'dismiss the appeal if they consider that no substantial miscarriage of justice has actually occurred'.

This wide notion of an unjust verdict contained in the Criminal Appeal Act 1907 can be conceived as demonstrative of an attempt by the legislature to provide a criminal appeal system that corresponded fully with a lay perspective on the correct functioning of the criminal justice system. That is, that only the factually guilty should be punished and the factually innocent should have a route to have their wrongful convictions overturned. More specifically, in allowing the Court of Criminal Appeal to rehear cases in their entirety and correct jury verdicts if they were deemed to have made the wrong decision, the 1907 Act, arguably, recognised that juries can and do make mistakes that may cause factually innocent individuals to be wrongly convicted, which is the key concern from a lay perspective. At the same time, although the Criminal Appeal Act 1907 allowed the Court of Criminal Appeal in theory to overturn convictions of potentially guilty offenders if the conviction was wrong in law, the proviso can be seen as nullifying this as convictions were to be upheld if the Court of Criminal Appeal did not think that a 'substantial miscarriage of justice has actually occurred', i.e. if the appellant was believed to be factually guilty. The final plank of s. 4 can be further conceived as focusing the Court of Criminal Appeal on the question of the possible factual innocence of appellants by allowing anything that it considered to be a miscarriage of justice to be overturned, again with the logical corollary that the notion of a miscarriage of justice in the proviso was not relating to factual guilt.

Indeed, although no precise statutory definition of a miscarriage of justice was provided by the 1907 Act, it is clear that the public crisis of confidence in the criminal justice system that was sparked by the Beck case at the time was precisely because of widespread concerns that he was a factually innocent victim of two wrongful convictions (see, for instance, Borchard, 1932, ch. 2; Irving, 1921: ch. 1; HC Deb, 1904). This was also reflected in the then Home Secretary's announcement to the House of Commons on the establishment of the Court of Criminal Appeal:

> [T]he only way to reverse the public belief that miscarriages of justice were an every-day occurrence ... was the establishment of a court capable of hearing appeals of fact, law and sentence. (Herbert Gladstone, cited in Pattenden, 1996: 31)

Moreover, and perhaps most indicative that the definition of a miscarriage of justice at the heart of the Criminal Appeal Act 1907 was based on a desire to assist potentially factually innocent victims of wrongful convictions, s. 9 gave the Court of Criminal Appeal extensive powers in its determinations of the truthfulness of the appellants' guilt. In summary, this included the authority to:

(a)   order the production of any document, exhibit or other thing connected with the proceedings;
(b)   order any witnesses who could have been compellable witnesses at the trial to attend and be examined before the court, whether they were or were not called at the trial, or order the examination of any such witnesses to be conducted;
(c)   receive the evidence, if tendered, of any witness (including the appellant) who was a competent but not compellable witness, also including the husband or wife of the appellant where such evidence could not have been given at the trial;
(d)   commission any scientific investigations that it saw fit; and
(e)   appoint any expert witnesses that it believed might assist it with its determinations. (see Criminal Appeal Act 1907, s. 9)

Despite the wide-ranging powers that were available to the Court of Criminal Appeal to assist factually innocent victims to overturn their convictions in theory, the strenuous resistance to the establishment of a court of appeal against criminal convictions by judges throughout the nineteenth century (see, for instance, Woffinden, 1987: 321) meant that court of appeal judges were disinclined from day one to overturn convictions on appeal that rested on facts that had already been heard and decided upon by the trial jury. As Richard Nobles (2012: 25) observed, even the first case before the Court of Criminal Appeal was rejected on the basis of a refusal to usurp the decision of the jury at the original trial, the logic given as: 'there ought not to be a [reconsideration of the jury verdict] where only admissible evidence went before the jury' (see R v Williamson). In another early unsuccessful appeal case in 1909 that had many similarities with the Beck case, Thomas Simpson was convicted of assault and robbery with two others following eyewitness identification that was accepted by the Court of Criminal Appeal as 'not very strong' (see R v Simpson, p. 128). However, his conviction was upheld, again on the basis that the Court of Criminal Appeal was not prepared to go against the verdict of the trial jury on facts that had already been decided upon:

All the difficulties as to identification were put to the jury. The judge said that he was satisfied with the verdict. The jury are the judges of fact. The … [Criminal Appeal] … Act … [1907] … was never meant to substitute another form of trial for trial by jury. The case was not a strong one. It would have been open to the jury to acquit, and no one could have called the verdict perverse. But the verdict which the jury have given must stand. (R v Simpson, p. 130)

However, from the perspective that the proper task of the criminal appeals system should focus on assisting potentially factually innocent victims to have 'miscarriages of justice' overturned, worse was to come with the administrative and legislative reforms that were introduced following the Interdepartmental Committee on the Court of Criminal Appeal in 1965. The Interdepartmental Committee on the Court of Criminal Appeal, or Donovan Committee, was established:

To consider and report (1) whether it would be in the public interest to transfer the hearing of all or some of the cases now heard by the Court of Criminal Appeal … to the Court of Appeal or some other Court; and if so as to the manner in which that Court should be constituted, the powers it should have and the procedure to be followed (2) If in the view of the committee the Court of Criminal Appeal should retain the whole or part of its current jurisdiction whether any and if so what changes are desirable.

Prior to the Donovan Committee, the Court of Criminal Appeal was a Puisne ('puny') Court compared with the Court of Appeal, which dealt only with appeals in civil matters. This meant that rather than Lords Justices of Appeal hearing cases in criminal appeals as they did in civil appeals, criminal appeals were heard by the same level of judges that sat in the original criminal trials from where the appeals came from. Criminal appeal judges, then, were tasked with the job of sitting in judgment of the decisions of their colleagues when they were hearing appeals. To attend to this, the Donovan Committee led to the merging of the Court of Criminal Appeal with the Court of Appeal, dividing it into the Civil Division and Criminal Division, staffed by the same order of judges so the criminal appeals system was no longer inferior.

The Donovan Committee also fed into the Criminal Appeal Act 1966, which critically removed the notion that the criminal appeals system was about quashing 'miscarriages of justice' from the criminal appeal statute books, although it left in tact the proviso that convictions should not be overturned if it was not felt that a miscarriage of justice had occurred:

Section 4(1) of the 1907 Act (which requires the Court of Criminal Appeal to allow an appeal inter alia, if they think that a verdict of the jury should be set aside on the ground that it is unreasonable or cannot be supported having regard to the evidence or that on any ground there had been a miscarriage of justice, subject, however, to the proviso that they may dismiss the appeal if they consider that no substantial miscarriage of justice has actually occurred) shall be amended as follows:

(a)   for the words from 'it is unreasonable' to 'evidence' there shall be substituted the words 'under all the circumstances of the case it is unsafe or unsatisfactory';

(b)   for the words 'on any ground there was a miscarriage of justice' there shall be substituted the words 'there was a material irregularity in the course of the trial'; and,

(c)   in the proviso the word 'substantial' shall cease to have effect.

This effect of this reform can be conceived as catastrophic for alleged factually innocent victims of wrongful convictions. Rather than problematising the Court of Criminal Appeal's refusal from its inception to comply with its governing statute, it instead served to legitimate its practice of non-compliance with the 1907 Act by amendments that fitted perfectly with its practice. This changed the focus of the newly formed CACD to hearing appeals on points of law and breaches of due process at the expense of the job that it was, arguably, originally established to undertake. That is, to provide an appeal mechanism to overturn 'miscarriages of justice', understood in terms of factual innocence.

The spiral away from a concern to assist factually innocent victims of wrongful convictions continued with the Criminal Appeal Act 1968, which consolidated the law on criminal appeals a mere two years after the 1966 Act. In particular, the 1968 Act enshrined s. 4(1) of the 1966 Act in s. 2(1) and introduced an even higher hurdle for potentially innocent victims of wrongful convictions to have their convictions quashed by the CACD. Pursuant to s. 23 of the Criminal Appeal Act 1968, except in exceptional circumstances, appellants were required to present fresh evidence that was not previously adduced at trial:

(1)   For the purposes of an appeal under this Part of this Act the Court of Appeal may, if they think it necessary or expedient in the interests of justice:

(c)   receive any evidence which was not adduced in the proceedings from which the appeal lies.

(2) The Court of Appeal shall, in considering whether to receive any evidence, have regard in particular to:

    (a)   whether the evidence appears to the Court to be capable of belief;

    (b)   whether it appears to the Court that the evidence may afford any ground for allowing the appeal;

    (c)   whether the evidence would have been admissible in the proceedings from which the appeal lies on an issue which is the subject of the appeal; and

    (d)   whether there is a reasonable explanation for the failure to adduce the evidence in those proceedings.

The Criminal Appeal Act 1995 further amended s. 2(1) of the Criminal Appeal Act 1968, making the role of the CACD solely to adjudicate whether any evidence that it deems to fulfil the admissibility clauses and is accepted as fresh evidence affects the legal safety of the conviction and to quash a conviction if it decides that the conviction is 'unsafe':

2(1)   Subject to the provisions of this Act, the Court of Appeal:

    (a)   shall allow an appeal against conviction if they think that the conviction is unsafe; and

    (b)   shall dismiss such an appeal in any other case.

Just as crucially, s.2(1)(b) of the 1995 Act above abolished the miscarriage-of-justice proviso, so that the CACD was no longer under an obligation to even consider not quashing convictions in cases where there were no doubts about the appellant's factual guilt. Instead, the proviso now in place is in line with the new standard for allowing appeals to the effect that the CACD may decide not to quash convictions if it does not think that the conviction was 'unsafe'.

These requirements demonstrate just how far removed the current criminal appeals system is from the system that *could have* operated under the 1907 Act. Most crucially, an incremental paradigm shift can be conceived to have occurred with the various steps of the reforming criminal appeal statutes since the 1907 Act. It has shifted from a system that was originally intended by Parliament (and believed by the public) to be concerned about factual innocence and factual guilt to one that is entirely concerned with compliance with the due processes of the prevailing criminal justice system.

One thing is certain: the CACD is less inclined to consider appeals that turn on the facts that may have been decided wrongly by a jury at trial than it is to consider and quash appeals on points of law, such as the judges' summing up, and those that satisfy the appeals criteria in the sense that they easily identifiable fresh evidence (see, for instance, Royal Commission on Criminal Justice, 1993: 162; Roberts, 2003). For Kate Malleson (1994: 158) the reasoning for this is twofold: 'One reason is pragmatic – the fear of being swamped and the lack of resources; the other is based on a belief that appeals undermine the purpose of the criminal justice process, in particular, the idea of finality.' John Spencer's (2006) analysis of the limits of the criminal appeals system leaves little doubt that the CACD is, indeed, overwhelmed. On the impact this has on factually innocent victims of wrongful convictions, he has this to say:

> The Court of Appeal is grotesquely overworked ... [which] is the reason why the Court of Appeal (Criminal Division), like the Court of Criminal Appeal before it, has always done its best to avoid getting involved in appeals that turn on disputed facts ... one of the consequences of which is that the defendant is in a weak position to appeal where he was wrongly convicted [meaning innocent] (as against convicted in proceedings vitiated by an error of procedure or of substantive law). (692–693)

This feeds into the overriding doctrine of finality referred to above by Malleson (1994: 158; see also, Nobles and Schiff, 2002: 679–684), which dictates that defendants in the Crown Court must forward their full defence at trial before a jury who are the ultimate arbiters of whether they are guilty or not guilty of the specific criminal offence that they are changed with on the basis of the evidence at trial. For Nobles and Schiff (2008: 464–472):

> An unstated but equally important consideration [of finality] is that this restriction frees a court to develop definitions of crimes and standards of fairness, without needing to consider the large number of convicted prisoners that, as a result, it might be likely to release into the community (with retrials becoming an increasingly remote possibility as time passes).

This was recently affirmed by Hughes LJ in R v Kenyon (paragraph 27):

> [T]he interests of justice lie in there being a single trial at which the Defendant and the Crown each presents the whole of its case. It is

apt to subvert the process of justice if it is open to a Defendant to rely on appeal on something which could have been relied upon at trial … There has to be fresh evidence which is strong enough to justify the conclusion that it is necessary or expedient in the interests of justice to override the interests which justice has in a single trial.

Just as crucially, the factually innocent must also satisfy the CACD's 'jury impact test' to have their conviction overturned, expressed by Bingham LJ in the following terms:

The Court of Appeal is a court of review, not a court of trial. It may not usurp the role of the jury as the body charged by law to resolve issues of fact and determine guilt. Where the Court of Appeal receives fresh evidence under section 23 of the 1968 Act it must assess the quality of the evidence and allow the appeal if it judges that the fresh evidence combined with the original evidence might have caused the jury, or a reasonable jury properly directed, to acquit. The test is what impact the evidence, if called at the trial, might have had on the jury. It is not permissible for appellate judges, who have not heard any of the rest of the evidence, to make their own decision on the significance or credibility of the fresh evidence … For these reasons it will usually be wise for the Court of Appeal, in a case of any difficulty, to test their own provisional view by asking whether the evidence, if given at the trial, might reasonably have affected the decision of the trial jury to convict. If it might, the conviction must be thought to be unsafe. (R v Pendleton, paragraphs 12–19)

What is unsafe for the CACD?

In place of statutory guidelines, the leading authority on the circumstances under which convictions might be deemed unsafe in the eyes of the CACD is R v CCRC, *ex parte* Pearson. Noting that the term 'unsafe' in s. 2(1)(a) of the Criminal Appeal Act 1968 does not lend itself to precise definition, Bingham LCJ saw the following situations as 'obvious' examples of unsafety:

1. Where it appears that someone other than the appellant committed the crime and the appellant did not;
2. Where the appellant had been convicted of an act that is not in law a crime;

3.   Where a conviction is shown to be vitiated by serious unfairness in the conduct of the trial or significant legal misdirection;
4.   Where the jury verdict, in the context of other jury verdicts, defies any rational explanation; and
5.   Where the Court of Appeal may have some 'lurking doubt' or uneasiness about whether an injustice has been done. (R v CCRC, *ex parte* Pearson, paragraph 10)

On its face, this presents an image of an appeal system that looks like it fits well with a lay perspective on how the CACD should function as reflected in Pattenden's (1996: 59) observation above that it is for righting a wide range of wrongs in criminal trials. Looked at more critically, however, the *Pearson* judgment can be described as a highly misleading form of judicial communication to the public domain that seeks to convey that it fits with a lay perspective which does not reflect the realities of the criminal appeal process.

Taking the scenarios in turn, scenario 1 is clearly about factual innocence, suggesting, wrongly, that the CACD is concerned with whether appellants did or did not commit the offences that they appeal against and, even, that the CACD is about identifying the real perpetrators in wrongful conviction cases. It can also be argued that it is significant that this is first in the list of likely scenarios of unsafety. This might be read as further indicating that assisting the factually innocent is the priority and the principal type of case that the CACD quashes. But, as has been shown above, appeals in the CACD are not about showing that someone else did the crime that the appellant was convicted of and is complaining about. Another reality is that a simple claim of factual innocence by a potential appellant who argues that the jury got it wrong or that they were let down by their legal team is unlikely to persuade the CACD to even hear the appeal, let alone overturn it. Rather, appeals are about showing a breach of process or showing with fresh evidence that the evidence that led to the conviction is no longer reliable. And, perhaps most significantly, this process is not concerned with whether appellants are factually innocent or factually guilty. This is evident in the successful appeal judgment of the M25 Three, in which Raphael Rowe, Michael Davis and Randolph Johnson were convicted of a series of robberies and violent attacks just off the M25 motorway near London in December 1988, where Mantell LJ held:

> In our view the case against all three appellants was formidable ... However we are bound to follow the approach set out earlier in this

judgment, namely assuming the irregularities which we have identified had not occurred would a reasonable jury have been bound to return verdicts of guilty? In all conscience we cannot say that it would … Accordingly we cannot say that any of these convictions is safe. They must be quashed and the appeals allowed … For the better understanding of those who have listened to this judgment and of those who may report it hereafter this is not a finding of innocence, far from it. (R v Davis, Johnson and Rowe)

Another good example is the case of Nicholas Mullen, which was cited in Chapter 2 as a notable breach-of-process case which was successful on appeal, despite the CACD not having doubts about his guilt for taking part in IRA bombing campaigns (BBC News, 1999). As Steyn LJ observed in Mullen's failed application for compensation:

> Mr Mullen was not innocent of the charge. On the contrary, the conclusion is inescapable that he knowingly lent assistance to an active IRA unit. (R (Mullen) v Secretary of State for the Home Department, paragraphs 56–57)

Yet Mullen's conviction was quashed because it was said by the CACD to have involved 'a blatant and extremely serious failure to adhere to the rule of law' (R v Mullen, paragraph 40). It will be recalled that Mullen's conviction had been deemed unsafe after ten years into his 30-year sentence. All involved in his deportation from Zimbabwe, the police, MI6, the Security Service and officials from the Foreign Office and the Home Office as well as the relevant authorities in Zimbabwe, had colluded to secure his extradition in circumstances in which he was denied access to a lawyer. This was contrary to Zimbabwean law and internationally recognised human rights, which the CACD felt amounted to a breach of due process that invalidated his conviction. The quashing of the conviction has been described as the CACD's way of denoting its condemnation of the behaviour of the prosecuting authorities in ever bringing the case of Mullen to trial (Roberts, 2003: 441). In quashing Mullen's conviction, Rose LJ was clear in his understanding that convictions that are obtained in breach of the prevailing procedures of the criminal justice system are to be seen as unsafe, notwithstanding the factual innocence or guilt of the appellant:

> [F]or a conviction to be safe, it must be lawful; and if it results from a trial which should never have taken place, it can hardly be regarded as safe. (R v Mullen, paragraph 66)

In quashing Mullen's conviction, Rose LJ was equally unequivocal about the need for convictions such as his to be quashed in the public interest so as to preserve the integrity of the criminal justice system:

> It is for the judge in the exercise of his discretion to decide whether there has been an abuse of process, which amounts to an affront to the public conscience ... not only where a fair trial is impossible but also where it would be contrary to the public interest in the integrity of the criminal justice system that a trial should take place. An infinite variety of cases could arise. General guidance as to how the discretion should be exercised in particular circumstances will not be useful. But it is possible to say that in a case such as the present the judge must weigh in the balance the public interest in ensuring that those who are charged with grave crimes should be tried and the competing public interest in not conveying the impression that the court will adopt the approach that the end justifies any means. (R v Mullen, paragraph 18, citing Steyn LJ in R v Latif)

At the same time, and at the other end of the factual innocence–factual guilt spectrum, are cases such as the Cardiff Three, Stefan Kiszko and Sean Hodgson, all factually innocent victims of wrongful conviction. Yet none of the cases were overturned because the appellants were factually innocent and the CACD wanted to correct an apparent wrong. On the contrary, in each of the cases the successful appellants had their convictions overturned because they could either show a breach of process or produce fresh evidence that was not or could not have been available at the time of the original trial. In either case the evidence against them was unreliable: the Cardiff Three showed that PACE had not been complied with in the police interviews of Stephen Miller; Stefan Kiszko had his conviction overturned when medical evidence showed that he could not have produced the sperm found on Lesley Molseed (see Walker, 1999: 50); and Sean Hodgson's conviction for the murder of Teresa de Simone was quashed when fresh DNA analysis of semen samples found at the crime scene showed that they did not come from him.

As for the remaining scenarios presented by Bingham LCJ in *Pearson*, scenario 2 is something of a misnomer. Convictions for acts that are not criminal offences are highly unlikely and individuals convicted of acts that are not crimes can also be conceived as factually innocent of the 'crime', which again reinforces the general idea that the CACD is in the business of assisting the innocent.

Scenario 3 indicates intentional abortions of justice, which the public might also accept as appropriate candidates for being quashed. However, a lay perspective may see scenario 3 as potentially problematic if the breach of process or legal misdirection by the trial judge did not also undermine the factual evidence of an appellant's guilt, which was the CACD proviso until 1995. Indeed, it is interesting to note that scenario 3 does not expressly mention that factually guilty offenders can have their convictions overturned when they can show an intentional breach of due process (as evident in the case of Mullen discussed above and the case of Michael Weir discussed in Chapter 2).

Scenario 4 signifies that the CACD will overturn jury verdicts if it thinks that convictions are unsafe, which is contrary to the jury impact test that the CACD abides. It is also contrary to the jury deference that the CACD and the Court of Criminal Appeal before it have shown since the criminal appeals system was created, although Spencer's (2007: 844) analysis interestingly cites successful appeals on the basis of forms of jury bias.

Finally, scenario 5 further implies that the CACD's function is to assist the innocent as it will, apparently, even quash convictions on occasions that it merely feels 'uneasy' that an injustice may have occurred. As an example of such a 'lurking doubt' successful appeal Bingham LCJ cited the case of R v Cooper that was overturned by the CACD in November 1968. This is an interesting example which might have been selected on the basis that the successful appellant in *Cooper* was almost certainly factually innocent, again arguably seeking to reinforce the message that the CACD fits with a lay perspective. More specifically, in R v Cooper the successful appellant, Sean Cooper, had his conviction overturned on the basis of a possible misidentification for an assault occasioning actual bodily harm. The appeal also featured plausible evidence that the real perpetrator was most likely a man named Peter Burke, to whom Cooper was said to have a striking resemblance, and who had allegedly confessed to the assault to a third party (see R v Cooper).

Moreover, Bingham LCJ erred in his choice of R v Cooper as example of a 'lurking doubt' successful appeal in the year 2001, the year that the *Pearson* judgment was delivered. *Cooper* was a very rare type of successful appeal and was overturned under the different appeal test in place at the time under the 1966 Criminal Appeal Act, as incorporated in the Criminal Appeal Act 1968, which instructed convictions to be overturned if they were thought to be 'unsafe and unsatisfactory' as opposed to the current test under the 1995 Criminal Appeal Act which is restricted to 'unsafe'. As Widgery LJ in R v Cooper noted:

The important thing about this case is that all the material to which I have referred was put before the jury. No one criticises the summing-up, and, indeed, counsel for the appellant has gone to some lengths to indicate that the summing-up was entirely fair and that everything which could possibly have been said in order to alert the jury to the difficulties of the case was clearly said by the presiding judge. It is, therefore, a case in which every issue was before the jury and in which the jury was properly instructed, and, accordingly, a case in which this court would be very reluctant indeed to intervene. It has been said over and over again throughout the years that this court must recognise the advantage which a jury has in seeing and hearing the witnesses, and if all the material was before the jury and the summing-up was impeccable, this court should not lightly interfere. Indeed, until the passing of the Criminal Appeal Act 1966 – provisions which are now to be found in s. 2 of the Criminal Appeal Act 1968 – it was almost unheard of for this court to interfere in such a case. However, now our powers are somewhat different, and we are indeed charged to allow an appeal against conviction if we think that the verdict of the jury should be set aside on the ground that under all the circumstances of the case it is unsafe or unsatisfactory. That means that in cases of this kind the court must in the end ask itself a subjective question, whether we are content to let the matter stand as it is, or whether there is not some lurking doubt in our minds which makes us wonder whether an injustice has been done … We have given earnest thought in this case to whether it is one in which we ought to set aside the verdict of the jury, notwithstanding the fact they had every advantage and, indeed, some advantages we do not enjoy. After due consideration, we have decided we do not regard this verdict as safe, and accordingly we shall allow the appeal and quash the conviction. As far as this matter is concerned the appellant is discharged. (Widgery LJ in R v Cooper, paragraph 36)

However, in 1999 in R v F, Roch LJ adjudged this position was no longer valid and that when considering an appeal against conviction the CACD should apply the simple and clear test expressed in the Criminal Appeal Act 1968 s. 2(1), as substituted by the Criminal Appeal Act 1995 s. 2, and allow the appeal only if it regarded the conviction as unsafe. For Roch LJ, while the CACD would always have regard to the individual circumstances of each case before it, there is no longer any room in its deliberations for concepts such as 'lurking doubt' in addition to the current statutory test of unsafe (see R v F). Despite this, Stephanie

Roberts' (2004) analysis of 300 successful appeals in 2002 found that seven had mentioned 'lurking doubt' either directly or indirectly, with one appeal being allowed and the other six dismissed or refused.

Is a test for unsafe a better protection for the factually innocent?

Despite the shift in criminal appeals from an explicit statutory focus on miscarriages of justice that was related to the possible factual innocence of appellants to determinations as to whether convictions are 'unsafe', a discernible due process perspective has been proffered in support of the current arrangements. In the most extensive analysis of the criminal appeals system in England and Wales ever undertaken, Rosemary Pattenden (1996: 57–58) argued that an important function of an appeal 'is to protect the defendant (whether guilty or not) to a fair trial conducted according to law', which simultaneously ensures the 'integrity of the criminal justice system':

> A lapse from due process may not only expose a defendant to the risk of wrongful conviction, but threatens the integrity of the criminal justice system. Most departures of due process are the fault of the trial judge. His errors can take a multitude of forms including misdirections of law or fact in the summing up, wrong decisions on the admissibility of evidence, mishandling of a submission of no case an unlawful exercise of discretion, procedural error, and bias ... The majority of appeals which reach the CACD have as their object the correction of due process errors. (Pattenden, 1996: 58)

Noting that criminal trials are a human process and human processes are apt to make mistakes, another benefit of the appeal system for Pattenden (1996: 59) is the legitimacy that it confers on the trial regime, specifically, and the criminal justice system, generally:

> The public knows that if something goes wrong something can be done about it ... Of course, the CACD does not always find error. More often it finds that the ruling complained of was correct. Affirmation, too, legitimizes the criminal justice process, it vindicates the trial judge and reinforces his authority.

There are several problems with such an analysis from the analysis presented above on the statutes that govern the workings of the CACD and from the previous chapters of this book. First, the due process argument fails to distinguish between due process rights for defendants in criminal trials as opposed to due process rights for potential appellants to the CACD. As I have argued elsewhere (Naughton, 2007: ch. 1), it is indeed appropriate to staunchly defend due process safeguards against wrongful convictions, however defined, at the pre-trial and trial stages of the criminal justice process, precisely on the basis of the intrinsic connection to the state's legitimacy of the criminal justice system. However, as shown above, due process at the CACD is currently structurally biased towards assisting appellants who can show a breach of due process in their conviction, or produce fresh evidence. As such, due process and a test for legal unsafety cannot guarantee that factually innocent victims of wrongful convictions will overturn their convictions. In particular, the present arrangements can exclude factually innocent appellants who may have been wrongly convicted by the jury on the facts or who were poorly represented by their lawyers who may not have presented evidence of their factual innocence at trial (see Naughton, 2010; Naughton with Tan, 2010: 56–59). Perhaps most crucially, and as was argued in Chapter 4, this calls for a more sophisticated approach to due process in terms of how it relates to the functioning of the CACD. It must be acknowledged that the way that the police investigate alleged crimes is to construct incriminating cases against suspects and that inherently unreliable forms of evidence are deemed admissible in criminal trials. Crucially, even where criminal trials are conducted in accordance with due process they can result in the conviction of the factually innocent (see also Spencer, 1989: 203; 2006: 683). The current appeal system cannot guarantee that all such convictions will be overturned.

Second, as the analysis in the previous section on the case law on CACD successful appeals showed, how the CACD understands and decides on convictions that it deems unsafe can mean that the factually guilty can have their convictions overturned if they can show a breach of due process, whether intentional or unintentional. At the same time, the CACD will not overturn convictions of potentially factually innocent victims of wrongful convictions if they cannot show such a breach of due process or do not possess fresh evidence of their factual innocence.

Third, this calls for a need for a further distinction of the concepts of 'fairness' and 'integrity' at play in the foregoing due process perspective. It is problematic to simply view adherence to the prevailing procedures of due process as making criminal trials 'fair' and that when the CACD overturns convictions that were obtained in breach of due process that the criminal justice system somehow retains its 'integrity'. Indeed, a lay perspective may not view a fallible criminal justice system as fair or as having integrity when factually innocent individuals can be and are convicted of crimes that they did not commit that they may never have overturned while the system overturns the convictions of guilty appellants who can show breaches of due process.

A final issue is linked to Pattenden's (1996: 59) assertions on the legitimacy conferred on the criminal justice system by the very existence of the CACD, which she argued transmits the message to the public that the wrongs of criminal trials can be fixed. The pertinent question is what kind of 'wrongs' does the CACD fix and how does this fit with a wider public (lay) perspective on the appropriate functioning of the CACD? I would agree that the CACD can be conceived as providing legitimacy to the criminal justice system in Pattenden's (1996: 59) second sense, that is when appeals are dismissed which communicates that convictions are 'safe'. However, the history of the criminal justice system shows that when convictions are overturned of victims of wrongful convictions who are believed to be factually innocent the legitimacy of the whole criminal justice system can be called into question. At such times, reforms are introduced so that the legitimacy is restored, as was the case with the Beck case that led to the setting up of the criminal appeal system (see Chapter 1 in this book; Naughton, 2007: ch. 4).

Conclusion

The criminal appeals system started life with a clear and simple vision: to provide a mechanism to assist factually innocent victims of wrongful convictions to have their convictions overturned. The only proviso was that the criminal appeal court would only quash a conviction where a miscarriage of justice had occurred. This corresponded entirely with a lay perspective on the criminal justice system in the nineteenth century and early twentieth century when the Court of Criminal Appeal was established, as much as it does today. Parliament attempted to make this possible with the passing of the Criminal Appeal Act 1907, which was armed with wide powers to get to the truth of claims of innocence by alleged victims of 'miscarriages of justice'. To this end, the Court of Criminal Appeal could conduct investigations, completely rehear cases and any convictions that were quashed were considered to be acquittals with no further criminal proceedings permissible, pursuant to s. 4(2) of the Act, which Spencer

(2007: 839) identified as a possible further factor in the reluctance of the Court of Criminal Appeal to quash convictions.

Despite this, justice (from a lay perspective) can be said to have been aborted from day one of the criminal appeals system by judges who collectively refused to overturn convictions on facts that had already been decided at the trial of first instance by the original finders of fact – the jury. In fairness to the judges, this might be explained by a desire not to act in a way that may be thought to be unconstitutional and generally outwith their remit. In common law systems the underpinning rationale is, normally, that judges decide the law and the jury decides on the facts. As such, to interfere with the sacredness of the role of the jury could be conceived by judges from a rule-of-law perspective as potentially undermining a central tenet of the criminal justice system, and possibly diminishing its legitimacy.

Whatever the reasons, and the thinking behind them, the criminal appeals system was significantly reformed over the course of the twentieth century to create the existing remit of the CACD. It has been shown that this is incommensurable with the origins of the criminal appeals system. Perhaps most significantly, with its focus on breaches of due process and points of law it can fail to see potentially factually innocent victims of wrongful convictions as having eligible grounds for an appeal if the evidence of their innocence was or could have been available at the time of the original trial.

The defence of the current arrangements is that the CACD has, 'understandably', adopted a pragmatic approach to appeals and that it has to focus on more 'straightforward' appeals or it would not be able to deal with its likely caseload. The 'floodgates' argument is a staple that is routinely trotted out by system defenders. It indicates that cost-effectiveness of court time is the key priority, rather than any potential hypothetical concern not to encroach on an area that is the proper domain of the jury. A further defence is that the factually innocent are better protected by a system that overturns convictions on breaches of due process, which simultaneously demonstrates the CACD's integrity and conveys it with legitimacy. This equally misses the point from a lay perspective, which would see a criminal appeal system that quashes convictions of factually guilty offenders and which is structurally prejudiced against the factually innocent as not legitimate at all. Moreover, due process advocates also fail to understand that while due process is a vital safeguard against abortions of justice it can simultaneously act as a procedural barrier against quashing the convictions of factually innocent victims where no breaches of due process have occurred. In this light, due process at the appeal stage may not be a solution for the innocent but part of the problem.

The foregoing analyses illustrate the power struggle that is constantly at play in the arena of criminal appeals and how factually innocent victims of wrongful convictions can lose out to legal arguments. They will continue to do so until the CACD is reconstituted to undertake the task that it was originally established for, and until the judges that reside in the CACD are prepared to make decisions that will truly deliver on that task.

7
The Criminal Cases Review Commission

Introduction

The last chapter showed how the Court of Appeal (Criminal Division) (CACD) does not fit with a lay perspective in terms of what would/should be the proper functioning of a criminal appeals system. Rather than a system to assist factually innocent victims to have wrongful convictions overturned, it operates on an altogether different plane to correct apparent breaches of process and to generally ensure that convictions are obtained in compliance with the prevailing legal rules and procedures of the criminal justice system. But, the history of wrongful convictions shows that alleged factually innocent victims may not give up their struggle to have their convictions overturned and clear their names just because the CACD decides that their conviction is not unsafe, or they are adjudged not to have admissible grounds of appeal. On the contrary, they may continue their fight with the formation of support groups and organisations and the launching of media and political campaigns to raise awareness of the alleged wrong in the hope that it might help to get the case reconsidered and overturned (see Chapter 1; Naughton, 2007: ch. 5).

In recent times, one of the most significant and successful campaigns ever mounted in the area of alleged wrongful convictions was on behalf of the 11 people, mostly family members, who were convicted for IRA terrorist offences in the cases of the Guildford Four (see Conlon, 1990) and the Maguire Seven (see Maguire with Gallagher, 1994). These cases combined with the cases of the Birmingham Six (see Hill and Hunt, 1995) and a string of other notable cases in which (mainly) Irish people who were believed to be factually innocent victims of wrongful convictions (see, for example, Woffinden, 1987; Mullin, 1986; Kee, 1986; JUSTICE, 1989,

1994; Ward, 1993; Callaghan and Mulready, 1993; Rose *et al.*, 1997; Walker and Starmer, 1999; Kennedy, 2002). They together caused a public crisis of confidence in the workings of the entire criminal justice system (see Colvin, 1994; Elks, 2008; Kyle, 2004).

The inquiries into the events surrounding the convictions of the Guildford Four and the Maguire Seven by Sir John May (see May, 1990, 1992, 1994) were extended by the RCCJ, which was announced on 14 March 1991, the day that the Birmingham Six had their convictions overturned in the CACD. In particular, the RCCJ found that successive home secretaries under the old system for investigating alleged miscarriages of justice were not proactive in weeding them out. They were even failing to refer potential cases back to the CACD for political, as opposed to legal, reasons.

On 1 April 1997, the CCRC was established under the Criminal Appeal Act 1995 following one of the main recommendations of the RCCJ. It replaced the Criminal Case Unit of C3 Division of the Home Office (hereafter referred to as C3) where the Home Secretary formerly had the power to order reinvestigations of alleged or suspected 'miscarriages of justice' and send them back to the CACD under s. 17 of the Criminal Appeal Act 1968. The CCRC receives applications from alleged victims of 'miscarriages of justice' in England, Wales and Northern Ireland (NI) who have previously failed in their appeals against conviction but continue to complain about those convictions (see CCRC, 2012a).

The CCRC is the world's first statutory publicly funded body charged with the task of reviewing alleged 'miscarriages of justice'. It was hard fought for and it is therefore perhaps not surprising that it has been the subject of much pride in certain quarters of its native jurisdiction (see, for instance, Quirk, 2007; McCartney *et al.*, 2008; Jessel, 2009; Elks, 2012). Its creation has also sparked a great deal of interest from other jurisdictions that see it as a possible extension to their own criminal justice system to solve their own perennial problem of wrongful convictions. For instance, the CCRC led to the setting up of the Scottish Criminal Cases Review Commission (SCCRC), which started its work in April 1999 under the terms of s. 194A of the Criminal Procedure (Scotland) Act 1995 (as amended by s. 25 of the Crime and Punishment (Scotland) Act 1997) (see Scottish Criminal Cases Review Commission, 2012) and the Norwegian Criminal Cases Review Commission (NCCRC), which came into force on 1 January 2004 (see Norwegian Criminal Cases Review Commission, 2012). Moreover, there is an ongoing debate for a CCRC-type body in the US (see Schehr, 2009; Scheck and Neufeld, 2002; Schehr and Weathered, 2004); Australia (see, for example, Weathered, 2007; Sangha and Moles, 2011a, b); Canada (see Walker and Campbell, 2009; Campbell, 2008: 130–133); and New Zealand (see, for instance, Ellis, 2007).

The interest in the CCRC in these other jurisdictions is no doubt bolstered by a general belief among legal scholars, most notably in the United States, that the CCRC is a state-sponsored innocence commission that was established to assist factually innocent victims of wrongful convictions to have their convictions overturned. Lissa Griffin (2001: 1243–1244), who defined a wrongful conviction as a 'conviction that is both factually and legally inaccurate', for instance, was an early voice that urged the US to look to the CCRC as a model forum to investigate claims of factual innocence by alleged victims of wrongful convictions:

> It is undeniable that public confidence in the ability of the US criminal justice system to render accurate results has eroded significantly in recent years. There is increasing concern that innocent people are being wrongfully convicted and that there is no systemic mechanism to correct these results. In determining how to respond to this concern, the US criminal justice system may look to its English counterpart for new approaches … there needs to be an effective forum for investigating and considering claims of innocence … [and] … the standards for considering claims of innocence need to be broadened … One such forum could be an independent governmental entity modelled after the English CCRC. (1301–1302)

The following year, Ronald Huff (2002: 14) echoed Griffin's call, arguing that:

> Criminal cases review commissions (or 'innocence commissions') should be established at the national and state levels in the United States … I believe that the time has come to do what the United Kingdom has done. We should establish commissions similar to their Criminal Cases Review Commission (CCRC) to review post-appellate claims of wrongful conviction.

Huff (2002: 1) was clear on his definition of what would constitute a 'wrongful conviction' and what would be the appropriate focus of such CCRC-style bodies that he thought should be created in the US:

> Convicted innocents ... people who have been arrested on criminal charges ... who have either pleaded guilty to the charge or have been tried and found guilty; and who, notwithstanding plea or verdict, are in fact innocent. (see also, Huff *et al.*, 1996: 10)

Shortly afterwards, the first innocence commission in the US was created in November 2002, claiming that it was, indeed, based on the CCRC. This was the North Carolina Actual Innocence Commission (NCIIC) (see Mumma, 2004; Maiatico, 2007). The US discourse that the CCRC is an innocence commission was strengthened by Jon Gould's (2008: 34) account of the creation and first years of the second innocence commission in the US, the Innocence Commission for Virginia (ICVA) that was established in 2003. Gould saw the CCRC as an example of how 'the United Kingdom' has 'institutionalize[d] innocence review'. More recently, it was further reinforced by David Wolitz's (2010: 20) analysis of innocence commissions and the future of post-conviction review in the US which cited the CCRC as the 'first innocence commission' (see also Petherick *et al.*, 2010: 339).

On the positive side, a belief that the CCRC exists to provide a mechanism to enable factually innocent victims to have their convictions overturned appears to have had a beneficial impact in the US in that such a belief has given traction to the setting up of commissions that indeed focus on the question of appellants' factual innocence or guilt. For instance, the NCIIC, the first of its kind anywhere in the world, was established by the North Carolina General Assembly in 2006 and began operating in 2007. It is a truth-seeking state agency for credible post-conviction claims of factual innocence in North Carolina. It is separate from the appeals process and applicants who are exonerated by the Commission process are declared innocent and cannot be retried for the same crime (see North Carolina Innocence Inquiry Commission, 2012). More specifically, if five of the eight voting members decide after an investigation of an alleged wrongful conviction that there is sufficient evidence of factual innocence to merit judicial review, the case is referred to a superior court judge who will in turn appoint a three-judge panel (not to include the original trial judge) to hold a hearing. The panel may compel the testimony of any witness, including the defendant. If the panel unanimously concludes that the convicted person is factually innocent by clear and convincing evidence, it must vacate the conviction and dismiss the charges (see, for instance, Griffin, 2009: 136).

Despite this, the downside of analyses that see the CCRC as an innocence commission or as a body that was created to assist factually innocent victims of wrongful convictions to have their convictions overturned is that they reveal a profound misunderstanding of, and are a misrepresentation of, the CCRC and how it operates. The CCRC is not to be mistaken as a panacea for the problem of the wrongful conviction of the factually innocent that it was widely thought to be. The main source for a comprehensive critique of the CCRC from the perspective of assisting allegedly factually innocent applicants is my edited book (Naughton, 2009a). It contains 16 chapters of analysis by a collective of 17 authors comprising leading criminal appeal practitioners, academics, investigative journalists and representatives from third-sector voluntary organisations that assist allegedly factually innocent victims of wrongful convictions. Most crucially, s. 13(1)(a) of the Criminal Appeal Act 1995 mandates that it can only refer a case back to the CACD if there is a 'real possibility that the conviction, verdict, finding or sentence would not be upheld were the reference to be made'. This 'real possibility test' that is required by its governing statute fatally compromises the CCRC's claim of 'independence' and with it its ability to assist factually innocent victims of wrongful conviction. It shackles the CCRC to the criteria of the CACD for quashing convictions. It means that the CCRC is always in the business of second-guessing how the CACD might decide any applications that it refers (see, for instance, Nobles and Schiff, 2001: 280–299). It means that the CCRC does not attempt to determine the truth of allegedly wrongful convictions in the way that the NCIIC does but, rather, whether convictions might be considered 'unsafe' by the CACD, on the terms discussed in the last chapter. This disconnects the CCRC, entirely, from what the RCCJ and the public envisaged. This is perhaps most apparent at the extremes of the CCRC's operations when it means assisting the factually guilty to have convictions overturned on points of law and breaches of due process – and turning a blind eye to potentially factually innocent victims who are unable to fulfil the 'real possibility test' to the satisfaction of the CCRC.

Against this background, this chapter considers the ability of the CCRC to assist applicants who claim that they are factually innocent of Crown Court convictions for serious criminal offences. In three parts, it first compares how far the working remit of the CCRC differs from what was recommended by the RCCJ. That is, a focus on whether there is a 'real possibility' that the CACD will see the conviction as legally unsafe rather than question whether applicants are factually innocent or guilty. It is shown that the CCRC's 'real possibility test' means that the factually innocent may be procedurally barred from having their convictions referred to the CACD, while the convictions of the factually guilty will be referred by the CCRC and overturned if they are believed to fulfil the test. Second, the type of cases that the CCRC reviews are considered in the context of its claimed 'success' rate. This reveals the wide range of matters that the CCRC deals with that C3 did not and that the CCRC's contribution to overturning Crown Court convictions is actually less than its predecessor, C3, if compared on a pro rata basis. This is despite having a budget that was nine times greater than C3 and a staff cohort which was six times greater that C3. Finally, there will be a critical engagement with four dominant lines of defence that have been routinely deployed in attempts to counter critiques of the CCRC's structural limitations in assisting the factually innocent.

How the CCRC deviates from what the RCCJ envisaged

The remit of the RCCJ was far reaching:

> [T]o examine the criminal justice system from the stage at which the police are investigating an alleged or reported criminal offence right through to the stage at which a defendant who has been found guilty of such an offence has exhausted his or her rights of appeal. (Royal Commission on Criminal Justice, 1993: 1)

Yet the RCCJ was concerned only with whether innocent defendants were convicted or guilty offenders were acquitted, as evident in the following quote from the RCCJ Report:

> [O]nly to the extent that they b[ore] on the risks of an innocent defendant being convicted or a guilty defendant being acquitted. (Royal Commission on Criminal Justice, 1993: 1; for a critical discussion, see Naughton, 2009c; 2007: 14–26)

These two short quotes give insight into the RCCJ's definition of what would constitute a miscarriage of justice and how the new body that it recommended should operate. In terms of definition, the RCCJ fully corresponded with a lay perspective: it was either the wrongful conviction of the factually innocent and/or the wrongful acquittal of the factually guilty. In terms of how the new body that it recommended, the CCRC, should operate, the RCCJ was expressly critical of the custom of successive home secretaries to show what it saw as undue deference to the CACD. It was critical of the apparent 'self-imposed restriction' employed by home secretaries in not referring cases back to the CACD where it was thought that there was no real possibility that it would take a different view than it did at the original appeal (Royal Commission on Criminal Justice, 1993: 181–182). It was on this basis that the RCCJ recommended that the public crisis in the criminal justice system at the time would be resolved by the:

> [C]reation of a new body independent of both the Government and the courts to be responsible for dealing with allegations that a miscarriage of justice [i.e. wrongful conviction of the factually innocent] has occurred. (Royal Commission on Criminal Justice, 1993: 183)

That the CCRC should be independent was crucial for the RCCJ. Although the RCCJ felt that the CACD ought to be able to quash the convictions of the factually innocent, it recognised that it operates within a realm of legal rules and procedures that mean it is neither 'the most suitable or the best qualified body to supervise investigations of this kind' (Royal Commission on Criminal Justice, 1993: 183). The RCCJ saw this as a shortcoming that could be attended to if the CCRC conducted thorough re-examinations of alleged miscarriages of justice. The CCRC was also recommended by the RCCJ to retain the authority of the Home Secretary under the previous C3 system. Any convictions referred back to the CACD were to be 'in the interests of justice' in the lay sense (see, for instance, Newby, 2009) and were to be, accordingly, considered as first appeals. As the RCCJ asserted:

> Where the result of the investigation indicated that there were reasons for supposing that a miscarriage of justice might have occurred, the [CCRC] would refer the case to the Court of Appeal, which would consider it as though it were an appeal referred to it by the Home Secretary under section 17 [of the Criminal Appeal Act 1968] now. (Royal Commission on Criminal Justice, 1993: 183)

In further recognition of the limits of the CACD under the existing criteria in overturning the convictions of factually innocent victims of miscarriages of justice, the RCCJ recommended that the free pardon under the Royal Prerogative of Mercy remain an available route for factually innocent victims of wrongful conviction to obtain justice:

> [I]f the Court of Appeal were to regard as inadmissible evidence which seemed to the [CCRC] to show that a [wrongful conviction of an innocent] might have occurred ... We therefore recommend that

the possible use of the Royal Prerogative be kept open for the exceptional case. (Royal Commission on Criminal Justice, 1993: 184)

This was incorporated into the Criminal Appeal Act 1995 as s. 16(2). This permits the CCRC to refer applications to the Secretary of State if it is of the opinion that the applicant is factually innocent but lacking the necessary legal grounds for the appeals system.

Contrary to this, the CCRC is not concerned with whether applicants are factually innocent or guilty and convictions that it refers are not considered as first appeals. It is mandated to also take account of the reasons why the conviction was not overturned in any failed appeals before the application to the CCRC. And, after almost 15 years of casework and the 14,778 applications that it has so far received, figures to 31 May 2012, it is yet to refer a single conviction for consideration for a free pardon under the Royal Prerogative of Mercy. This is in stark contrast with the situation prior to the creation of the CCRC when free pardons under the Royal Prerogative of Mercy were fairly frequent when the evidence of applicants' factual innocence fell outside of the scope of the CACD's grounds of appeal, that is, it was not fresh evidence (for a discussion, see Naughton, 2009c: 30–37).

As indicated above, the crux of the problem from the perspective of the CCRC's ability to assist the factually innocent, is the requirement under s. 13 of the Criminal Appeal Act 1995 that it has to employ a 'real possibility test' in deciding whether convictions referred are likely to be overturned. This subordinates the CCRC to the appeals criteria of the CACD in a way that is contrary to what was envisaged by the RCCJ (for a critical discussion, see Naughton, 2009b). The legal authority on how the CCRC should interpret the 'real possibility test' is R v Criminal Cases Review Commission, *ex parte* Pearson, in which Bingham LCJ defined the prescribed test as:

[I]imprecise but plainly denot[ing] a contingency which, in the Commission's judgment, is more than an outside chance or a bare possibility but which may be less than a probability or a likelihood or a racing certainty. The Commission must judge that there is at least a reasonable prospect of a conviction, if referred, not being upheld. The threshold test is carefully chosen: if the Commission were almost automatically to refer all but the most obviously threadbare cases, its function would be mechanical rather than judgmental and the Court of Appeal would be burdened with a mass of hopeless appeals; if, on the other hand, the Commission were not to refer any case unless it judged the applicant's prospect of success on appeal to be assured, the cases of some deserving applicants would not be referred to the Court and the beneficial object which the Commission was established to achieve would be to that extent defeated. The Commission is entrusted with the power and the duty to judge which cases cross the threshold and which do not. (paragraph 17)

The following quote from the CCRC website aptly illustrates the impact of the 'real possibility test' on how it understands its remit and scope:

If you are asking us to review your conviction, we will not be looking again at the facts of your case in the way that the jury did to decide if you are guilty or innocent. Our concern will only be with the question which the Court of Appeal would ask, which is whether your conviction is unsafe. This can mean us considering issues such as:

- was the trial as a whole fair?
- did the trial Judge make the correct legal rulings during the course of the trial (for example, in relation to disclosure of evidence, the admissibility of evidence or a submission of no case to answer)?
- did the trial Judge fairly sum up the case to the jury and assist the jury with the appropriate legal directions?
- very importantly, is there now fresh evidence that was not presented at trial? (CCRC, 2012b)

This highlights the extent to which the CCRC deviates from what was recommended by the RCCJ and its total lack of independence from the CACD. It calls for further distinctions to be made between what the RCCJ recommended and the part that the CCRC plays as an integral part of the criminal appeals system.

For instance, the RCCJ's perspective on a 'fair trial' as mentioned in the first bullet point was in terms of 'fairness of the outcome' and whether a factually innocent defendant was convicted. Contrary to this, the CCRC sees it as about 'fairness of process' in terms of compliance with the prevailing criminal justice procedures. This links with the references to the 'correctness' and 'fairness' of legal rulings and summing up by the trial judge in the second and third bullet points, which further detaches the work of the CCRC from the perspective of the RCCJ. The CCRC, then, is best viewed as a bolt-on quality control mechanism to the existing criminal appeals system that works to ensure that the decisions of the CACD meet with its own rules and procedures in the global interests of upholding its (the CACD) vision of criminal justice system integrity; it seeks to determine whether convictions are lawful, not whether they are just in the lay sense of factual innocence and guilt.

The knock-on effect of this is that the CCRC does not undertake thorough investigations to determine whether claims of innocence are true. It does not undertake the kind of public enquiries of claims of innocence by alleged victims of miscarriages of justice in the way that was pictured by the RCCJ. Instead, the 'real possibility test' means that it seeks to determine whether alleged wrongful convictions might be legally unsafe by the CACD. This renders its reviews for the most part as mere 'desktop reviews' of applications (see Newby, 2010; also Naughton, 2010: 30–32). The CCRC seeks to determine whether there is an apparent breach of process, or whether there is any possible fresh evidence that might undermine the evidence that led to the conviction. This fails to recognise that factually innocent victims can be wrongly convicted even in the absence of any transgressions of due process (see analysis in Chapter 4; Naughton, 2007: ch. 3; 2011a: 40–54; 2012; Spencer, 1989: 203; 2006: 683). This runs counter to how the CCRC was imagined by the RCCJ: that is, that it would reinvestigate claims of factual innocence thoroughly to determine whether they are valid or not and assist factually innocent victims of wrongful conviction to obtain justice in the CACD or by a free pardon under the Royal Prerogative of Mercy.

Finally, the CCRC's reference to it being 'very important' that applicants have fresh evidence in bullet point four above demonstrates, further, how far its operations are at odds with the RCCJ and a lay perspective on its role. It means that the CCRC will emulate the CACD in assisting factually guilty offenders to overturn their convictions. A pertinent example of a CCRC referral in which the applicants were factually guilty is the joint appeals of R v Clarke and McDaid (see R v Clarke and R v McDaid). There was no doubt that Clarke and McDaid were guilty as charged and the CACD dismissed their convictions at their first appeal. Despite this, the CCRC referred their convictions for GBH back to the CACD solely on the ground that the bill of indictment was not signed. The CACD again dismissed their appeals. However, their convictions were subsequently quashed by the House of Lords on the basis that the absence of a signature on their indictment invalidated their trial and hence their convictions could not stand (see R v Clarke and R v McDaid).

At the same time, the CCRC may not refer the cases of factually innocent victims of wrongful conviction if the review is unable to adduce fresh evidence and the conviction is not felt to fulfil the 'real possibility test', described by Bingham LCJ in *Pearson* as follows:

> The exercise of the power to refer accordingly depends on the judgment of the Commission, and it cannot be too strongly emphasised that this is a judgment entrusted to the Commission and to no one else ... the Commission cannot therefore invite the court to review issues or evidence upon which there has already been a ruling ... The Commission has, in effect, to predict how the Court of Appeal is likely to answer the question which arises under section 23, as formulated above. In a conviction case depending on the reception of fresh evidence, the Commission must ask itself a double question: do we consider that if the reference is made there is a real possibility that the Court of Appeal will receive the fresh evidence? If so, do we consider that there is a real possibility that the Court of Appeal will not uphold the conviction? The Commission would not in such a case refer unless it gave an affirmative answer to both questions. (see R v Criminal Cases Review Commission, *ex parte* Pearson, paragraphs 16–18)

As evidence of the limitations of the CCRC's 'real possibility test' as it impacts on applicants who claim factual innocence, a dossier of 45 cases of potentially factually innocent alleged victims of wrongful convictions were made public by the Innocence Network UK (INUK) in March 2012. They were part of its campaign for the reform of the CCRC so that it might be better placed to assist factually innocent applicants. All of the cases have been refused a referral back to the CACD at least once by the CCRC on the basis that they do not meet the 'real possibility test' despite continuing doubts about the evidence that led to their convictions. The cases included in the dossier comprised mainly prisoners who are serving life or long-term sentences for serious offences, including gangland murders, armed robbery, rape and other sexual offences. In all of the cases the alleged victims continue to maintain that they had no involvement at all in the offences they were convicted of. They assert that they were wrongly convicted due to reasons including fabricated confessions, eyewitness misidentification, police misconduct and flawed expert evidence (Innocence Network UK, 2012c).

'Success' rate

To 31 May 2012, the CCRC had received 14,778 applications, including the 279 cases that were transferred from the Home Office when the CCRC was set up, approximately a thousand each year. Of these, it had completed its reviews of 14,133 cases, of which it had referred 503 to the relevant appeal court. This equates to an average referral rate over the period of 3.6 per cent, although in 2010–2011, the CCRC referred only 22 cases or 2.3 per cent of the 947 cases that it completed reviews on (see CCRC, 2011: 7; 15). Of the total number of cases referred, 461 appeals had been heard and 324 were reported to have been 'quashed' and 137 were reported to have been upheld. On a straightforward reading this suggests a 'success' rate of approximately 20 cases a year that have been 'quashed' following a referral by the CCRC, or around 65 per cent of the applications that it has so far referred. On face value, this certainly appears to be an increase on the previous system under C3, which contributed to an annual average of five convictions being quashed upon referral between 1980 and 1992, for instance (Pattenden, 1996: 363).

Such a crude statistical comparison between the CCRC and C3, however, is methodologically problematic as the CCRC and C3 are not directly comparable: they did different things, with different resources at their disposal. First, the CCRC has six times more staff than C3 had, and the budget of the CCRC is nine times greater than that of C3, so more referrals might well be expected. In 1994, for instance, C3 had 12 caseworkers and two and a half senior staff working full-time on alleged miscarriages of justice and related issues (Pattenden, 1996: 349). This compares with a current (June 2012) cohort of about 90 staff at the CCRC, including nine commissioners (although this is contrary to the s. 8(3) of the Criminal Appeal Act 1995 which mandates that the CCRC has a no fewer than 11 commissioners), and a core of about 50 caseworkers, who are supported by administrative staff (see Ministry of Justice, 2012c). The annual staff costs of C3 in 1991 were £357,000. Using Retail Price Index tables Nobles and Schiff (2009: 151) showed that this translates into a staff cost budget in 2006, for instance, of £530,290. In contrast, the staff budget for the CCRC for 2005–2006 was £4,930,439, nine times greater than C3.

Second, the remits of C3 and the CCRC are different. C3 was remitted:

1. To assist Ministers in discharging the Home Secretary's duties and powers under the Mental Health Act 1983 and the Criminal

Procedure (Insanity) Acts 1964 and 1991 in relation to offenders detained in psychiatric hospitals whose leave, transfer or discharge is subject to Home Office consent. To co-ordinate the development of policies designed to improve the response of the criminal justice system to mentally disordered offenders.

2. To assist Ministers in discharging the Home Secretary's responsibilities in relation to the royal prerogative of mercy and references to the Court of Appeal under section 17 of the Criminal Appeal Act and the payment of compensation to persons wrongfully convicted; and to keep the law and practice relating to the investigation and correction of wrongful convictions under review. (HC Deb, 1992)

Unlike C3, then, the CCRC is not required to undertake any policy or law reform work in the area of law and practice, nor does it assist with compensation to victims of wrongful convictions. Also unlike C3, the remit of the CCRC as determined by ss. 9–12 (inclusive) of the Criminal Appeal Act 1995 is much wider than a restriction to a consideration of Crown Court convictions. The CCRC deals with any convictions verdicts, findings and/or sentences given either on indictment in the Crown Court or in summary hearings in magistrates' courts in England, Wales and NI. However, pursuant to s. 16 of the Criminal Appeal Act 1995 the CCRC, similar to C3, does assist with Royal Prerogative of Mercy work, either by way of a referral to/from the Secretary of State. Unpacking this further to make the problem of comparison between C3 and the CCRC clearer, as its remit related to the criminal justice system C3 dealt only with alleged wrongful convictions for serious criminal offences given in the Crown Court. It did not deal with appeals against length of sentence and it did not deal with appeals against convictions and/or sentences in magistrates' courts in the way that the CCRC does.

This links to a third related point, which further reveals how the CCRC is, arguably, not fulfilling its expected public mandate from a lay perspective, namely that it should exist to help factually innocent victims of serious wrongful convictions to overturn their convictions. In terms of criminal convictions, C3 was petitioned by human rights and civil liberties organisations such as JUSTICE following its own investigations that led it to belief that the people it represented were factually innocent victims of wrongful conviction and imprisonment. It was the success of such innocence-oriented efforts that induced the public crisis of confidence in the entire criminal justice system and prompted the government of the day to establish the RCCJ. However, and as already indicated, in working entirely within the realm of legal rules and procedures the CCRC deals with applicants irrespective of their factual innocence or guilt and can be said to act as a filter for the appeal courts. In so doing, it effectively sanctions the successful appeals against conviction of factually guilty offenders or reductions of their sentences if their applications are deemed to satisfy the requirements of the appeal courts. At the same time, if it turns up evidence that indicates an applicant's factual innocence that was available at the original trial it may not constitute grounds for a referral (see also Nobles and Schiff, 2001: 280–299). As such, despite its apparent shortcomings, C3 operated in a way that was, arguably, more in line with public notions of the interests of justice as it was concerned with whether alleged victims of miscarriages of justice were factually innocent. The CCRC, on the other hand, is akin to a legal watchdog body that seeks to ensure that the decisions of criminal justice system meet with its stated rules of due process. On this point it is interesting to note that focus group research with CCRC commissioners and case review managers (CRMs) found that those who participated in the session did not see it as problematic that they are not independent from the CACD, proudly describing themselves as 'gatekeepers for the Court of Appeal' (see Maddocks and Tan, 2009: 128). This confirmed earlier commentary by CCRC Commissioner, Leonard Leigh, who asserted:

> It is not the function of the Commission, as gatekeeper to the Court of Appeal, to revisit findings of fact made at trial. The Commission must conclude that by reason of new evidence or argument there is a real possibility that the conviction or sentence, if referred, will be quashed by the appellate court. (Leigh, 2004)

Finally, the CCRC's definition of 'quashed' needs to be clarified. Perhaps most crucially, the CCRC data on 'quashed' cases is not to be read as synonymous with C3 quashed convictions. First, by 'quashed', the CCRC includes conviction referrals that are quashed by the CACD that are sent for retrial and in which the appellants are subsequently reconvicted. Second, it also includes sentences that are 'quashed' and replaced with a lower sentence and the appellant remains in prison Third, the CCRC also counts as successes those cases where alternative convictions are substituted, for instance manslaughter for murder (on these three categories, see Naughton, 2003a: 7). Fourth, the CCRC engages in multiple counting, rating its 'success' not in terms of individual cases but numbers of convictions (see Woffinden, 2010). For instance, the case of the Bridgewater Four would be recorded as four successful cases and the case of the M25 Three as three, making a total of seven 'successes' for two cases. Finally, the CCRC statistics include cases in magistrates' courts (see Kerrigan, 2006) for such things as road traffic offences, parking tickets and the notorious case of Dino the German shepherd dog. The CCRC helped to reprieve Dino from 'death row' in September 2004 after he was put under a destruction order, imposed under the Dangerous Dogs Act 1991, three years earlier by Northampton Magistrates' Court in July 2001. Dino had bitten Elizabeth Coull who tried to intervene in a fight between him and her pet terrier, Ralph. The legal battle over Dino's case passed from the magistrates' court to Northampton Crown Court, to the High Court, the House of Lords, the European Court of Human Rights and finally the CCRC. The CCRC looked into the case and referred it back to Northampton Crown Court, whereupon the destruction order was rescinded (see Rozenberg, 2004; Endangered Dogs Defence and Rescue, 2004; Naughton, 2009b: 2, 14).

The foregoing is not meant as advocating for the return of C3, which clearly presented a constitutional problem, which was correctly resolved with the separation of post-appeal investigations of alleged wrongful conviction from politics. Rather, it is to make clear that comparing the work of the CCRC and that of C3 is akin to comparing apples and oranges: they each have/had different premises on what actually constitutes a miscarriage of justice, which determined that they deal/dealt with alleged miscarriages of justice in different ways and they had different referral powers at their disposal. To be sure, the aim here is to outline some of the key characteristics of the CCRC and introduce the idea that the replacement of C3 with the CCRC is not the final solution to the overturning of the convictions of the factually innocent that was hoped for and many believe it is. Moreover, when assessed in the context of the foregoing analysis, the CCRC's performance in serious wrongful conviction cases does not look so favourable when compared with that of C3. In fact, C3's average of five cases a year with six times less staff and nine times less resources stands up well against the CCRC's average of 1.4 cases a year since 2005 on the basis of multiple counting, as detailed by Woffinden (2010). Things are not always what they appear to be on the surface. It appears from a deeper analysis that we have shifted from a problem with the political sphere failing to refer the cases of potentially factually innocent individuals convicted of serious criminal offences in the Crown Court back to the CACD if those cases were thought to conflict with political interests to a problem with the CCRC failing to refer and overturn cases of the potentially factually innocent if they are believed to conflict with the dictates of the legal system.

The CCRC's response

The foregoing has detailed the extent to which the CCRC does not fit with what was recommended by the RCCJ. It is not the kind of post-appeal investigatory body to conduct thorough investigations of claims of factual innocence that the RCCJ anticipated. It is not a state-sponsored innocence commission akin to those that have been spawned in the US, whatever those wishing to implement innocence commissions and international scholars may believe or may want to believe. And, yet, CCRC spokespeople and academic lawyers have argued in defence of the CCRC along the following four lines:

1. that the CCRC and the CACD need to be have the same test;
2. that the integrity of the criminal justice system is paramount and the wrongly convicted are better protected by a test for unsafety rather than a test for provable innocence;
3. that the concern with the limitations of the CCRC in assisting victims of wrongful conviction who may be factually innocent risks further eroding due process rights afforded to suspects of crime; and
4. that Parliament requires the CCRC to work to the CACD test so it is wrong to blame the CCRC for its failures in assisting the factually innocent.

Each will now be critically considered in turn.

The CCRC and the CACD need to have the same test?

A common argument in defence of the CCRC is that it should have the same test as the CACD, as there is no point at all in referring cases that have no chance of being overturned. It is argued that to create an asymmetrical system would be 'absurd', as such a practice would raise expectations among applicants, cause a tension and much confusion between the CCRC and the CACD, and would not be in the public interest:

> Whatever statutory test Parliament … imposed it has to be one that articulates with the test that the Court of Appeal itself has to apply. If you break that link and you establish an asymmetry between the two tests, you will be creating an absurd situation. It would create

tension between the Court of Appeal and the Commission, it would raise expectations, it would cause confusion, and it is difficult to see what possible public interest could be served by referring cases on a basis that had no relation to the test employed by the court itself. (the then Chair of the CCRC, Professor Graham Zellick, 2004, cited in R v Cottrell and Fletcher, paragraph 55; see also Zellick, 2005b; Newby, 2009: 104; Kerrigan, 2009)

The first problem with this line of defence is that it overlooks the historical context of the establishment of the CCRC. The CCRC was set up in the wake of a public crisis of confidence in the criminal justice system precisely because of the symmetry that was identified by the RCCJ between the C3 system and the CACD and its apparent failures in overturning the wrongful conviction of people believed to be factually innocent (see Naughton, 2009c; Nobles and Schiff, 2008: 472). Moreover, the RCCJ, which gave life to the CCRC, was set up on the day that the Birmingham Six had their convictions overturned in the CACD and it is both geographically and politically symbolic that the CCRC is based in Birmingham rather than the capital, London. It is an enduring reminder that it was set up in governmental response to one of the most notorious miscarriages of justice in British legal history. Its purpose was to restore public confidence that the criminal justice system could rectify wrongful convictions given to those widely believed to be factually innocent.

Second, this position fails to recognise other possible impacts and wider benefits that sending such cases back to the appeal courts might have, even if they were not to be overturned. Such cases could, for instance, raise public awareness of the inability or unwillingness of the CACD to overturn cases of appellants thought, even by the CCRC after its impartial investigations, to be factually innocent but who do not fulfil the current CACD criteria (see Naughton 2009b: 5).

Contrary to this, the perspective that the CCRC and the CACD should work to the same test (legal unsafety) works to prevent public knowledge of the limits of the CACD in dealing with factual innocence claims by alleged victims of wrongful conviction. It fails to understand that the RCCJ intended that the CCRC be independent of the courts, precisely, so that it would be asymmetrical with the CACD in its investigations of alleged miscarriages of justice, defined as the wrongful conviction of the factually innocent. The CCRC was not anticipated to be an addition to the criminal appeals system that was deferential to the CACD. For the RCCJ, it was to be a body to provide a remedy for factually innocent victims of wrongful convictions either though the CACD or if innocent victims were not thought to have legal grounds via the avenue of the Royal Prerogative of Mercy. In its dealings with the CACD, factual innocence is not a live issue due to the 'real possibility test'. As for the Royal Prerogative of Mercy, the CCRC is yet to refer a case for consideration and is unlikely to ever do so because reviews to determine whether applications might be legally unsafe are not to be equated with investigations that seek to determine whether claims of factual innocence are valid or not (see Naughton, 2009c: 36).

The integrity of the system is paramount and the factually innocent are better protected by a test for unsafety?

A second line of defence of the CCRC's statutory link with the CACD responds directly to the establishment of the Innocence Network UK (INUK) and its member innocence projects, which are seen as unnecessary in a jurisdiction with the CCRC. There are three planks to this defence:

1. that it is dangerous to argue that the CCRC is not concerned with factual innocence, as if it was widely known, it could lead to the further marginalisation of miscarriages of justice by the public and politicians;
2. that the wrongly convicted are actually better served by a test for legal unsafety as fewer innocent people would have their convictions overturned if the legal criterion was provable factual innocence, if only because factual innocence is often impossible to prove; and
3. that the integrity of the criminal justice system is of primary importance and to consider the safety of a conviction provides a more demanding test for the system is the surest way to assist the factually innocent in overturning their convictions. (for examples of this perspective, see Quirk, 2007; Jessel, 2009)

Put simply, the very emergence of innocence projects in the UK in a post-CCRC system indicates that the CCRC may not be the panacea for wrongful convictions that this line of argument supposes. Moreover, the CCRC's own website (as cited above) makes it abundantly clear that it not concerned with whether applicants are factually innocent or guilty but, rather, with whether the CACD might find the conviction unsafe. Indeed, the evidence is irrefutable. As shown above, the CCRC assists in the quashing of criminal convictions given to factually guilty offenders when there has been an apparent breach of due process. Yet the 'real possibility test' restricts it from undertaking thorough investigations of claims of factual innocence if the evidence of factual innocence is unlikely to be considered to be fresh evidence on the basis that it was or could have been available at the time of the original trial.

However, I do agree with the idea that if this was more widely known it is likely that there would be the kind of public and political backlash that is feared by adherents to this line of defence. This is precisely what occurred prior to the setting up of the RCCJ amid the fallout from the cases of the Guildford Four, Birmingham Six, and so on, and was the reason for the establishment of the CCRC. This would likely happen not because the public and politicians would want to sideline miscarriages of justice but, rather, because they care about miscarriages of justice, understood in a lay sense of the RCCJ as the wrongful conviction of the factually innocent and the factually guilty escaping justice (also understood in the lay sense) on breaches of due process.

Second, the argument that the wrongly convicted are actually better served by a test for legal safety as fewer innocent people would overturn their convictions if they had to prove factual innocence rather than unsafety of conviction reveals a profound misunderstanding of what it means to be innocence oriented: it is about the *quality* of convictions overturned, not the *quantity*. Moreover, an innocence-oriented approach does not necessarily seek to prove that alleged victims of wrongful convictions are in fact innocent, although if it is possible to prove factual innocence all attempts will be made to prove it. Indeed, the methodology of an innocence-oriented approach is two-pronged. There is an interrogation of the process that to the conviction (police investigation and prosecutorial conduct, for instance) and the evidence that is claimed to prove that the alleged innocent victim is factually guilty. Simultaneously, ways are sought to determine whether the claim of factual innocence by the alleged victim can be validated. Such an approach operates akin to the kind of public enquiries that the RCCJ thought the CCRC would undertake.

The case of Simon Hall (see Naughton and Tan, 2010: 328–331) investigated by the University of Bristol Innocence Project and referred back to the CACD by the CCRC, provides a good illustration. The investigation questioned the reliability of the fibre evidence that was claimed to link Simon Hall to the murder of 79-year-old Joan Albert (see University of Bristol, 2010). It also suggested that DNA testing be undertaken on the handle of the murder weapon (knife) to either incriminate or exclude him (see University of Bristol, 2011). However, if the possibility of proving factual innocence is not available, say in a case where a rape conviction is based on the testimony of the accuser and the investigation can show that the alleged victim of the rape lied, the person should be regarded as factually innocent. This is dictated by the presumption of innocence, as there would be no reliable evidence that the victim of the wrongful conviction is factually guilty of the alleged criminal offence. A good example is the case of Warren Blackwell who was convicted of sexual assault in 1999 following allegations by the complainant that he had attacked her outside a social club (see Chapter 3, for fuller discussion). After spending three years in prison, Blackwell's conviction was overturned when it emerged that the complainant had a history of making false allegations of sexual assault against other men and frequently changed her name so that she could not be identified by the police (see Greenhill, 2006b).

Third, the idea that the integrity of the criminal justice system is paramount and provides the surest way to assist the factually innocent in having their convictions overturned conflates the test for legal safety with factual innocence. It misrepresents the CCRC's 'real possibility test' and the basis on which the CACD overturns criminal convictions. It seeks to justify the test for legal unsafety on the assumed basis that it acts to assist factually innocent victims of wrongful conviction. Just as crucially, as discussed in Chapter 6 in relation to the CACD, it calls for a distinction between a legal notion of 'integrity', defined as strict compliance with criminal appeals procedures, and a lay understanding of 'integrity'. The latter would distinguish between successful appeals overturned on the basis of factual innocence, such as Sean Hodgson (see R v Hodgson) the first DNA exoneration in the UK, and successful appeals that are overturned on apparent breaches of due process, for example cases such as Mullen, Weir and Clarke and McDaid cited above.

In this context, it is interesting to reflect on a recent statement to the press by the current Chair of the CCRC, who was formerly the Chief Executive of the Crown Prosecution Service (CPS) (see Naughton, 2008b), in response to critiques of its handling of claims of factual innocence by applicants:

> If we came across any new evidence that we thought suggested somebody was innocent we'd move heaven and earth to look into it. I've got people who'd lie down in the street to stop the traffic if they thought it would help. (Richard Foster, cited in Robins, 2010)

Such statements are regularly mobilised when the CCRC engages in public debate. They are both revealing and profoundly misleading of the role of the CCRC and how it reviews alleged wrongful convictions. The CCRC, evidently, want the public to see it as fulfilling its public mandate as recommended by the RCCJ, as a 'champion of justice' (see Jessel, 2009), to give the impression that it assists factually innocent victims of wrongful convictions. But, the reference to 'new evidence' in the foregoing quote highlights that the CCRC is restricted to second-guessing the CACD criteria. Just as crucially, evidence of potential factual innocence has to be unearthed by an investigation that is looking for it. It is not just happened across in a (mainly desk top) review of whether the conviction might be legally unsafe (see Naughton, 2009c: 20–35).

A due process defence

A third line of defence argues that a critique of the limitations of the CCRC in dealing with applications by potentially factually innocent victims of wrongful convictions risks further eroding due process rights for suspects of crime. This perspective argues that such 'innocence campaigners fail to take sufficient account' of the fact that in 'legal terms, all defendants, even those caught red-handed ... are to be presumed innocent until proven guilty' (Quirk, 2007: 767). The main fear for proponents of this perspective seems to be that to raise the CACD's test to factual innocence would not protect those individuals who are convicted following 'irregularities in the arrest, investigation or trial procedure' who may not be innocent, which 'would mean the loss of an important safeguard for the integrity of the process, as much as for the liberties of individuals' (Quirk, 2007: 769). It is argued that:

> At a time when the due process protections offered to defendants are under attack, it is misguided and intemperate to ... argue for reform, in terms of protecting the innocent. Such an approach neglects the wider protective principle of such safeguards and, at least, implies that protection for some suspects is less important than others. (Quirk, 2007: 762)

It is argued that given the extensive powers that the state holds over the liberties of citizens, it is imperative that they are exercised appropriately so as to avoid compromising confidence in the administration of justice (Quirk (2007: 780).

This perspective fails to acknowledge that it is the discourse of factual innocence that has been instrumental in effecting landmark due process safeguards in response to widespread public crises of confidence in workings of the criminal justice system that were prompted by the belief that factually innocent people had been wrongfully convicted and imprisoned. For instance, a raft of established and globally respected due process safeguards against the conviction of the factually innocent derived from the *Confait* affair in which three suspects believed to be factually innocent were found to have been wrongly convicted by the police, and the subsequent recommendations of the Royal Commission on Criminal Procedure (RCCP) (discussed in Chapters 1 and 3 of this book). These included PACE, which provides protections for suspects in police investigations; the national duty solicitor scheme, so that suspects can have access to legal advice in police stations; and the separation of police investigations from decisions to prosecute with the establishment of the CPS. Moreover, the CACD, itself, which adherents to the due process defence of the CCRC argue as appropriately having judicial supremacy over the CCRC, has its origins in the public crisis of confidence in the criminal justice system that was caused by the case of Adolf Beck (discussed in Chapter 6).

Second, it is a fact of social, political and legal life that successful appeals in the CACD *are* different and that some *are* more important than others. That is why there is public, political and legal criticism when convictions such as Mullen, Weir and Clarke and McDaid, successful appellants believed to have been guilty, are overturned, which can also spark campaigns for the reform of the existing criminal justice system arrangements. As will be shown in Chapter 9, Mullen is at the heart of debates and reforms about whether successful appellants thought to be guilty should be entitled to statutory compensation for victims of miscarriages of justice. Moreover, in response to Weir's successful appeal, the CPS made a public apology for its failures (see Steele, 2000). The fallout from the Weir successful appeal case also feed into the reforms of the 800-year-old double jeopardy rule under the Criminal Justice Act 2003, which now allows acquitted individuals to be tried again for certain serious offences if there is 'new and compelling evidence' of factual guilt (Part 9 of the Act). Successful appeals overturned on a breach of process that is not thought to undermine the evidence of factual guilt, such as Clarke and McDaid, Mullen and Weir, are simply of a different order and not to be equated with successful appeals in which the factual evidence of guilt is completely discredited.

Third, the due process defence of the CCRC also errs in its under-standing of the basic thrust and motivation of Herbert Packer's (1968) models that it relies upon for its framing. Packer will for ever be immortalised in criminal justice studies the world over by virtue of the influence of his models of the underlying values and operational remit of the US criminal justice process – 'due process' and 'crime control'. They do not need to be rehearsed here, save to emphasise that Packer's models were entirely oriented to the lay concern for factual innocence and factual guilt. The values of the 'due process' model were, in essence, described as prioritising civil liberties in order to protect against 'miscarriages of justice', understood as the wrongful conviction of the factually innocent. On the other hand, the underpinning values of his 'crime control' model were depicted as prioritising the conviction of the factually guilty. In short, for Packer's analytic (as well as from a lay perspective and the RCCJ) there is nothing wrong per se with crime control, nor a criminal justice system that seeks to convict factually guilty offenders, so long as it protects, as far it can, against the wrongful conviction of the factually innocent. It is in the public interest that factually guilty offenders are convicted, which is, after all, the intended purpose and function of the criminal justice system. Contrary to this, arguments for legal safety over factual innocence, as shown above, serve to support the current arrangements whereby factually guilty offenders can have convictions for murder and terrorist offences overturned, while potentially factually innocent victims of wrongful conviction are unable to do so because the CCRC is deferential to the CACD criteria.

Finally, the due defence of the CCRC confuses *suspects'* rights *within* the criminal justice process and the rights of alleged factually innocent *applicants* to the CCRC *outside* of the criminal justice process. Due process safeguards, indeed, seek to protect all suspects, whether factually innocent or guilty, at the police investigation stage, defendants at the trial stage, and appellants at the first appeal stage. However, the CCRC was established with an expectation by the RCCJ to be an extension to due process safeguards operating at the external post-appeal stage. It was expected to assist the potentially factually innocent who fail to have their conviction overturned within the normal appeals system: some applicants to the CCRC may be able to find fresh evidence that was not available at the time of the original trial that can prove they are factually innocent, such as Sean Hodgson who benefited from advancements in DNA science; some applicants might be able to muster fresh evidence to show that an accuser lied, such as Warren Blackwell; but, as recognised by the RCCJ, some applicants who are potentially factually innocent (for instance, Simon Hall) need the CCRC to investigate their claim of innocence thoroughly and if the evidence against them is shown to be unreliable or they are found to be factually innocent but do not have admissible grounds of appeal to have their cases referred through the other method available for a free pardon under the Royal Prerogative of Mercy. As such, it is not appropriate to criticise critiques of the limits of the CCRC in assisting the factually innocent on the basis of a possible eradication of the due process rights of suspects *within* the criminal justice process. The CCRC does not deal with *suspects* of crime but, rather, with the alleged factually innocent victims of wrongful conviction who have not been able to have their convictions overturned within the normal appeals system, quite often because there has been no identifiable breach of due process rights in the police investigation or the trial proceedings.

Is the CACD to blame?

A final defence of the CCRC in the literature is the attempt to deflect critical attention away from the CCRC altogether. It seeks to lay the blame for the ongoing difficulties that the factually innocent face in trying to overturn their convictions with the CACD. This was expressed by the then Chair of the CCRC Graham Zellick (2006) as follows:

> It may be that what really lies at the root of the problem is not the test we apply but the test that the Court of Appeal applies, the test of safety, because, of course, any change to that test would have corresponding implications for us; we would have to adjust our approach accordingly.

From this perspective, it is argued that the CCRC must work within the statute set by Parliament and that the problem of the CCRC cannot be addressed independently of the CACD (see, for instance, Robins, 2010; Kerrigan, 2009).

The failure of this perspective is that the statute that governs the workings of the CCRC is wider than its just working with the CACD. As already indicated in the last section, while the CCRC will work within the parameters of the CACD test with certain applications that it is appropriate to do so, it is required by its governing statute to use other available avenues when the applicant is innocent but does not have admissible grounds for appeal – the Royal Prerogative. Moreover, applicants to the CCRC will in the main have already failed in a normal appeal at the CACD where alleged breaches of due process and fresh evidence can be dealt with and the CCRC was supposed to conduct external in-depth investigations of claims of innocence. The CCRC was not established because the public were concerned that the Guildford Four, the Birmingham Six, among others, were unable to have their convictions overturned because of the flagrant breaches of due process in their convictions. It was because they were believed to be factually innocent victims of wrongful conviction and imprisonment and the existing system for dealing with such alleged wrongful convictions could not or would not refer their cases back to the CACD.

Conclusion

The wrongful conviction of the factually innocent is a perennial problem that plagues criminal justice systems the world over. The wrongful convictions of the Guildford Four, Birmingham Six and the Maguire Seven that were overturned in the late 1980s and early 1990s revealed the inner workings of all that can go wrong with a criminal justice system. The cases caused a public crisis of confidence in the entire criminal justice system, not only at home but around the globe. The RCCJ was established to show that something was being done to fix the problem and address the public crisis. And, although the CCRC does not correspond with the recommendations of the RCCJ, its limitations in dealing with continuing claims of factual innocence by alleged victims of wrongful convictions are less widely known. In this context, it is unsurprising that the CCRC may seem attractive to other jurisdictions seeking their own solution to the problem of wrongful convictions. It is widely believed that it is a proven ready-made remedy that can simply be added on to other criminal justice systems.

Another aspect of the CCRC's casework that often causes surprise is that it also deals with a range of other issues that its predecessor C3 did not. This includes sentence matters, technical wrongful convictions such as cases where murder convictions are replaced with manslaughter convictions; cases that are relatively more trivial, such as road traffic offences and destruction orders under the Dangerous Dogs Act 1991. This is another departure from what the RCCJ recommended and from what other jurisdictions believe the CCRC exists to do.

Whatever the intentions behind the arguments in defence of the CCRC's subordination to the CACD, they do not withstand critical scrutiny. It may make the relationship between the CCRC and the CACD more workable (see, for instance, Nobles and Schiff, 2002:

692–693) to have a test that is in harmony. But the problem identified by the RCCJ was that the previous system for dealing with claims of factual innocence by alleged victims of wrongful convictions was failing precisely because of the symmetrical deference of C3 to the CACD.

The argument for the integrity of the criminal justice system to be the principal concern for the CCRC and the test for legal unsafety over factual innocence puts forward a notion of 'integrity' as understood in the strict legal sense. It puts forward a blind adherence to legal rules and procedures, even if it means overturning the convictions of factually guilty terrorists, murderers and violent offenders that may present an ongoing threat to public safety. An example is the case of Mullen who was charged with an IRA blackmail plot after his successful appeal for IRA terrorist offences because of the apparent breach of due process in his extradition from Zimbabwe (see BBC News, 2009a).

By contrast, 'integrity' as understood from a lay perspective would arguably distinguish between criminal convictions that are quashed in light of evidence of procedural irregularities and/or breaches of due process that do not undermine the factual guilt of the appellant, which can be sent for retrial, and those that are or should be overturned when the evidence that indicates factual guilt is entirely discredited, whether it is fresh evidence or not. This is the task that the CCRC is widely believed to undertake and, no doubt, a principle reason why other jurisdictions are interested in exploring the establishment of their very own CCRC-style body.

The due process defence is similarly unconvincing and ineffective. It is not appropriate to argue against the concern for potentially factually innocent victims of wrongful convictions and imprisonment at the post-appeal stage to somehow retain rights for suspects of crime within the criminal justice process. Moreover, the whole point of due process as modelled by Packer is to protect the factually innocent from wrongful conviction. So, to argue for retaining the current system that leaves potentially factually innocent victims of wrongful convictions procedurally barred from having their convictions overturned seems bizarre in the extreme.

The argument that the CACD is the site of the real problem misses the point entirely. The CCRC was set up because of apparent flaws with the CACD in dealing with alleged factual innocence appeals when the evidence was not fresh. It deals with alleged miscarriages of justice at the post-appeal stage for that very reason: the RCCJ meant it to deal with the difficult cases that the CACD is not best placed to deal with; not to be subordinate to the CACD.

This chapter has detailed the statutory limitations of the CCRC in assisting the factually innocent and the failings of the defences of the CCRC that are routinely deployed. The intention was to provide an understanding of the structural underpinnings of the CCRC that governs how it deals with applications and the kind of applicant it is most inclined to assist: those that have an identifiable breach of process or fresh evidence at the expense of an investigation into claims of factual innocence by alleged victims of wrongful convictions to determine their validity.

PART III

The Harmful Consequences of Wrongful Convictions and the Limits of Redress

8
Victimology

Introduction

Official statistics are a common starting point for sociological research in attempts to get some sense of the scale of the problem to be investigated, and those on successful appeals are helpful in this regard, too. For instance, between 2004 and 2008 the Crown Court overturned an annual average of 2,056 criminal convictions given in magistrates' courts (Ministry of Justice, 2009). In the same period an annual average of 207 criminal convictions given in the Crown Court for more serious offences were quashed in the Court of Appeal (Criminal Division) (CACD) (Ministry of Justice, 2009). On top of this, the appeal courts overturn between approximately 15–20 convictions referred by the Criminal Cases Review Commission (CCRC) each year (CCRC, 2010). In broad terms, then, the official statistics on successful appeals show that convictions overturned in the Crown Court represent approximately 90 per cent of all successful appeals in England and Wales per annum in recent years (which is perhaps not so surprising given that the overwhelming majority of criminal convictions are given in magistrates' courts); that those overturned in the CACD represent in the region of 10 per cent; and, that the convictions overturned following a referral back to an appeal court by the CCRC form around 1 per cent of all successful appeals each year.

In assessing such data, it is important to note that official statistics are not objective facts. On the contrary, they are the products of the power relations at play in the criminal justice process. They are based on the decisions by appeal courts within the terms of their prevailing rules to determine whether alleged wrongful convictions should be upheld or be quashed. As such, the official statistics on successful appeals reflect the criminal justice system's perspective and do not include those victims of miscarriages and abortions of justice who are unable to overturn their convictions because they are deemed to not fulfil the criteria of the appeals system. As discussed in the previous two chapters, this can include factually innocent victims if the evidence of their factual innocence was available at the time of the original trial and is therefore not deemed to be the kind of fresh evidence required by CACD, for instance.

Yet, despite these shortcomings the official statistics on successful appeals do give a strong discursive base to work from in critical socio-logical analyses of the criminal justice system. They are all official acknowledgements that cannot easily be sidestepped – that the criminal conviction was wrong in a legal sense in some way or other. Official sta-tistics on successful appeals thus allow an analytical framework to be constructed that captures sight of the thousands of successful appellants and the additional thousands of secondary victims (wives, husbands, parents, children, and so on) that can be conceived to be affected by the problems of miscarriages and abortions of justice for sociological inquiry. Indeed, although precise statistics on the number of secondary victims that are affected by miscarriages and abortions of justice are not available, as with other social problems such as alcoholism, drug abuse or domestic violence, for instance, for every victim that is represented in the official statistics on successful appeals many more secondary vic-tims can be extrapolated who are also indirectly harmed in multiple ways. On this basis, as I have argued elsewhere (see Naughton, 2003a; 2007: ch. 2), a sociological analysis would include all successful appeals to gain an understanding of the officially acknowledged 'errors' of the criminal justice system and the wide range of harms that are associated with miscarriages and abortions of justice as defined by successful appeals.

As convictions for serious criminal offences in the Crown Court carry greater punishments than offences dealt with in magistrates' courts, my first step towards a more nuanced sociological analysis of the harmful consequences associated with successful appeals to primary victims and their families was to separate the different types of successful appeals in the official statistics. The derived 'Typology of Successful Appeals' can be utilised as a heuristic device to define successful appeals by appeal courts and whether they were overturned on a first appeal within the normal criminal appeals system, or on an appeal following a referral back to an appeal court by the external workings of the CCRC. It denotes those convictions overturned in the Crown Court for less seri-ous criminal offences in magistrates' courts as 'mundane' in recognition of their greater number and regularity or everydayness; those cases over-turned within the normal appeals process in the CACD for serious offences as 'routine'; and those far fewer in number successful appeals that are overturned by the external post-appeal mechanisms of CCRC as 'exceptional' in a statistical sense.

Against this background, the following three sections of this chapter puts the Typology of Successful Appeals to work to explore the harmful impacts to exceptional, routine and mundane victims of wrongful con-victions and their families (see also Naughton, 2003a, 2004b; 2007: ch. 8). In so doing, it undertakes individual and comparative sociological analyses of and between the mundane and routine successful appeals that are overturned within the criminal appeals system and those excep-tional successful appeals that fail to be overturned by a normal appeal. For this task, case studies are used to illustrate the kind of harmful impacts that victims and their families can experience, thereby includ-ing secondary victims in the sociological gaze. As such, the following is not intended to be definitive. Nor is it claimed that all victims will expe-rience the impacts of successful appeals in the same or even similar ways. Rather, the aim here is to put forward a framework for a holistic victimology of successful appeals that takes into account the harms that can befall all successful appellants in whichever appeal court the con-viction is overturned and whether it is within or outside of the normal appeals process. Finally, an alternative perspective is critically analysed that conflicts with the sociological perspective adopted and applied here. This highlights how the criminal justice system and its adherents operate within a restrictive analytical framework that is so narrowly focused on exceptional successful appeals that are overturned following a referral by the CCRC that it excludes almost all of the harmful impacts that can occur in the sum total of successful appeals in England and Wales.

Exceptional successful appeals

The existing literature on the harm of wrongful convictions has focused on those victims who spent years or even decades incarcerated before having their convictions overturned. Such victims tend to fall within the 'exceptional' category as their extended imprisonment is often a result of the failure of the criminal justice system to overturn their con-victions through the normal appeals process. Research has found that many victims of long-term wrongful imprisonment find it difficult if not virtually impossible for them to fit back into society and rebuild their lives. This is due to the resultant permanent and disabling psychological and emotional disorders, including a unique form of post-traumatic stress disorder (PTSD). This renders them difficult to live with post-release and prone to mood swings, emotional outbursts; unable to form bonds with their wives and children and a general climate of familial estrangement (see Grounds, 2004; 2005; Jamieson and Grounds, 2005; Grounds and Jamieson 2003; Campbell and Denov, 2004; Denov and Campbell, 2005).

Paddy Joe Hill of the Birmingham Six had his conviction overturned after 16 years in prison on his third appeal following a referral back to the CACD by the Home Secretary under the C3 system. He exemplifies, perhaps, the worst kind of social impacts to families. In a major interview with *The Guardian*, he gave an insightful account of how family bonds come under pressure and can break down under the strain of wrongful imprisonment:

> Once you go into a prison and you're innocent, every fucking part of your relationship is based on fucking lies. Families come to see you and you're given the biggest load of bollocks, everything is all right, blah blah. And you're doing exactly the same thing, telling your family, 'everything is all right, yes, yes, don't worry'. How can everything be all right when you're serving fucking 21 life sentences for nothing? ... You don't tell them the truth, for the simple reason is they've got enough on their plate outside and you've got enough on your plate inside. You're lying for the best of reasons: to protect your family. (Paddy Joe Hill, cited in Hattenstone, 2002)

In common with many other exceptional victims, Hill's wife divorced him while he was in prison (see Naughton, 2007: 155). His children grew up in care homes, themselves being subjected to forms of bullying and abuse by virtue of being the children of a convicted IRA terrorist murderer, which included 'being locked up in homes, being spat at, being locked in cupboards, being thrown into baths of cold water' (cited in Hattenstone, 2002).

Talking about his relationships with his children since his release, he observed that:

> [Y]ou find your family has all grown up without you. You feel like an intruder, you're completely isolated. They talk about things they can relate to, and the only fucking thing you can relate to is four walls, a door, and a fucking barred fucking window. So it's like two strangers

from different countries, one speaking in his language, and you're speaking in yours, and you don't understand each other. (Paddy Joe Hill, cited in Hattenstone, 2002)

In fact, Hill says that due to his detachment from his children that he feels no emotional connection to them at all:

My kids are like strangers to me ... and I don't feel nothing ... I feel sorry for my kids because they are never ever going to have a real father-and-son or father-and-daughter relationship with me. (cited in Hattenstone, 2002)

The longer exceptional victims of wrongful imprisonment spend in prison, the harder it will be for them to get a job as a way of starting to rebuild their lives. It might be true to say that the difficulties of read-justment would equally apply to the guilty prisoners who served long-term custodial sentences. However, crucial distinctions exist between the experiences of victims of wrongful imprisonment who maintain their innocence in prison and those who are guilty. The psychological trauma that victims of wrongful imprisonment suffer, for instance, is compounded by their sense of injustice of being in prison for some-thing that they have not done (see, for instance, Jamieson and Grounds, 2002: 65). Further, as discussed in detail in Chapter 5, prisoners main-taining innocence who have been given life or indeterminate sentences are frequently confronted by a situation known as the 'parole deal', which disadvantages them in numerous ways compared with prisoners who accept their guilt and comply with the prison regime.

The 'parole deal' accounts for a combination of impacts that work together to ratchet up the difficulties for exceptional successful appel-lants post-release. They spend longer in prison than prisoners who admit their guilt as they rarely achieve release on their tariff dates – the date set by the courts as to when the prisoner is eligible for release on parole. Examples include Stephen Downing (see Hale, 2002) and Robert Brown (see R v Brown) who each served approximately a decade past their given tariff and may still be in prison today if they had not had their convictions of murder overturned in the CACD.

Unlike guilty offenders, prisoners maintaining innocence are not usually prepared for release. Guilty offenders will normally have a step-by-step programme towards release. This will include support from the prison and probation services as well as voluntary organisa-tions to help them prepare for life after prison. It will include advice about state benefits, training, education, work experience and preparation for release. It will likely involve a period of a couple of years in an open prison where they experience a less regulated regime and may work in the community during the day like regular citizens, only returning to the prison after work. The objective is to help prisoners return to normal life, get a job and home, and cope with life without reoffending (HM Prison Service, 2011).

On the other hand, prisoners maintaining innocence who have their convictions overturned in the CACD are often released abruptly without any preparation or support at all. Johnny Kamara, for instance, spent 16 of his 20-year sentence in solitary confinement for the murder of John Suffield Jnr, a Liverpool bookmaker. When he had his conviction overturned he was left to fend for himself with no support structures to help him to reintegrate back into the community (see Traynor, 2006). Perhaps not surprisingly, this experience had impacts, too, upon Kamara's ability to relate to others long after he was released:

> Even now, six years on, I still like being on my own. Sometimes I still go out all hours of the night driving. I still get a bit panicky in crowds. (John Kamara, cited in BBC News, 2006a)

The lack of support for such prisoners deepens their difficulties in reintegration into society. They are released from the CACD with no pre-release preparation plan and with no ongoing support from probation as they are not deemed to be eligible. They can also lose contact with their families while they were in prison they have no family support either. Four years after his release, having served 14 years' imprisonment, for instance, Andrew Adams was reported as struggling to cope with life outside prison. Convicted for the murder of Jack Royal, his conviction was overturned on the basis of poor defence at trial, among other identified causes (R v Andrew Adams). As he refused to accept his guilt in prison, he did not receive any advice about training, education, housing and employment, nor given counselling for problems such as alcoholism or depression. As his mother died while he was in prison and his father is suffering from Alzheimer's, Adams had no home to go back to and found himself homeless, unemployed, with no means of income as he was deemed ineligible for compensation (see Laville, 2011).

In concluding this section on the kinds of harm that can affect exceptional successful appellants and their families it must be noted that not all successful appellants who have their cases overturned following a referral back to the appeal courts by the CCRC serve a long-term custodial sentence. Indeed, the CCRC also refers convictions given in the Crown Court to the CACD where applicants have not received a custodial sentence and to the Crown Court for less serious criminal convictions given in magistrates' courts. As such, the harms experienced by exceptional successful appellants who do not receive a prison sentence are likely to fit better with the analysis of the harms that accompany routine and/or mundane successful appeals that will be discussed below. However, exceptional successful appellants who do not receive a custodial sentence, whether they had their conviction quashed by the CACD or the Crown Court, will likely spend longer in their struggle to overturn their convictions and at a greater financial, social and psychological cost to them and their families than conventional routine and mundane successful appellants.

Routine successful appeals

Convictions in the Crown Court are for serious criminal offences such as murder, rape or robbery. Although not all convictions given in the Crown Court carry a prison sentence, the majority of convictions do. In 2009, for instance, approximately two-thirds of defendants found guilty in the Crown Court were given a custodial sentence. The precise statistics for 2009 were that 73,419 defendants were found guilty in the Crown Court and 50,241 defendants sentenced in the Crown Court were given a custodial sentence. This figure includes defendants who were convicted in a magistrates' court but were passed on to the Crown Court for sentencing (see Ministry of Justice, 2010). As such, the majority of routine successful appellants who were convicted in the Crown Court and had their conviction overturned on a normal appeal in the CACD are likely to have served a prison sentence.

In saying this, a crucial distinction between exceptional and routine successful appellants is that routine victims who serve prison sentences are likely to serve shorter sentences by virtue of their convictions being overturned through the normal appeals system. Yet many of the harmful impacts that can apply to victims and their families in exceptional successful appeals are likely to also feature in routine convictions overturned by the CACD. Even though they might not have spent long periods in prison, routine successful appellants can spend many years consumed by the struggle to contest the initial allegation, defend the charges at trial, appeal and overturn the conviction, and seek redress for the damage caused to them and their families. Routine successful appellants who were convicted in the Crown Court for serious criminal offences will also be subject to the stigma that such convictions carry. This often continues long after they have had their convictions overturned and can have knock-on effects in terms of impacts on family life and the ability to rebuild their lives, following a successful appeal.

A pertinent comparison of the similar impacts that can befall routine successful appellants compared with exceptional successful appellants are the cases of Sally Clark (see Batt, 2005) and Angela Cannings (see Cannings with Davies, 2006) who were among a number of women who were wrongly convicted and imprisoned for murdering their children when they died in unexplained circumstances (Doward, 2005).

Sally Clark

Sally Clark was convicted in Chester Crown Court in November 1999 for the murders of her two sons, Christopher who was found dead in his cot at 11 weeks old in December 1996, and Harry who died at 8 weeks old in November 1997. Dr Alan Williams conducted post-mortems on both babies. His original assessment of Christopher's death was that it was due to a lower respiratory tract infection. It was treated as a case of Sudden Infant Death Syndrome (SIDS), or 'cot death'. However, he believed that Harry's death was non-accidental and consistent with shaking on several occasions over several days. This prompted Dr Williams to conduct further tests in relation to Christopher and a change of his original opinion. In line with his belief that Harry had been murdered, he now concluded that Christopher's death had also been unnatural and that the evidence was suggestive of smothering (R v Clark, paragraphs 2–3).

Sally Clark's first appeal was unsuccessful. However, her conviction was overturned following a referral back to the CACD for a second time by the CCRC when fresh microbiology evidence emerged that Dr Williams had not made available to the defence or the prosecution at the time of the trial. It indicated that Harry might have died from natural causes. This led to a further re-evaluation of the cause of Christopher's death by the CACD to a finding that he may also have died of natural causes:

> [W]e are of the firm view that if Harry's death may have been from natural causes, it follows that no safe conclusion could be reached that Christopher was killed unnaturally. Accordingly the conclusion that the verdict in respect of Harry's death is unsafe necessarily leads to a conclusion that the verdict in respect of Christopher's death is

also unsafe and it too must be quashed. (R v Clark, paragraphs 135–136)

As discussed in Chapter 4, the other main plank of the evidence against Sally Clark was the expert opinions of the then highly distinguished paediatrician Professor Sir Roy Meadow and his now discredited theory of SIDS that posited that one SIDS death is a tragedy, two is suspicious and three is murder unless there is proof to the contrary (Meadow, 1989; Moss, 2004). In quashing the convictions, the CACD was also furnished with evidence from the Royal Statistical Society, among other experts, that was highly critical of the statistical evidence that was given by Professor Meadow (see R v Clark).

Angela Cannings

Angela Cannings was convicted in Winchester Crown Court in April 2002 for the murders of her two sons, 7-week-old Jason who died in 1991 and 18-week-old Matthew who died in 1999. Cannings was also initially charged with the murder of her first child Gemma who died in 1989 at the age of 13 weeks, but the charge was dropped at the start of the trial. The prosecution's case against Angela Cannings hinged on the testimonies of two main experts. The first was Professor Meadow who gave similar evidence to his previous evidence in the case of Sally Clark: because three unexplained child deaths in a family is such a very rare event, in the absence of a natural explanation for their deaths, the children had most likely died as a result of smothering:

> It was a terrible tragedy first of all and an awful tragedy and very unusual – the third death in the family, that's a rare event, very rare … the unusual feature is death so soon after being seen well, the fact that there had been previous deaths in the family and the fact that he [Matthew] had had an episode of some sort only nine days before he died … those features are ones that are found really quite commonly in children who have been smothered by their mothers. (Meadows, cited in Cannings with Davies, 2006: 130)

Dr Ward Platt, the second main prosecution expert, was of the opinion that although three infant deaths in the same family is not itself evidence of murder, the pattern revealed by these deaths as a whole was compelling evidence that Angela Cannings had smothered her children (R v Cannings, paragraphs 134–137):

> [H]aving looked at the other possibilities, having considered the whole situation ... it is my opinion that they were caused deliberately and in this case by smothering. (Platt, cited in Cannings with Davies, 2006: 133)

By the time Cannings' appeal was heard, the credibility of Professor Meadow's evidence had been seriously undermined with the quashing of Sally Clark's conviction. It was accepted in Cannings' appeal that the fact that a sudden infant death had occurred more than once in the same family is not itself evidence that the deaths were deliberately inflicted. In short, Professor Meadow's opinion was just that – an opinion which had not been sufficiently researched and was not substantiated by any evidence at all. Further, the CACD also heard and accepted evidence of further infant deaths in Canning's extended family, which suggested a possible genetic link to her children's deaths. In quashing Angela Cannings' convictions, Judge LJ emphasised that murder should not be inferred simply because the exact cause of death cannot be found and suggested that Cannings should not have been tried in the first place:

> Experts in many fields will acknowledge the possibility that later research may undermine the accepted wisdom of today ... That does not normally provide a basis for rejecting the expert evidence, or indeed for conjuring up fanciful doubts about the possible impact of later research. With unexplained infant deaths ... in many important respects we are still at the frontiers of knowledge ... for the time being, where a full investigation into two or more sudden unexplained infant deaths in the same family is followed by a serious disagreement between reputable experts about the cause of death, and a body of such expert opinion concludes that natural causes, whether explained or unexplained, cannot be excluded as a reasonable (and not a fanciful) possibility, the prosecution of a parent or parents for murder should not be started, or continued, unless there is additional cogent evidence, extraneous to the expert evidence ... In cases like the present, if the outcome of the trial depends exclusively or almost exclusively on a serious disagreement between distinguished and reputable experts, it will often be unwise, and therefore unsafe, to proceed. (R v Cannings, paragraph 178)

The foregoing case studies illustrate the marked similarities between the wrongful convictions of Sally Clark and Angela Cannings in terms of evidence that convicted them and led to their convictions being over-turned. The similarities between the cases also extend to the shared harms that they and their families suffered pre- and post-successful appeal. First, both women were denied the chance to grieve for their recently dead children, as they faced criminal investigations into the deaths amid suspicions that they were culpable. Second, both women had their remaining children removed from them for fear that they may harm them: Sally Clark's third son (who cannot be named for legal reasons) was taken from her when he was just days old when she was convicted (Batt, 2005: 58–76); Angela Cannings had to leave the family home in November 1999 when she was on bail or risk having her remaining daughter Jade, who was 3 years old at the time, being taken into care. Third, both women were vilified in prison for being child killers, or 'nonces', and were the targets of hatred and regular assaults from other prisoners. As Angela Cannings said:

> I was a target for other prisoners within those walls. As a child-killer, my conviction made me the lowest of the low among inmates and many would relish the chance to attack me, to express their hatred of my supposed crime in punches and blows. (Cannings with Davies, 2006: 161)

Fourth, both women found it virtually impossible to resume their old lives after release, being permanently scarred by their experiences. In March 2007, Sally Clark died from acute alcohol intoxication. At the inquest, it emerged that she never recovered from her ordeal and that she suffered a number of serious psychiatric problems, including endur-ing personality change after her catastrophic experience, protracted grief reaction and alcohol dependency syndrome (Gibb, 2007). As for Angela Cannings, the four years of separation from her husband and daughter irreparably damaged the bonds between them. It was attrib-uted as the reason for her divorce from Terry after 25 years of marriage and also to Jade suffering from 'acute separation anxiety' and resisting her mother's attempt to pick up her parental role when she was released (Weathers, 2008).

Indeed, we must also take account of the knock-on impacts felt by the spouses of Sally Clark and Angela Cannings and their remaining children. Steve Clark was also unable to grieve for his dead son. He was forced to sell their home to meet huge legal bills following Sally's trial and unsuccessful first appeal, to avoid bankruptcy. He gave up his part-nership in a leading corporate law firm when Sally's first appeal was unsuccessful and took a position as a legal assistant with a firm close to Bullwood Hall prison, near Southend, so that he and their son could visit more regularly (*The Telegraph*, 2007). At one point their third son was taken into care (Roberts and Tozer, 2007). Similarly, Terry Cannings was forced to give up a job that he said he loved to care for Jade when Angela was arrested. He also had to sell the family home and move into a council house, as he was no longer able to pay the mortgage. Reflecting on the impacts of his wife's wrongful conviction Terry Cannings stated:

> Before all of this I was a very lucky man. I had a great job, a great marriage and a great family. Now things are very different. Angela has confirmed divorce is the only way forward ... It is all down to the four years' separation. After she came out of prison we were two different people ... I am signed off work for depression and there are so many personal things I haven't been allowed to deal with properly, like grieving for my son. It has been one hell of a struggle. (Terry Cannings, cited in *Daily Mail*, 2009)

Mundane successful appeals

Convictions in magistrates' courts are for relatively less serious summary offences, such as common assault or motoring offences, to more serious 'either way' offences for theft, burglary, sexual offences and actual bodily harm (ABH) assault. The punishment suffered as a result of wrongful convictions in magistrates' courts can also be significant. Magistrates' courts have the power to impose a range of sentencing options from community orders, fines (up to £5,000) and imprisonment of up to 6 months for one offence and 12 months for more than one offence. In addition, convictions in magistrates' courts can result in more severe sentences if they are committed to the Crown Court for sentencing. Although convictions in magistrates' courts can carry a prison sentence, the reality is that punishments are normally non-custodial fines and community sentence orders (for details, see Magistrates' Court Act, 1980).

Moreover, while the crimes that they were convicted of and the sentences received by mundane successful appellants are relatively less serious and lower when compared with routine and exceptional successful appellants who receive long-term prison sentences, they too can be subjected to a range of harmful impacts that detrimentally affect their lives and those of their families. Indeed, mundane successful appeals, in common with routine and exceptional successful appeals, can also involve stain to reputation. Further, loss of jobs and life savings, spent trying to overturn wrongful convictions, may occur.

For instance, Edmond Taylor was convicted of dangerous driving at Redhill Magistrates' Court in 2005. He was banned from driving for a year and fined £430. Taylor, who always maintained that he was innocent of the offence, faced losing his job as a cash handler for Securitas if he failed in his appeal against the conviction. After a year-long battle to clear his name, involving four hearings, Taylor's conviction was finally overturned by Guildford Crown Court in October 2006 when Judge John Crocker was shown a CCTV picture of the moment of arrest of the offending driver who was a white man, whereas Taylor is black. It transpired that, unknown to Taylor, his car, a Vauxhall Corsa, was seen reversing along the hard shoulder of the M23. It and his identity had been stolen. When PC Paul James of Surrey Police arrived to investigate the offence the driver gave his name as Edmond Taylor and produced a document to prove his identity and that he owned the car. A fixed penalty notice was issued and a notice for Taylor to produce his insurance and other documents at a police station within three days. The driver was then permitted to drive on. He returned the car to where he had stolen it from: outside Taylor's home in south London (see Teed and Cassidy, 2006).

Another case that illustrates the wide-ranging harms that may occur in mundane successful appeals is that of David Rucker, a teacher wrongly convicted for common assault at Northallerton Magistrates' Court in October 2006 following false allegations by his school pupils. Prior to his conviction, Rucker, who had been a teacher for 15 years, was described by Ofsted inspectors as an 'outstanding' teacher. His conviction meant that he had to give up his job. He then ran up thousands of pounds of debt, which he claimed he and his family could ill afford, to try to clear his name. His legal costs were paid using compensation his wife had received for treatment after a car accident. After a 19-month struggle to clear his name, his conviction was quashed at Teesside Crown Court in January 2008, when the court heard how Rucker had been the fourth teacher at his school to have been accused of wrongdoing by children in the same year group (see Editorial, 2008). Indeed, although not the direct subject of this analysis, false allegations against those working in the teaching and caring professions are a common phenomenon (see Falsely Accused Carers and Teachers, 2012; False Allegations Support Organisation, 2012).

The loss of livelihood is likely to apply to a greater or lesser extent to all successful appellants, whether mundane, routine or exceptional, if they want to return to a career or profession that requires a Criminal Records Bureau (CRB) check. There are two types of checks. A Standard Disclosure normally pertains to applicants for jobs in financial services, which will reveal an applicant's current and spent convictions, cautions, reprimands and warnings. An Enhanced Disclosure is the highest level of check, required for all those wanting to work with children and vulnerable adults. They contain the same information as the Standard Disclosure, but with the addition of any information deemed relevant by the local police forces. This includes allegations of sexual and physical offences against children and vulnerable adults, even when charges and convictions were not given. If there are any doubts about the relevancy of 'soft information' on suspects who were accused but not charged, the policy is to lean towards inclusion. Although quashed convictions should restore the presumption of innocence and erase the criminal record, the fear that successful appellants may commit future crimes renders them at a disadvantage in returning to the careers that they were educated and trained for. This arguably also impacts on society more generally in terms of the loss of skills and experiences to the economy that such professionals could contribute.

Indeed, the stigma that accompanies a criminal conviction often persists even when convictions are overturned. The 'no smoke without fire' discourse can haunt successful appellants post-conviction whatever the offence they were convicted of, whichever appeal court overturned their conviction, and whether that was by way of normal appeal or CCRC referral (see Naughton, 2004b; 2007: ch. 8).

In contemporary society, social status, psychological significance and economic well-being are intimately connected to whether a person is in paid employment and the kind of employment that they are engaged in. Successful appellants who are unable to gain employment due to the ongoing discrimination and stigma of their convictions will suffer in terms of loss of earnings. They will also likely suffer the forms of social exclusion that affects the unemployed, with the inevitable knock-on consequences on their psychological well-being and how they are viewed by their family members and communities.

An alternative perspective

The sociological perspective applied here seeks to understand the harm caused by the criminal justice system to individuals who have criminal convictions overturned on appeal. Contrary to this, the criminal justice system's perspective, evident in the statute for compensation for victims of miscarriages of justice – s. 133 of the Criminal Justice Act 1988 (explored in detail in the next chapter) – includes only those who have a conviction overturned outside of the normal criminal appeals system as problematic. This strictly limits the number of victims that can be conceptualised from the sum total of successful appeals. The logic seems to be that the criminal appeals system is akin to complaints procedures generally: that convictions overturned by the normal appeals are internal to the workings of the criminal justice system and are not proof of a systemic problematic but, rather, that the system works. As such, it is argued that the focus should instead be restricted to those successful appeals that fail to be overturned within the normal appeals process. This perspective is summarised by leading advocates in the following terms:

> [W]e would argue that the appeal process works effectively for those 'routine' and 'mundane' cases and it does not work effectively for those cases ... term[ed] 'exceptional'. Instead of focusing on the 'mundane' and 'routine' appeals, we would argue that ... [we] ... should focus on why the 'exceptional' appeals are exceptional and why they take so long to succeed on appeal, these usually being factual innocence cases. (Roberts and Weathered, 2009: 51–55)

This perspective is profoundly problematic for the following reasons. First, there is no evidence to support the empirical assertion that successful appeals that follow a referral by the CCRC are 'usually' factual innocence cases, which suggests that the CCRC deals mainly with wrongful convictions by allegedly factually innocent victims of wrongful convictions. Moreover, and as shown in the last chapter, in addition to alleged wrongful convictions, the CCRC also deals with a range of other issues, including: sentence matters – cases where murder convictions are referred back to the CACD on the ground that they should be quashed and replaced with manslaughter convictions; convictions in magistrates' courts for less serious criminal convictions such as road traffic offences; destruction orders given to dangerous dogs. And when the CCRC reviews criminal convictions it is entirely subordinated to the criteria of the appeal courts and can only refer cases if they are deemed to have a 'real possibility' of being overturned in terms of s. 13 of the Criminal Appeal Act 1995. As such, the CCRC is always working in the realm of trying to predict how the appeal courts will respond to cases that it refers. This means that the CCRC's rationale and operations seek to determine whether convictions are safe in law; it does not question whether applicants are factual innocent or guilty.

Second, limiting the number of successful appeals to approximately 1 per cent of the total number of successful appeals promotes a research agenda that is anathema to the sociological enterprise. Sociology is as much about problematising and seeking to understand the impacts and effects of the normal, routine and mundane workings of social and legal systems and how they impact on the population, as it is with restricted analyses of exceptional occurrences and phenomena. Contrary to this, the adherents and advocates of the criminal justice system perspective are likely to produce forms of knowledge of just one type of successful appeal that merely glimpses the causes and effects of successful appeals as a total social and legal phenomenon, albeit arguably the most harmful type that victims and their families can endure. However, they turn a blind eye to the harms and victimisation that can be inflicted on routine and mundane successful appellants such as Cannings, Taylor and Rucker (discussed above).

Third, it has been further suggested that to include all successful appeals in critical analyses of miscarriages of justice 'elid[es] the legal and political interpretations of miscarriages of justice and ... risks expanding the term into irrelevance' (Quirk, 2009: 419). On the contrary, the foregoing analysis acknowledges the nuances between the different types of successful appeals. Yet it simultaneously highlights the limitations of criminal justice system definitions of miscarriages of justice that fail to recognise, and perhaps more crucially take responsibility for, the cumulative harms that apply to 99 per cent of successful appellants, which are part and parcel of the normal workings of criminal justice process. As such, the narrow focus on exceptional successful appeals can be conceived as an extremely conservative project that serves to maintain the existing power relations of the criminal justice system. It legitimises and leaves unabated the wide-ranging and profound forms of harm that the existing arrangements cause to thousands of primary victims and many more thousands of secondary victims each year.

Conclusion

This chapter has sketched the harms that can be gleaned from analyses of case studies of successful appeals and how they might impact on primary and secondary victims. By including the official statistics on successful appeals as systemic evidence of wrongful convictions, it has shown that the 'errors' of the criminal justice system can destroy lives and ruin careers. Further, there can be permanent ongoing social stigma, psychological trauma and financial hardship, all of which can affect thousands of successful appellants and their families. This is true whether the successful appellants in the cases discussed had their convictions overturned in the Crown Court or the CACD on a normal appeal or on a referral back to the appeal courts by the CCRC.

Of course, the 'elephant in the room' of the foregoing analysis is that not all successful appellants are factually innocent. Indeed, the cases selected for analysis may not be representative of the population of successful appellants as a whole, which include cases of guilty successful appellants such as Weir and Mullen (discussed in Chapter 2); Clarke and McDaid (discussed in Chapter 6). From a lay perspective, it is difficult to argue that such successful appellants are victims at all and the impacts on their lives and even their families are harmful. On the contrary, public morality from a lay perspective might consider guilty successful appellants as escaping punishment that is deserved for the harms that they caused to victims of crime and to the families of such victims. As such, a sociological approach to successful appeals opens up a fundamental tension between the lay perspective and the workings of the criminal justice system. The criminal justice system is governed by rules and procedures that do not relate to public morals from a lay perspective. Those rules dictate that whether appellants are factually innocent or guilty is not the issue. Rather, appellants must have their convictions quashed if they are 'unsafe'. This is a broad notion that encompasses a range of situations from fresh evidence that renders convictions unreliable to serious breaches of process that are deemed to undermine the integrity of the criminal justice system. However, from a lay perspective, successful appellants are only seen as victims, and the impacts, no matter how wide-ranging and deep, are only seen as harms if they are considered to be factually innocent.

This brings us back to the discussion in Chapter 2 and the reality that it is only on rare occasions that the factual innocence or factual guilt of successful appellants is definitively established. This leaves the majority of successful appellants, whether they are the victims of unintended miscarriages or intended abortions of justice, in limbo, with the public uncertain as to whether they have been harmed by the criminal justice system or whether they have escaped their just punishments by having their convictions overturning. However, this tension should not undermine the attempt to ascertain the victimhood of victims of miscarriages and abortions of justice as evidenced by successful appeals from a sociological perspective. Rather, critical discussion of these conceptual conflicts should be seen as part of, and not external to, a productive socio-legal project of defining what is a miscarriage of justice; how miscarriages differ from intentional abortions of justice; the likely scale of the problem; and how they impact on individuals and their families.

9

Compensation

Introduction

The issue of compensation is a salient feature of media coverage when wrongful convictions are discussed. *The Guardian*'s report on Paul Blackburn's (see Naylor, 2004: Chapter 5) successful appeal 27 years after he was convicted for the attempted murder and sexual assault of a 9-year-old boy (see Duffield, 1994), for instance, included the following statement from his solicitor, Glyn Maddocks: 'He will be entitled to a substantial amount of compensation' (cited in *The Guardian*, 2005). Similarly, *The Telegraph*'s coverage of Robert Brown's successful appeal, after having spent 25 years in prison for the murder of Annie Walsh, included a statement from his solicitor, Robert Lizar, that 'compensation could run into millions' (cited in Pook, 2002). Likewise, in the case of Stephen Downing, convicted for the murder of Wendy Sewell (see Hale, 2002) the first sentence of *The Guardian*'s report of his successful appeal the day after the CACD quashed his conviction read as follows: 'Stephen Downing, the victim of Britain's longest-running miscarriage of justice, began the fight for massive compensation for his 27 years in prison after his murder conviction was quashed yesterday' (see Vasagar, 2002). The article went on to state that Downing was expected to claim in excess of £2m in compensation, with further claims for psychological damage and loss of earnings (Vasagar, 2002; *The Guardian*, 2002).

However, Blackburn, Brown (see Mackay, 2004) and Downing (see BBC News, 2006b) may be considered 'fortunate' – despite having spent 25 years in wrongful imprisonment – in that they were all eligible for state compensation. More recently, the ex-gratia scheme has been abolished and a more restrictive approach has been adopted. This is reflected in amendments to the statutory compensation scheme for victims of miscarriages of justice (see Criminal Justice and Immigration Act 2008).

Collectively, the implications of these changes are drastic: fewer success-ful appellants are now deemed eligible and those that are will receive relatively lower awards than previously awarded.

Against this background, this chapter assesses the existing statutory compensation scheme for victims of miscarriages of justice in England and Wales under s. 133 of the Criminal Justice Act 1988, noting that in place of an official definition this expresses the state's vision of what constitutes a miscarriage of justice in England and Wales (see Roberts, 2003). In three parts it, first, considers the now terminated ex-gratia scheme to show the important part that it played providing financial redress to factually innocent people who overturned their convictions through the normal appeals process and the harm caused to victims of police misconduct and other public officials more generally. Second, it shows that due to the narrow definition of what constitutes a miscar-riage of justice under the statutory compensation scheme most success-ful appellants who have their convictions quashed in an appeal court will not be eligible for compensation. Finally, it assesses the caps that now apply and the deductions routinely taken from the awards to eligi-ble applicants. This reveals that those who do receive compensation from the statutory scheme may not be adequately compensated for the harms and losses that they suffer. It shows that the existing statutory compensation scheme for victims of miscarriages of justice operates to vitiate public concern for successful appellants who overwhelmingly are deemed to fall outside of the scheme and do not receive compensation for the losses and harms that they and their families suffer.

The ex-gratia scheme

Victims of wrongful convictions in England and Wales have received compensation for over 100 years. The first recipient was Adolf Beck in 1904, who was twice wrongly convicted for larceny on erroneous eye-witness identification evidence. The case of Beck was instrumental in the creation of the Court of Criminal Appeal in 1907 (as discussed in Chapters 1 and 6). Beck was awarded £5,000 by the government of the day for the harm that he experienced. Using the Historic Inflation Calculator this equates to approximately £450,000 in terms of its cur-rent purchasing power, or around £90,000 in today's money for each of his 5 years of wrongful imprisonment (see Historic Inflation Calculator, 2012; Naughton, 2003b). However, his compensation was awarded on a discretionary basis initiating an ex-gratia scheme that was the only route to compensation for victims of wrongful convictions until the introduction of a domestic statutory scheme by the Criminal Justice Act 1988. This, simultaneously, fulfilled the UK's obligation in international law to compensate victims of wrongful convictions following the ratification of s. 14(6) of the International Covenant on Civil and Political Rights (ICCPR) on 23 March 1976.

The importance of the ex-gratia scheme, which ran alongside the statutory scheme for almost 20 years after it was introduced, was that it gave discretion to the Home Secretary to award compensation to certain successful appellants and others who fell outside of the scope of the statutory scheme, mainly victims of abortions of justice. Douglas Hurd, the Home Secretary at the time, outlined the circumstances under which an ex-gratia payment would be awarded as follows:

> [T]o people … who have spent a period in custody following a wrongful conviction or charge … that … resulted from serious default on the part of a member of a police force or of some other public authority. There may be exceptional circumstances that justify compensation in cases outside these categories. In particular, facts may emerge at trial, or on appeal within time, that completely exonerate the accused person. I am prepared, in principle, to pay compensation to people who have spent a period in custody or have been imprisoned in cases such as this. I will not, however, be prepared to pay compensation simply because at the trial or an appeal the prosecution was unable to sustain the burden of proof beyond a reasonable doubt in relation to the specific charge that was brought. (HC Deb, 1985)

However, the discretionary scheme was abruptly abolished by Charles Clarke, when he was Home Secretary, in a written ministerial statement in April 2006 (Clarke, 2006). This was to save an estimated £5 million per annum, this being the sum total awarded to a small number of qualifying recipients from the £10 billion that is spent annually on the criminal justice system. Tim Worstall's (2006) criticism of the scheme's abolition puts the alleged saving for the public purse into context:

> The proffered reason, to save £5 million a year, is simply beyond satire. The Government, in its infinite wisdom, annually disposes of about £500 billion of the nation's production: denying those … unjustly banged up will save some 0.001 per cent of public expenditure. Just to provide some context, the £5 million saving is less than the £5.7 million spent in 2003 on subsidising the swill bins at the Houses of Parliament.

Yet the abolition of the ex gratia scheme can be conceived as having more far-reaching and profound consequences than merely saving the state £5 million. Severing state compensation for misconduct by police officers and other public officials effectively communicated the message that the state was no longer willing to take responsibility for and – crucially for the discussion here – willing to pay compensation for the misdoings, intentional or otherwise, by its agents who cause miscarriages or abortions of justice.

At the same time, the abolition of the scheme put an end to state compensation for factually innocent victims of wrongful convictions who have their convictions overturned in a normal, in-time appeal as they do not fall within the scope of the statutory compensation scheme. As will be elaborated below, it meant that all successful appellants who have their convictions overturned within the normal appeals system are left with no remedy at all for harms sustained. Equally, those who spend time on remand or are charged and not convicted will not be eligible for compensation under the statutory scheme (see Spencer, 2010: 805).

Finally, and although it is beyond the scope of this chapter, it must be noted that alleged victims of wrongful convictions can also seek financial redress through the civil route by bringing legal actions for compensation against police authorities, individual police officers, witnesses who gave false testimony, expert witnesses, and so on. These matters were considered by Keith Stanton (2010) who concluded that a major stumbling block to such attempts, however, is the difficulty in establishing the causation, a problem that is also experienced by successful appellants in the United States (see Avery, 2008; Ravenell, 2010; Bernhard, 1999), and so it is unlikely that other theoretical routes to financial redress will bear fruit.

Eligibility for the statutory scheme

The Criminal Justice Act 1988, s.133 contains the statutory compensation scheme for victims of miscarriages of justice states:

> (1) … when a person has been convicted of a criminal offence and when subsequently his conviction has been reversed [quashed] or he has been pardoned on the ground that a new or newly discovered fact shows beyond reasonable doubt that there has been a miscarriage of justice, the Secretary of State shall pay compensation for the miscarriage of justice to the person who has suffered punishment as a result of such conviction or, if he is dead, to his personal representatives,

unless the non-disclosure of the unknown fact was wholly or partly
attributable to the person convicted
    ...
(5) In this section 'reversed' shall be construed as referring to a conviction having been quashed –
    (a)   on an appeal out of time ...
    (b)   on a reference – under the Criminal Appeal Act 1995 [i.e. fol-
          lowing a referral by the Criminal Cases Review Commission]
(6) For the purposes of this section a person suffers punishment as a
result of a conviction when sentence is passed on him for the offence
of which he was convicted.

This section of the chapter unpacks the central tenets of the eligibility criteria outlined in s. 133 of the Act. It argues that the definition of miscarriage of justice is narrow. It considers the consequences of this – for
example, how s. 133 restricts which applicants (i.e., those having had a
conviction overturned) might thereby qualify for statutory compensation.

Only certain successful appeals will do

It is immediately apparent that s. 133 does not apply to those routine
or mundane successful appeals that were discussed in the last chapter;
such cases are ineligible for state compensation for harm suffered.
Rather, only those successful appellants – termed exceptional in the last
chapter – who fail to have their convictions overturned by the normal
appeal process have a hope of qualifying for compensation. They must
have their convictions overturned on an 'out-of-time' appeal, e.g., having their cases referred back to the appeal courts by the post-appeal
machinations of the CCRC.

  As such, the definition of a miscarriage of justice contained in s. 133
effectively limits eligibility for compensation under the statutory scheme
to approximately 1 per cent of those whose convictions have been overturned in England and Wales. The logic seems to be that routine and
mundane convictions overturned by the normal appeals process are
proof that the appeal system works (for an example of this logic, see
Roberts and Weathered, 2009: 51–55). This applies even when there is
evidence of police or prosecutorial misconduct or factual innocence that
would have previously been compensated by the ex gratia scheme.

  A major problem with such a perspective, however, is that it fails to
engage with the sociological reasoning that all convictions overturned

in a criminal appeal court should be acknowledged as instances of official miscarriages of justice and/or abortions of justice. That is, such an approach fails to take account of – indeed, is arguably indifferent to – the harms that can be caused to successful appellants and their families by the very criminal justice system that is supposed to protect citizens from harm (see discussion in Chapter 8).

Beyond a reasonable doubt?

Appellants who have successfully had their convictions overturned must then prove that they are a miscarriage of justice 'beyond a reasonable doubt'.

The definition of beyond reasonable doubt was a central debate in whether Nicholas Mullen (R v Mullen) was a victim of a miscarriage of justice and therefore entitled to statutory compensation. This also sparked a governmental consultation on whether convictions should be overturned if the appeal courts are satisfied that an appellant is factually guilty (see Ministry of Justice, 2006). In 1990, Mullen was convicted of conspiracy to cause explosions and endanger life. After he had been in prison for nearly ten years, however, his conviction was quashed on an out-of-time appeal on the ground that his deportation from Zimbabwe to the UK involved a breach of due process rendering the conviction unsafe. It transpired that the British Secret Intelligence Service, assisted by the British police, had colluded with the Zimbabwean authorities in Mullen's deportation, which was contrary to the law of Zimbabwe and international law (discussed in Chapters 2 and 6).

Following his successful appeal, Mullen applied for compensation, although it was not part of his appeal case that he was factually innocent of the offence of which he was convicted, or, that, apart from the breach of process, his trial was in any way flawed. Mullen's battle for compensation spawned three judgments. First, the Queen's Bench Divisional Court did not see compensation as payable under the statutory scheme. This was then reversed in the Court of Appeal which thought is was. This was in turn appealed by the Secretary of State to the House of Lords (HL) (R (Mullen) v Secretary of State for the Home Department; see also Nobles and Schiff, 2006: 80–91).

The HL reinstated the Divisional Court's ruling that Mullen was not eligible for compensation, although there was a divide in the precise reasoning of the five Law Lords involved. For Steyn LJ, compensation was only appropriate where there is clear evidence of innocence for the following reasons:

[T]he autonomous meaning of the words 'a miscarriage of justice' extends only to 'clear cases of miscarriage of justice, in the sense that there would be acknowledgement that the person concerned was clearly innocent' ... This is the international meaning which Parliament adopted when it enacted section 133 of the 1988 Act. Mr Mullen can certainly say that he was a victim of a failure of the trial process inasmuch as the circumstances in which he was deported from Zimbabwe were deliberately concealed from him before and at his trial. If it had been disclosed the trial would have been stopped. But Mr Mullen was not innocent of the charge. On the contrary, the conclusion is inescapable that he knowingly lent assistance to an active IRA unit. He is therefore not entitled to compensation under section 133. (R (Mullen) v Secretary of State for the Home Department, paragraphs 56–57. Lord Roger agreed with this interpretation)

From a different perspective, but also seeing compensation as inappropriate to a successful appellant who is unlikely to be innocent and, in fact, likely to be guilty, Bingham LJ argued that, while the CACD was correct to quash Mullen's conviction:

[T]he default did not affect the fairness of the trial or throw doubt on the verdict which the jury, by a majority, returned. Secondly, the Secretary of State was in my view entitled to treat as exceptional a case in which there appeared to him to be no reason to doubt Mr Mullen's guilt. (R (Mullen) v Secretary of State for the Home Department, paragraph 12. This perspective was favoured by Lord Scott and Lord Walker)

Following the *Mullen* debacle, Sion Jenkins (Jenkins and Woffinden, 2008) was refused compensation under the statutory scheme on the grounds that a miscarriage of justice beyond a reasonable doubt required evidence of factual innocence. Jenkins was convicted in 1998 for the murder of his stepdaughter Billie-Jo Jenkins. His first appeal was unsuccessful in 1999, but his second appeal in August 2004 was successful, and the CACD ordered a retrial, with Jenkins being released on bail. The juries in two subsequent retrials were unable to reach majority verdicts at the Central Criminal Court (Old Bailey) in London. In February 2006, the CPS announced that it would seek no further retrials and Jenkins was officially declared not guilty and acquitted. Jenkins applied for compensation for his six years of imprisonment, but was refused in

August 2010. A spokesperson from the Ministry of Justice was quoted as follows:

> The Court of Appeal has made clear that, in the court's view, the right test to adopt in deciding whether someone is entitled to compensation is whether they have been shown to be clearly innocent. (cited BBC News, 2010)

The state's definition of a miscarriage of justice and factual innocence requirement to be eligible for statutory compensation was further clarified in the refusal of Andrew Adams' application under s. 133 for his 14 years of wrongful imprisonment (R (Adams) v Secretary of State for Justice). Convicted in May 1993 for the murder of Jack Royal in March 1990, Adams had his conviction overturned in January 2007 when a series of errors made by his defence team at trial was revealed. In particular, due to their inadequate preparation for Adams' trial, numerous pieces of crucial evidence which could have undermined the prosecution's case against him were overlooked and his conviction was deemed to be unsafe and quashed (R v Andrew Adams). In turning down Adams' appeal against the refusal to award him compensation, Dyson LJ distinguished four categories of fresh evidence successful appeal in the CACD, with only the first category relating to innocence and thereby eligibility for compensation:

> [T]here are at least three classes of case where the CACD allows an appeal against conviction on the basis of fresh evidence ... A category 1 case is where the court is sure that the defendant is innocent of the crime of which he has been convicted. An obvious example is where DNA evidence, not obtainable at the time of trial, shows beyond doubt that the defendant was not guilty of the offence. A category 2 case is where the fresh evidence shows that he was wrongly convicted in the sense that, had the fresh evidence been available at the trial, no reasonable jury could properly have convicted. An example is where the prosecution case rested entirely on the evidence of a witness who was put forward as a witness of truth and fresh evidence undermines the creditworthiness of that witness, so that no fair-minded jury could properly have convicted on the evidence of that witness. It does not follow in a category 2 case that the defendant was innocent. A category 3 case is where the fresh evidence is such that the conviction cannot be regarded as safe, but the court cannot say that no fair-minded jury could properly convict if there were to

be a trial which included the fresh evidence. The court concludes that a fair-minded jury might convict or it might acquit. There is a fourth category of case to which Lord Bingham referred in *Mullen*. This is where a conviction is quashed because something has gone seriously wrong in the investigation of the offence or the conduct of the trial, resulting in the conviction of someone who should not have been convicted. (R (Adams) v Secretary of State for Justice, paragraph 19)

John Spencer's (2010: 820–822) analysis offers three categories which roughly tallied with Dyson LJ's categorisation. He departs from Dyson, however in seeing Dyson's second and third categories (which Spencer simply sees as category b cases) as eligible for compensation along with Dyson's first category (factual innocence cases) (Spencer's category a cases). Spencer agrees with Dyson, however, in seeing successful appellants who are factually guilty as ineligible for compensation, which he calls category c cases.

An apparent reluctance to award state compensation to successful appellants who may be or are factually guilty is arguably understandable, even if they were convicted in breach of the rule of law, not least for fear of a backlash in terms of public disapproval. Although it does beg the question from a 'black letter' perspective as to what kind of integrity is being upheld. If the criminal appeals system sees it appropriate to quash such convictions and release people believed to be terrorists, then it seems legally illogical to not follow through and see such successful appellants who, in the words of Dyson LJ, 'should not have been convicted' – and who have spent a decade incarcerated – as eligible for compensation.

Perhaps most crucially, however, Dyson LJ in *Adams* set criteria for eligibility for statutory compensation for miscarriages of justice on the basis of two highly exceptional cases that do not fit with the reality of the criminal appeals system. *Mullen* is a rare case in England and Wales of a successful appellant believed to be factually guilty, and, to date, England and Wales has only had one clear-cut DNA exoneration – the case of Sean Hodgson (R v Hodgson). Hodgson, convicted for the murder of 22-year-old Teresa de Simone in 1979, had his conviction overturned in March 2009 after 27 years of wrongful imprisonment when DNA testing of the semen sample collected at the crime scene did not match his profile (BBC News, 2009b). Six months after his successful appeal, Hodgson was completely exonerated from any involvement in the murder when DNA testing on the exhumed body of the original police suspect, David Lace, resulted in a complete match with biological samples from the crime scene (Jamieson, 2009; also discussed in Chapters 2 and 7 in this book).

As such, a major problem with the way that Dyson LJ categorised successful appeals at the post-appeal stage is that it requires successful appellants to provide something that most will not be able to – proof of factual innocence – which is also something that the criminal justice system does not require. As discussed in Chapter 4, although defendants in criminal trials are formally presumed to be innocent and the burden is on the prosecution to prove the charges against them beyond a reasonable doubt, the notion of innocence is very much a red herring in criminal trials. Proof of factual innocence is not required in criminal trials, which seek to determine, rather, whether defendants are guilty or not guilty of the criminal offences that they are charged with. Similarly, criminal appeals do not seek to determine whether appellants are, in fact, innocent or guilty. On the contrary, as shown in Chapter 6, appeals in the CACD for serious convictions given in the Crown Court under s. 23 of the Criminal Appeal Act 1968 normally only accept new evidence or argument that was not available at the time of the original trial or a previous appeal, seeking to determine whether convictions are 'unsafe' according to the specific terms of the Criminal Appeal Act 1995. In this context, appellants strive to find such fresh evidence to discredit the evidence that led to their conviction, in order that it be deemed unsafe and therefore overturned. Appellants as such do not seek to establish their factual innocence. If it is decided that the conviction is unsafe, the CACD will allow the appeal and quash the conviction (s. 2 Criminal Appeal Act 1968; s.7 of the Act also provides that the CACD has the power to order a retrial at the Crown Court). Crucially in this process, however, evidence of factual innocence that was available at the time of the original trial or a previous appeal may not be deemed to be grounds for appeal to the appeal courts or the CCRC.

Moreover, Dyson LJ's analysis also runs counter to the presumption of innocence which Roch LJ previously reasoned should be returned to the successful appellants in the judgment that quashed the convictions of the Bridgewater Four. It is worth repeating here:

> If we conclude … that the convictions were unsafe then the convictions would be quashed and the presumption of innocence which exists in favour of all unconvicted persons would be re-established … We shall consequently allow these appeals and quash the convictions … in respect of all four appellants … Consequently the presumption

of innocence in respect of the four appellants will be re-established. (R v Hickey and Others)

Contrary to this, and despite the fact that almost all out-of-time successful appeals will fall into categories 2 and 3 of his typology and should be presumed to be innocent until proven guilty, Dyson LJ did not see such successful appellants as eligible for miscarriage-of-justice compensation from the state.

Matters came to a head in May 2011 when the Supreme Court handed down its landmark judgment on what currently constitutes a 'miscarriage of justice' for the purposes of statutory compensation (see R (on the application of Adams) (FC) v Secretary of State for Justice). In two separate appeals, Andrew Adams, and Eamonn MacDermott and Raymond McCartney were given permission to appeal against the refusal by the Secretary of State to award compensation on the basis that their successful appeals did not show that they were 'clearly innocent'. All three had had their murder convictions overturned, following a referral back to the appeal courts by the CCRC.

In particular, the Supreme Court noted that s. 133 provides no fixed meaning for the term miscarriage of justice and held that claimants for statutory miscarriage-of-justice compensation do not need to prove that they are factually innocent. Instead, it ruled that out-of-time successful appellants will have to show that on the basis of the new or newly discovered fact that they should not have been convicted, or that a conviction could not possibly be based on those facts.

On this basis, it was held by a majority that MacDermott and McCartney were eligible for compensation, as their confessions, the only evidence that led to their convictions, were unreliable. Adams' appeal was unanimously dismissed. Although it was accepted that incompetent defence representation deprived him of a fair trial and it was correct therefore for his conviction to be quashed, the Supreme Court asserted that it did not mean that the jury would inevitably have acquitted him.

The Supreme Court judgment is to be welcomed for establishing that clear proof of factual innocence is not a requirement for compensation under the statutory scheme. However, there remains scope for further debate on what constitutes a miscarriage of justice and who should fall within the ambit of the statutory scheme (see Naughton, 2011b). For instance, the judgment fails to settle contentious cases such as that of Barry George (R v Barry George), who spent eight years in prison for the murder of television presenter Jill Dando until he was acquitted in a retrial in August 2008. His initial application for compensation was also refused because of his failure to prove his factual innocence at his appeal. Despite the fact that when he was acquitted at his retrial, the CPS declared that he had every right to be considered an innocent man.

However, responding to the news that George was to renew his application for statutory compensation in light of the Supreme Court judgment, a spokesperson from the Ministry of Justice said: 'We will continue to fight the Barry George case. We still think that under the new measure he would still not be entitled to compensation' (cited in Bowcott and Laville, 2011).

Amount

Formerly, there was no limit on how much compensation could be paid to eligible successful appellants, whether the application was deemed eligible under the statutory or the ex gratia scheme. Rather, awards were calculated in accordance with the normal principles of compensation for civil damages. However, amendments to s. 133 of the Criminal Justice Act 1988 by the Criminal Justice and Immigration Act 2008 curtailed in crucial ways the amount of compensation payable to those successful appellants that are accepted as victims of miscarriages of justice. The amendments also introduced further deductions to those applications that already existed (s. 61 Criminal Justice and Immigration Act 2008). In specific terms, the 2008 Act introduced the following amendments to s. 133 of the Criminal Justice Act 1988 that, together with the existing deductions for saved living expenses, will form the backdrop for this analysis:

- a limit on the level of compensation payable to £500,000 for those serving fewer than 10 years in relevant detention and to £1,000,000 for those serving over 10 years in relevant detention;
- a limit on the loss of earnings for any one year to 1.5 times the median annual gross earnings;
- allowing the Assessor to make deductions for other criminality and conduct from the overall award; and
- allowing the Assessor to make deductions for the contributory conduct of the applicant.

To better illustrate the likely impact of these caps and deductions, the analysis in this section compares critically the facts of the case of Sean Hodgson, identified in the previous section as an eligible applicant for compensation under the terms of the statutory scheme, against recipients of compensation under the previous statutory and ex-gratia schemes.

Caps

The underlying principle for the calculation of tort/civil damages, which statutory compensation for miscarriages of justice used to follow, is that the amount awarded should restore claimants to the position that they would have been in had the tort/wrong not occurred. It means awarding successful claimants an amount that reflects the harms and damages incurred as a result of the tort/wrong. The classic formulation of this is in the case of Livingstone v Rawyards Coal Company where Blackburn LJ stated that the measure of damages was:

> [T]he sum of money to be given for reparation of damages ... should as nearly as possible get at that sum of money which will put the party who has been injured, or who has suffered, in the same position as he would have been in if he had not sustained the wrong for which he is now getting his compensation or reparation. (at 7; see also Burrows, 1987: 16)

Fiona Mactaggart (HC Deb, 2005), the then Parliamentary Under-Secretary of the Home Office, outlined the remit and scope of the compensation scheme for miscarriages of justice before the amendments as follows:

> The compensation process involves two separate and distinct concepts of loss: pecuniary and non-pecuniary loss. The pecuniary element, the quantifiable financial loss, is intended to put the applicant back into the financial position they would have been in but for their wrongful conviction, but not to a position better than that ... The non-pecuniary loss award ... is in recognition of, for example, loss of reputation, loss of liberty, hardship, mental suffering, injury to feelings, and inconvenience. It is an award in recognition of the miscarriage of justice itself.

Contrary to this, the artificial caps put on the statutory compensation scheme for miscarriages of justice by the Criminal Justice and Immigration Act 2008 detaches it from normal tort principles. In consequence, the amount being awarded may not reflect the entirety of the harm suffered by eligible victims.

This is acutely evident in the case of Hodgson, as the caps introduced to the statutory compensation scheme by the 2008 Act means that the maximum amount of compensation payable is no greater than £1 million for his 27 years of wrongful imprisonment. Indeed, limiting statutory compensation for miscarriages of justice to either £500,000 or £1 million also seems unjust and inconsistent when compared with relatively greater awards paid out prior to the amendments under the 2008 Act or under the ex-gratia scheme before it was abolished. For instance, Mike O'Brien of the Cardiff Newsagent Three case (see O'Brien with Lewis, 2008: 198–199) was awarded £685,058 (before deductions for 'saved living expenses' – discussed below) in 2002 for his 11 years of imprisonment for the murder of Philip Saunders. This equates to £62,325 per annum, meaning that, all things being equal, Hodgson would have to receive at least £1,682,787 for his 27 years of imprisonment if calculated on the same terms as O'Brien's award.

The caps will also mean that victims of wrongful convictions who lose successful businesses will not receive adequate remedy for their extensive financial losses. Reginald Dunk and Alexander Schlesinger, for instance, were wrongly convicted in 1983 for allegedly attempting to smuggle machine-guns to Iraq and ordered to pay £63,000 in fines and costs (see Abrams, 1999). They were each awarded £2 million plus costs in 1999 in recognition of their wrongful convictions, loss of business and personal distress (see Norton-Taylor, 2000). If Dunk and Schlesinger were deemed eligible under the existing scheme, they would receive a maximum of £500,000 each (as they did not spend time in prison), around one-quarter of the assessment of their actual losses before the caps were introduced, as they did not serve a custodial sentence over 10 years.

This impacts, too, on the amendments to the statutory compensation scheme by the Criminal Justice and Immigration Act 2008 that limit the loss of earnings that can be awarded for any one year to 1.5 times the median annual gross earnings according to the latest figures published by the Office for National Statistics at the time of the assessment. As such, the existing statutory compensation regime cannot adequately compensate those, like Dunk and Schlesinger, who lose successful businesses or those with high salaried professional careers who are victims of wrongful convictions. In this sense, the existing scheme can be conceived as having a certain type of ideal victim at the award stage, i.e. one that is likely to be adequately compensated within the confines of the imposed caps, such as a person who was unemployed at the time of their wrongful conviction or in a low-paid job.

Another relevant example is the case of Colin Stagg who would not be eligible for compensation under the existing statutory scheme, as he was never convicted and did not have a conviction overturned a on an out of time appeal. Stagg received £706,000 in 2008 under the ex-gratia scheme for the 13 months that he spent on remand for the alleged murder of Rachel Nickell when Robert Napper was identified with DNA testing as the real murderer (Stevenson, 2008). If Hodgson's compensation were calculated on this basis, the award would be in the region of £18 million. This sum would be on a par with the level of awards that some victims of wrongful convictions receive in the United States. For instance, Edmond Ovasapyan received $1.7 million from the City of Glendale, Los Angeles County, California, for being wrongly detained for eight months as part of a murder investigation (see Hicken, 2011).

Deductions for other criminality

In the absence of established legal authorities, and as compensation awards to victims of miscarriages of justice are not publicly available information (Ministry of Justice, 2008: paragraph 18), we do not know how deductions are calculated or the impact that they have on the overall amounts awarded. Rather, the information that we have is gleaned from those who receive awards disclosing details of same to the media. However, we can say that in addition to the limits on the total amount payable to eligible recipients of compensation, the statutory compensation scheme also departs from normal tort calculations in making deductions for other criminality. As mentioned, tort awards for wrongful convictions should, at least in theory, relate to the harm that was suffered when a victim was wrongly convicted for a crime that they did not commit. They should not relate to previous criminal offences or separate criminal offences that may be committed subsequent to the wrongful convictions being overturned.

An analogy with claims for road traffic incidences seems apposite. Insurance premiums take into account previous motor incidents and give discounts to drivers without convictions for motoring offences or with clean driving licences, for instance. However, claims for compensation are not reduced because of previous offences or accidents that were the fault of the driver who is a victim of a road traffic accident.

Contrary to this, under the existing statutory scheme for miscarriage-of-justice compensation eligible applicants are assessed holistically in terms of past and future criminality. This appears to be an explicit strategy to shift the culpability for miscarriages and abortions of justice from the agencies or agents of the criminal justice system that caused them onto the victims themselves. It effectively further distinguishes between deserving and undeserving eligible successful appellants to limit the awards payable by the state.

In making deductions for other, past or future, criminality, the assessment of awards under the statutory compensation scheme could be said to be doubly punishing eligible claimants. The harm that they and their families suffer because of their wrongful conviction is seemingly deemed to be less harmful or less worthy of financial redress by the state simply by virtue of their past or future criminality. Yet the idea that victims of wrongful convictions are less harmed if they have a previous criminal record runs counter to the victimology studies. It has been shown, for instance, how the experience of wrongful imprisonment is unique; and, arguably, much more challenging than the experiences of prisoners who are guilty and serving sentences for crimes that they did commit (Tan, 2011).

Moreover, deducting compensation for previous criminality also fails to take account of the fact that previous criminal convictions have been implicated as a 'major factor in the conviction of the innocent' (Huff *et al.*, 1996: 79). As these authors noted, a criminal record renders defendants vulnerable to wrongful conviction for a range of reasons. In particular, defendants with criminal records are less inclined to testify in court for fear that they will be incriminated if their previous criminal convictions are revealed during cross-examination. Moreover, juries tend to see previous convictions as evidence of 'bad character' and thus tend to disbelieve the evidence given by such defendants. In such cases, juries take less care over returning guilty verdicts (Huff *et al.*, 1996: 80).

Saved living expenses

The Home Office Assessor may also make a deduction from awards under the statutory compensation scheme for miscarriages of justice in respect of the saved living expenses, or for what has colloquially been termed 'bed and board'. That is, the costs an applicant would have been required to pay out of their net income, for example rent or mortgage payments, had they not been (wrongly) imprisoned as a result of a wrongful conviction (Ministry of Justice, 2008: paragraphs 11–14).

From reports in the press we know that Michael O'Brien of the Cardiff Newsagent Three, for instance, had £37,158 deducted from his award for what was claimed he would have 'saved' on things like rent and rates had he not been in prison for 11 years (see O'Brien with Lewis,

2008). John Kamara's compensation award was also deducted by £75,000 for his 'savings' during the 20 years he was imprisoned (see Shorter, 2010). Two of the Bridgewater Four, cousins Michael and Vincent Hickey, each had £60,000 deducted from their final awards for 17 years of imprisonment (see Naughton, 2003b). Although an imprecise calculation, the four cases cited each incurred a deduction of approximately £3,500 for each year of wrongful imprisonment, irrespective of the overall award each received.

If such a deduction is incurred by Hodgson, his award is possibly going to be reduced by a further £100,000 for so-called saved living expenses. This would be less problematic if awards were not capped. But it means that the longer that victims such as Hodgson spend in prison, the greater the impact of deductions for savings while in prison on final awards that they will receive: deductions for saved living expenses alone will potentially reduce the maximum that Hodgson will receive from £1 million to an upper limit of £900,000.

The possibility of making deductions for saved mortgage payments raises an additional critical issue, especially for victims who served long terms of wrongful imprisonment and were unable to purchase a property and pay a mortgage during their imprisonment. As this relates to Hodgson's claim, the Average House Prices in the UK (2012) index shows that had he purchased a property in 1982, the year that he was wrongly convicted, at the national average house price of £24,177, the value of his property would have increased by £155,186 to £179,363 by 2008, the year before he was released (figures were not available for 2009 the year that Sean Hodgson had his conviction overturned). If such rises were also taken into account in assessing compensation awards they could arguably act to balance deductions taken for saved living expenses and result in awards that more appropriately put victims of wrongful convictions back into the position that they might have been in had they not been wrongly convicted.

Conclusion

When a person suffers an injury through no fault of their own due to medical negligence, a violation of industrial health and safety guidelines or a motor car incident, for instance, we might expect that the injured person receives compensation that seeks to put them back into the position that they were in or would have been in had the injury not occurred. In the same way, it may seem intuitive to think that when a person has a conviction for a criminal offence in a criminal appeal court

overturned that they would, and morally should, be eligible for financial remedy from the state for the harms inflicted as a result of justice
gone wrong.

Contrary to this, the overall conclusion to be drawn from the foregoing analysis is that the existing statutory compensation scheme for miscarriages of justice functions as a system of filters and cuts that fails to
acknowledge the harm caused to the majority of successful appellants
in terms of loss of jobs, reputation, time spent in prison, and so on. First
it sieves out the vast majority of successful appellants, having had their
convictions overturned in the normal appeal process. It then requires
the exceptional successful appellants to have had their convictions
overturned on the basis of new or newly discovered facts that show that
they should not have been convicted, or that a conviction could not
possibly be based on those facts. After this, it subjects the awards of
those rare few who are deemed to be eligible to caps on the maximum
amount that they can receive, and routine deductions that further
diminishes their awards. All of which means that they may not receive
an award that adequately reflects the harm they have experienced.

As such, even though the UK fully complies with its international
obligations to have a statutory compensation scheme for victims of miscarriages of justice, it is submitted that the remedy provided to victims
of wrongful convictions is unsatisfactory. The majority of successful
appellants do not qualify and those successful appellants that do receive
compensation may receive insufficient award to provide for their ongoing medical needs, such as specialist counselling for the often irre-
versible PTSD from which some victims have been found to suffer (see,
for instance, Grounds, 2004, 2005; Hill, 2010).

Moreover, successful appellants who spend years or even decades in
prison are often released with no family or financial support at all. It is
therefore vital that, first, the harm that they have experienced is recognised. Second, that they receive adequate financial provisions to enable
them to rebuild their lives, without which the harms are exacerbated
and unlikely to ever be overcome (see Tan, 2011). Of course, financial
compensation can never fully remedy the loss of freedom and stain to
reputation suffered by those who have been wrongly convicted and
imprisoned. It is equally hard to measure how much compensation
would adequately reflect the harms inflicted on victims of miscarriages
and abortions of justice as much depends on the harm caused to the victim in question. What is clear though is that the state is increasingly
unsympathetic to the plight of wrongful conviction victims, seeing the
majority of successful appellants as ineligible and undeserving and

demonstrating a mean-spirited attitude to those that are eligible to reduce the amount that it has to pay.

An adage that is commonly used in critical analyses of the criminal justice system is that the ultimate test of its justness is not that it should never make mistakes but, rather, what is done in response to apparent wrongs and the extent to which speedy attempts are made to make proper amends. A wrongful conviction is not corrected simply by the act of overturning the conviction in an appeal court. It requires a commitment to provide a fast and fair remedy to victims, so that their harms and losses can start to be alleviated. The existing statutory compensation scheme for miscarriages of justice is failing the majority of successful appellants who ought to have their victimhood acknowledged and their losses compensated.

PART IV

Conclusion

10

Troubleshooting the Black Spots of the Criminal Justice System

Using the analogy of a factory maintenance engineer, the introductory chapter made a case for a diagnostic sociological analysis of failings in the criminal justice system. These are manifest in successful appeals against criminal conviction as part of a troubleshooting project in the maintenance of the criminal justice system. The overall aim of such a diagnostic endeavour is to identify the black spots of the criminal justice process that emerge in post-mortem analysis of successful appeal cases. It was proffered that only when we are armed with an understanding of the key areas and aspects of the criminal justice system which are vulnerable to causing wrongful convictions can suitable attempts then be made to fix such black spots in the hope that such causes of wrongful convictions can be prevented in the future.

The first step in any such troubleshooting endeavour is to understand the nature of the problematic to be studied as a precursor to any attempted remedies: maintenance engineers need to know what the problem is before they can attempt to fix it. To this end, the concept of intent was employed in Chapter 2 to distinguish between intentional abortions of justice and unintentional miscarriages of justice and how each of these categories relates to the issue of whether the successful appellant is factually innocent or factually guilt. This firmly grounded the analysis within a lay perspective on the proper functioning of the criminal justice system. It resulted in a sixfold typology of abortions of justice and miscarriages of justice that clarified the different phenomena which are normally included together under the nebulous catch-all: 'miscarriages of justice'.

An extensive exploration of the causation of abortions of justice and miscarriages of justice in Chapters 3 and 4 revealed that because of the

extent of abortions of justice and miscarriages of justice factually innocent people are vulnerable to being wrongly convicted. In terms of miscarriages of justice, the factually innocent can fall prey to witnesses who
give evidence in good faith. They are also vulnerable to being wrongly
convicted by police officers and prosecutors in a system that can facilitate the wrongful conviction of factually innocent individuals without
a breach of the prevailing rules of due process

Of course, factually guilty people will also be convicted by the existing criminal justice system, which is not necessarily automatically a
good thing either. As cases such as Mullen, Weir and Clarke and McDaid
show, if the factually guilty can show an intentional breach of due
process, i.e. that they are victims of abortions of justice, they can have
their convictions overturned, which can lead to public crises of confidence in the criminal justice system comparable to those that occur
when the factually innocent are convicted. Moreover, crises of confidence in the criminal justice system that are induced by successful
appeals of the factually guilty can lead to reforms that can render the
factually innocent more vulnerable to wrongful convictions, as in the
case of Michael Weir – and the reform of double jeopardy under the
Criminal Justice Act 2003.

This provides a basis for thinking about troubleshooting strategies
that might respond to the two very different socio-legal phenomena of
abortions of justice and miscarriages of justice. Taking abortions of justice first, it is evident that the effectiveness of safeguards against wrongful convictions such as PACE, the Criminal Procedure and
Investigations Act 1996, the Code for Crown Prosecutors, and so on, is
compromised by lack of accountability when police officers and prosecutors intentionally breach them. An obvious solution would be to vig-
orously pursue criminal charges against any public official who
intentionally breaches a statute or code of conduct that is expressly
intended to protect against wrongful convictions. This might include
bringing charges for perverting the course of justice against police officers who are shown in successful appeals to have intentionally fabricated evidence against suspects and against prosecutors who knowingly
and intentionally failed to disclose evidence to the defence. It would
also include charges for contempt of court against witnesses who intentionally mislead the court by giving false evidence.

A far more sophisticated approach to remedy the causes of miscarriages of justice is required, however, as they are systemic and rooted
in the routine operations of the criminal justice process at the pre-trial
and trial stages. If there is a serious commitment to protect against

wrongful convictions, there needs be a rethink on how the police investigate alleged crimes; how alleged crimes are prosecuted; how inherently unreliable forms of evidence are deemed to be admissible in criminal trials. Police officers can no longer simply build incriminating cases against suspects, something that has been identified in various research studies over the last 30 to 40 years. What is required instead is a more objective approach that takes seriously the possibility that the accused or the suspect may be factually innocent.

An illustration that clarifies this point is the following scenario that I regularly present to my students: a woman walks into a police station with two black eyes and claims that she had been assaulted; what do you see? In ten years of teaching, the immediate response from almost all of the students that I have taught, including several former police officers, is that they see a victim of assault. And, therein lies the problem. The instinctive starting point is a presumption of guilt – to see the alleged victim as a victim and the alleged offender as an offender. This bias is evidently problematic in the context of the wealth of reasons and motivations for false allegations that were presented in Chapter 3. As was shown, this kind of thinking can lead the police and the prosecution to fail to conduct proper investigations to ascertain whether allegations made are sufficiently credible, as in the cases of Warren Blackwell, Mike Lawson and Basil Williams-Rigby, Darryl Gee and Roger Beardmore.

Of course, it is not only a problem in the area of false allegations and cases such as Sally Clark, Angela Cannings and Barry George reveal that routine police investigations that do not breach due process can also lead to wrongful convictions for other alleged offences. This indicates that the problem with police methodology goes beyond what can be addressed with piecemeal reforms. Indeed, there is a need for a cultural shift towards a more objective method of policing and prosecuting alleged crimes that is more in line with the spirit of the presumption of innocence. There also needs to be a rethink on the question of the admissibility of inherently unreliable forms of evidence, such as untested expert opinions, uncorroborated witness testimonies, weak eyewitness identification evidence, dubious forensic science, and so on, which are also implicated in causing unintentional miscarriages of justice.

Following on from this, the analysis turned to how the existing criminal justice system deals with alleged wrongful convictions, with a particular focus on claims of factual innocence by alleged victims. Starting with the issue of prisoners maintaining innocence in Chapter 5, it was shown that the current system of risk assessment and the parole deal is incompatible with the realities of the criminal justice system in which factually innocent individuals can be convicted and can fail to have their convictions overturn in the appeals system or through the CCRC. As such, the Parole Board is currently disadvantaging potentially factually innocent victims of wrongful convictions, seeing them as 'deniers' of the crimes that they are alleged to have committed when some claims of factual innocence by prisoners may be genuine. While it is not wholly unreasonable for the Parole Board to argue that it is legally obliged to work on the basis that prisoners are guilty, there are moral, practical and policy justifications for devising an alternative method of assessing prisoners who say that they are innocent so that they are not disadvantaged vis-à-vis prisoners who acknowledge their guilt. Overall, the status of a prisoner as an innocence maintainer cannot continue to be used as a risk factor in predictions of future criminality.

The limits of the Parole Board in terms of alleged innocent victims of wrongful convictions emphasises the importance of an appeal system that can assist the factually innocent to have their convictions overturned. This was indeed the intention of Parliament when it established the Court of Criminal Appeal a little over a century ago. However, as was shown in Chapter 6, the refusal of Court of Criminal Appeal judges to go behind jury verdicts in favour of appeals that rested on points of law, claims of breaches of due process and fresh evidence meant that the potential of the appeal system to assist the factually innocent was fatally compromised from the start. Added to this, the various reforms over the years, most notably the Criminal Appeal Acts of 1968 and 1995, gave statutory legitimacy to an appeal system that may overturn the convictions of the factually guilty and may not see potentially factually innocent victims of wrongful convictions as having admissible grounds of appeal if the evidence is not deemed to be fresh. Overall, if the role of the Court of Appeal (Criminal Division) (CACD) is truly to safeguard the integrity of the criminal justice system, then integrity must be understood as not solely related to notions of the procedural fairness but to its social justice outcomes as well. This requires that principles of finality and jury deference cannot be allowed to act as barriers to the overturning of convictions given to those who may be factually innocent.

It was, in large part, in recognition of the barriers of the CACD in dealing with claims of factual innocence by alleged victims of wrongful convictions that the Criminal Cases Review Commission (CCRC) was created and why it was supposed to be independent from the legal system. Widely believed to be an innocence commission, the CCRC was shown in Chapter 7 to be failing in its public mandate as recommended by the Royal Commission on Criminal Justice (RCCJ) as it mimics the appeal courts in restricting itself to seeing only those cases thought to have a real possibility of being quashed, as appropriate for a referral. The analysis also showed that when compared with C3, the previous system for alleged wrongful convictions post-appeal, the CCRC is better resourced and staffed. Despite this, the CCRC plays a lesser part in overturning convictions for serious offences than C3 did if compared on a pro rata basis. The various defences of the operations of the CCRC, the need for symmetry between the CCRC and the CACD and arguments around the primacy of due process, miss the point that the CCRC was established precisely because the CACD can fail to overturn the convictions of the factually innocent – and the fact that something else was needed. Overall, the CCRC needs to be an independent investigatory (as opposed to a desktop review) body that can act as a pressure on the CACD to overturn cases where the factually innocent might have been wrongly convicted, rather than being led by the CACD in terms of its review procedure and referral decisions.

The analysis then turned to the harmful consequences of wrongful convictions and the limits of existing forms of redress by the state. The victimology of wrongful convictions in Chapter 8 drew on official statistics on successful appeals as systemic evidence of official miscarriages of justice and/or abortions of justice. It showed that if all successful appeals in the Crown Court and the CACD are included in critical sociological analyses that many thousands of direct and secondary victims can be shown to be harmed when the criminal justice system gets it wrong: lives are destroyed, careers are ruined, individuals and families can sustain permanent and ongoing psychological damage and social stigma.

Despite this, as shown in Chapter 9, the existing statutory scheme for compensating victims of miscarriages of justice is so narrowly focused that it fails to recognise successful appellants who have their convictions overturned in a normal appeal as eligible for any form of financial redress from the state at all for the harms that they have suffered; nor does it recognise secondary victims. Rather, only those who have their convictions overturned outside of the normal appeals system are potentially eligible, amounting to a maximum of 1 per cent of successful appellants in England and Wales each year. Added to this, the further hurdles that applicants to the statutory compensation scheme must overcome, in particular, that the conviction must have been overturned on a new or newly discovered fact that shows that a conviction could not possibly be based on those facts, means that less than the 1 per cent actually qualify. Turning to quantum, the system of caps and deductions means that even those who are eligible for state relief may not be adequately compensated for the harms that they and their families experienced. The existing statutory compensation scheme is structured in such a way that almost all victims of wrongful convictions will not receive any compensation from the state at all. Moreover, those who are accepted as eligible for the statutory scheme may not receive awards along the lines of normal tort principles that aim to put successful claimants back in the position that they would have been in had the wrongful conviction not occurred.

Overall, the foregoing substantive analyses have shown that the existing criminal justice system is profoundly flawed from a lay perspective that sees its fundamental role as the conviction of the factually guilty and the role of the appeal courts and the CCRC as assisting factually innocent victims of wrongful convictions to have their convictions overturned.

Continuing the analogy of an engineering factory, in light of the foregoing it seems apposite to conceive the victims of wrongful convictions as the throwaway scrap parts of the processes of the criminal justice machinery. Indeed, for the most part, successful appellants who stand as evidence of the black spots of the criminal justice system are treated as mere collateral damage in the 'war against crime'. They are discarded without apology, accountability, relief or remedy from the state for the harm suffered by them and their families. And yet there is a marked difference between how an engineering factory relates to the possibility of scrap parts and how the criminal justice system relates to wrongful convictions.

The possibility of scrap parts in a manufacturing context is taken very seriously and steps are taken so that they can be avoided. This involves a major commitment to inspection procedures and the implementation of all manner of quality control systems that aim to identify scrap parts in-house. Typically, centre lathe turners and milling machine operators, for instance, who make parts for the aerospace industry, however skilled and experienced they may be, are not permitted to start to produce their batches of components unless and until the first-off inspector is satisfied that they conform to the required dimensions and tolerances of the drawings that they work from. As they make their components, the operators are required to inspect a random sample. There will also be periodic inspection by the inspector. And all components will be rechecked in the final inspection department before they leave the factory.

On the surface it looks like the criminal justice system is likewise replete with quality control mechanisms and systems. At the pre-trial stage there is PACE, the Code for Crown Prosecutors and the Criminal Procedure and Investigations Act 1996, for instance. There is also an appeals system and we have the CCRC, the world's first post-appeal body for investigating alleged miscarriages of justice that fail to be overturned by the appeal system.

But, as this book has shown, delving deeper we can see that the quality control safeguards of the criminal justice system routinely fail to protect against wrongful convictions. Factually innocent people can even be convicted without breaches of due process having occurred, and which may never be overturned by the appeal system and/or referred by the CCRC.

The conclusion of this troubleshooting analysis of the criminal justice system is simply that the prevention, identification and rectification of wrongful convictions, whether intentional abortions of justice or unintentional miscarriages of justice, has to be hardwired into the criminal justice system and become a pervasive goal of every part of the criminal justice system and every agent who works for and within it. Until such time as safeguarding the innocent becomes the overriding objective of the criminal justice system, the black spots that have been identified in the successful appeal cases cited throughout this book will remain as vulnerable sites that can cause victims to be wrongly convicted.

References

Abrahams, G. (1964) *Police Questioning and the Judges' Rules*, London: Oyez.

Abrams, F. (1999) '"Arms to Iraq" men to be paid £125,000 damages', *The Independent*, 8 December.

Allen, N. (2006) 'George Orwell was right: spy cameras see Britons' every move', *Bloomberg*, 22 December.

Ashworth, A. (2003) *Principles of Criminal Law* (4th edn) Oxford: Oxford University Press.

Auld, R. (2001) 'Review of the Criminal Courts of England and Wales' <http://webarchive.nationalarchives.gov.uk/+/http://www.criminal-courts-review.org.uk/auldconts.htm> 24 June 2012.

Average House Prices in the UK (2012) [online] <http://www.mortgageguideuk.co.uk/housing/average-house-prices.html> Accessed 26 June 2012.

Avery, M. (2008) 'Obstacles to Litigating Civil Claims for Wrongful Conviction: An Overview', *Boston University Public Interest Law Journal* 18: 439–451.

Baldwin, J, and McConville, M. (1979) 'Plea Bargaining and the Court of Appeal', *British Journal of Law and Society*, 6(2): 200–218.

Baldwin, J. (1992) 'Legal Advice in the Police Station', *New Law Journal*, 142(6581): 1762.

Baldwin, J. and McConville, M. (1977) *Negotiated Justice: Pressures to Plead Guilty*, London: Martin Robertson.

Barnsley, M. (2000) 'Repression in British prisons', *Chain Reaction*, August.

Batt, J. (2005) *Stolen Innocence: The Sally Clark Story – A Mother's Fight for Justice*, London: Ebury Press.

Batty, D. (2006) 'Sir Roy Meadow', *The Guardian*, 17 February.

BBC News (1998a) 'Why murder evidence was flawed' 12 June.

BBC News (1998b) 'Bomb atrocity rocks Northern Ireland', 16 August.

BBC News (1999) 'IRA Prisoner wins appeal', 4 February.

BBC News (2000) '"Murderer" freed after 20 years', 30 March.

BBC News (2001) 'Murder police could face discipline', 19 February.

BBC News (2002a) 'Police chief sued over fatal arson', 17 December.

BBC News (2002b) 'David Asbury', 15 August.

BBC News (2003) 'Mysteries unlocked by DNA', 4 July.

BBC News (2005a) 'The problem with eye witnesses', 24 August.

BBC News (2005b) 'Sir Roy Meadow struck off by GMC', 15 July.

BBC News (2005c) 'Care home convictions are quashed', 30 June.

BBC News (2006a) 'A prison within a prison', 8 April.

BBC News (2006b) 'Downing given final compensation', 16 October.

BBC News (2006c) 'Damages claim over arson jailing', 9 March.

BBC News (2006d) 'Pathologist resigns from register', 22 September.

BBC News (2007) 'The speck that convicted George', 7 November.

BBC News (2009a) 'Man shocked by "IRA blackmail"', 8 January.

BBC News (2009b) 'Man's 1979 murder verdict quashed', 18 March.

BBC News (2009c) 'Court quashes murder conviction', 16 June.

BBC News (2009d) 'Ex-pathologist "admits arrogance"', 11 June.

BBC News (2010) 'Sion Jenkins fails in compensation bid', 10 August.

BBC News (2011a) 'Lynette White case: Angela Psaila "directed by police"', 20 July.

BBC News (2011b) 'Lynette White case: Police "rewrote witness statements"', 11 October.

BBC News (2012) 'Warning over prison release delay', 14 May.

BBC Press Office (2007) 'Panorama: Jill Dando – the jury's out' [online] http://www.bbc.co.uk/pressoffice/pressreleases/stories/2007/10_october/29/dando.shtml> Accessed 16 June 2012.

Bennetto, J. (2003) 'Convicted after 15 years: The prostitute's killer who watched three men go to jail for his crime', *The Independent*, 5 July.

Beynon, J. (1986) 'Powers and Proprieties in the Police Station', in J. Beynon and C. Bourn (eds), *The Police: Powers, Procedures and Proprieties*, New York, Pergamon Press.

Berlins, M. (2002) 'When innocence and death don't count', *The Guardian*, 18 June.

Bernhard A. (1999) 'When Justice Fails: Indemnification for Unjust Conviction', *Pace Law Faculty Publications*, Paper 4 [online] <http://digitalcommons.pace.edu/lawfaculty/4> Accessed 24 June 2012.

Bingham, T. (2000) *The Business of Judging: Selected Essays and Speeches: 1985–1999*, Oxford: Oxford University Press.

Blackstone, W. (1765–1769) *Commentaries on the Laws of England*, Oxford: Clarendon.

Blair, T. (2002) 'Prime Minister's Speech on "Re-balancing of Criminal Justice System"' 18 June [online] <http://www.pm.gov.uk/output/Page1717.asp> Accessed 23 June 2012.

Blakemore Brown, L. (2009) 'Sir Roy Meadow Removes Himself from the General Medical Council Register' [online] <http://www.theoneclickgroup.co.uk/documents/vaccines/Sir%20Roy%20Meadow%20Removes%20Himself%20From%20GMC%20Register,%20Blakemore%20Brown.pdf> Accessed 20 June 2012.

Bloxham, A. (2008) 'Barry George: I was stalking another woman at time of Jill Dando Murder', *The Telegraph*, 3 August.

Boggan, S. (2001) 'Dando's killer put gun barrel to the side of her head', *The Independent*, 5 May.

Bond-Kaplan, P. (1998) 'Causative Aspects of "Suggestibility"', *New Law Journal*, 148(6841): 740.

Borchard, E. M. (1932) *Convicting the Innocent: Sixty-Five Actual Errors of Criminal Justice*, New Haven, CT: Yale University Press.

Bowcott, O. and Laville, S. (2011) 'Supreme court ruling redefines miscarriages of justice' *The Guardian*, 11 May.

Brandon, R. and Davies, C. (1973) *Wrongful Imprisonment: Mistaken Convictions and their Consequences*, London: George Allen & Unwin.

Bridges, L. and Hodgson, J. (1995) 'Improving Custodial legal Advice', *Criminal Law Review*, February: 101–113.

Bridges, L. and Sanders, A. (1990) 'Access to Legal Advice and Police Malpractice', *Criminal Law Review*, July: 494–509.

Bromley, A. (2009) 'Innocence a handicap to progression', *Inside Time: The National Monthly Newspaper for Prisoners*, June.

Brown, D., Ellis, T. and Larcombe, K. (1992) *Changing the Code: Police Detention under the Revised PACE Codes of Practice*, Home Office Research Study No. 129, London: HMSO.

Bruce, V. (1998) 'Fleeting Images ff Shade Identifying People Caught on Video', *Psychologist*, July.

Bucke, T. and Brown, D. (1997) 'In Police Custody: Police Powers and Suspects' Rights under the Revised PACE Codes of Practice', Home Office Research Study No.174. London: Home Office.

Buckleton, J. Curran, J. and Gill, P. (2007) 'Towards Understanding the Effect of Uncertainty in the Number of Contributors to DNA Stains', *Forensic Science International: Genetics*, 1(1): 20–8.

BUPA (2010) 'Factsheet: Cot death and sudden infant death syndrome (SIDS)' [online] <http://www.bupa.co.uk/individuals/health-information/directory/c/sids> Accessed 20 April 2012.

Burrell, I. (2000) 'The trusted system that wrongly fingered a detective', *The Independent*, 20 October.

Burrell, I. and Bennetto, J. (1999) 'Police unit to blame for "dozens more injustices"', *The Independent*, 1 November.

Burrows, A. S. (1987) *Remedies for Torts and Breach of Contract*, London: Butterworths.

Burton, F. and Carlen, P. (1979) *Official discourse: On Discourse Analysis, Government Publications, Ideology and The State*, London: Routledge & Keegan Paul.

Callaghan, H. and Mulready, S. (1993) *Cruel Fate: One Man's Triumph over Injustice*, Dublin: Poolbeg.

Callan, K. (1997) *Kevin Callan's Story*, London: Little, Brown and Company.

Camber, R. (2010) 'Innocent man jailed for 3 years over false rape claim – despite police knowing "victim" was a fantasist', *Daily Mail*, 18 June.

Campbell, D. (2002) 'Fall guys', *The Guardian*, 10 July.

Campbell, K. (2008) 'The Fallibility of Justice in Canada: A Critical Examination of Conviction Review', in M. Kilias, and R. Huff (eds), *Wrongful Conviction: International Perspectives on Miscarriages of Justice* Philadelphia, PA: Temple University Press.

Campbell, K. and Denov, M. (2004) 'The Burden of Innocence: Coping with a Wrongful Imprisonment', *Canadian Journal of Criminology and Criminal Justice*, 46(2): 139–164.

Cannings, A. with Davies, M. L. (2006) *Against All Odds the Angela Cannings Story: A Mother's Fight to Prove her Innocence*, London: Time Warner.

Cassell, P. (1998) 'Protecting the Innocent from False Confessions and Lost Confessions: and from "Miranda"', *Journal of Criminal Law and Criminology*, 88(2): 497–556.

Chakrabarti, S. (2008) 'A Thinning Blue Line? Police Independence and the Rule of Law', *Policing*, 2(3): 367–374.

Chalmers, R. (2012) 'Jonathan King: "The only apology I have is to say that I was good at seduction"', *The Independent*, 22 April.

Chan, S. (1994) 'Scores of convictions reviewed as chemist faces perjury accusations', *Los Angeles Times*, 21 August.

Choongh, S. (1997) *Policing as Social Discipline*, Oxford: Clarendon.

Clarke, C. (2006) 'Compensation for miscarriages of justice', written ministerial statement by the Home Secretary, 19 April [online] <http://press.home office.gov.uk/Speeches/compensation-miscarriage-justice> Accessed 24 June 2012.

Coates, T. (2001) *The Strange Case of Adolph Beck*, London: Stationery Office.

Cole, S. (1999) 'What Counts for Identity? The Historical Origins of the Methodology of Latent Fingerprint Identification', *Science in Context*, 12(1): 139–172.

Cole, S. (2001) *Suspect Identities: A History of Fingerprinting and Criminal Identification*, Cambridge, MA: Harvard University Press.

Cole, S. (2005) 'More than Zero: Accounting for Error in Latent Fingerprint Identification', *Journal of Criminal Law & Criminology*, 95: 985–1078.

Coleman, C. Dixon, D. Bottomley, K. (1993) 'Police Investigative Procedures: Researching the Impact of PACE', in Walker, C. and Starmer, K. (eds), *Justice in Error*, London: Blackstone Press.

Colvin, M. (1994) 'Miscarriages of Justice: The Appeal Process', in M. McConville, and L. Bridges (eds), *Criminal Justice in Crisis*, Aldershot: Edward Elgar.

Conlon, G. (1990) *Proved Innocent*, London: Hamish Hamilton.

Cookson, R. (2008) 'Prison suicide inquiry could cast doubt on Lin Russell murder verdict', *The Independent*, 1 June.

Cookson, R. and Campbell, D. (2006) 'Parents' claims prompt new inquiry into jail death of police informant', *The Guardian*, 9 June.

Criminal Cases Review Commission (2011) 'Annual Report and Accounts 2010/11' HC1225, London: HMSO.

Criminal Cases Review Commission (2012a) 'Our History' [online] <http://www.ccrc.gov.uk/about/about_28.htm> Accessed 20 June 2012.

Criminal Cases Review Commission (2012b) 'What We Can Do for You' [online] <http://www.ccrc.gov.uk/canwe/canwe_32.htm> Accessed 20 June 2012.

Criminal Procedure Rules (2011) 'Part 33 Expert Evidence' [online] <http://www.justice.gov.uk/courts/procedure-rules/criminal/rulesmenu/part_33> Accessed 2o June 2012.

Crown Prosecution Service (2010a) 'The Code for Crown Prosecutors', London: CPS Communication Division.

Crown Prosecution Service (2010c) 'Low Copy Number DNA Testing in the Criminal Justice System' [online] <http://www.cps.gov.uk/publications/prosecution/lcn_testing.html> Accessed 24 June 2012.

Crown Prosecution Service (2010d) 'Adventitious (Chance) DNA Matches' [online] <http://www.cps.gov.uk/legal/s_to_u/scientific_evidence/adventitious_dna_matches/> Accessed 24 June 2012.

Crown Prosecution Service (2011) 'Self-Defence and the Prevention of Crime' [online]   <http://www.cps.gov.uk/legal/s_to_u/self_defence/#Principle> Accessed 26 June 2012.

Crown Prosecution Service (2012) 'The Principles We Follow' [online] <http://www.cps.gov.uk/about/principles.html> Accessed 26 June 2012.

Crown Prosecution Service, 'Summary of National DNA Database from the Prosecution Perspective' (2010b) [online] <http://cps.gov.uk/legal/s_to_u/scientific_evidence/summary_of_national_dna_database/> Accessed 24 June 2012.

Daily Mail (2009) 'Angela Cannings, who was wrongly jailed for murdering her children, finds happiness with a new man', 14 September.

Davies, A. (2003) 'Talking Cop: Discourses of Change and Policing Identities', *Public Administration*, 81(4): 681–699.

Dennis, I. (2005) 'Reverse Onuses and the Presumption of Innocence: In Search of Principle', *Criminal Law Review*, December: 901–936.

Denov, M. and Campbell, K. (2005) 'Criminal Injustice: Understanding the Causes, Effects and Responses to Wrongful Convictions in Canada', *Journal of Contemporary Criminal Justice*, 21(3): 224–249.

Devlin, P. (1976) 'Report to the Secretary of State for the Home Department on the Departmental Committee on Evidence of Identification in Criminal Cases', London: HMSO.

Dixon, D., Coleman, C. and Bottomley, K. (1990) 'Consent and the Legal Regulation of Policing', *Journal of Law and Society*, 17(3): 345–362.

Doughty, S. (2011) 'Daughter of racehorse trainer at centre of custody battle was coached to claim her father had sexually abused her', *Daily Mail*, 23 August.

Doward, J. (2005) '"My home is now my prison cell"', *The Observer*, 20 February.

Dror, I., Charlton, D. and Peron, A. (2006) 'Contextual Information Renders Experts Vulnerable to Making Erroneous Identifications', *Forensic Science International*, 156: 4–78.

Dudley, R. (2002) 'We were victims too', *The Observer*, 7 July.

Duffield, B. (1994) 'Paul Blackburn – Work in Progress', in Jessel, D., *Trial and Error*, London: Channel 4.

Dyer, C. (1999) 'Lord Denning, controversial "people's judge", dies aged 100', *The Guardian*, March 6.

Eades, D. (2010) *Sociolinguistics and the Legal Process*, Bristol: Multilingual Matters.

Easterbrook, F. H. (1992) 'Plea Bargaining as Compromise', *Yale Law Journal*, 101(8): 1969–1978.

Eddowes, M. (1955) *The Man on Your Conscience: An Investigation of the Evans Murder Trial*, London: Cassell.

Editorial (2008) 'Teacher's assault conviction is quashed after 19 months of "hell"', *Daily Mail*, 20 January.

Editorial (2012) 'My ex-girlfriend claimed I raped her – now she's in jail for lying', *Daily Mirror*, 1 February.

Elks, L. (2008) *Righting Miscarriages of Justice? Ten Years of the Criminal Cases Review Commission*, London: Justice.

Elks, L. (2010) 'Miscarriages of Justice: A Challenging View', *Justice Journal*, 7(1): 6–21.

Elks, L. (2012) 'Our criminal review body has led to dozens of convictions quashed', *The Guardian*, 19 April.

Ellicott, C. and Kisiel, R. (2011) 'Jailed: the soldier's cheating wife who claimed she was raped to cover up pregnancy while husband was in Afghanistan', *Daily Mail*, 1 March.

Ellis, P. (2007) 'Criminal Cases Review Commission' [online] <http://www.peterellis.org.nz/MediaReleases/2007–0514_peterellis_CriminalCases.htm> Accessed 22 June 2012.

Endangered Dogs Defence and Rescue (2004) 'Dino – The Legal Struggle' [online] <http://www.endangereddogs.com/EDDRDinoLegalHistory.htm> Accessed 23 June 2012.

Epstein, R. (2002) 'Fingerprints Meet Daubert: The Myth of Fingerprint Science is Revealed', *Southern California Law Review*, 75(3): 605–657.

Fallon, A. (2011) 'Police officers escaping punishment by resigning', *The Guardian*, 31 October.

False Allegations Support Organisation (FASO) (2012) website [online] <http://www.false-allegations.org.uk> Accessed 12 July 2012.

Falsely Accused Carers and Teachers (FACT) (2012) website [online] <http://www.factuk.org> Accessed 12 July 2012.

Fenton, N. and Neil, M. (2000) 'The Jury Observation Fallacy and the Use of Bayesian Networks to Present Probabilistic Legal Arguments', *Mathematics Today*, 36(6): 180–187.

Findlay, K. A., and Scott, M. S. (2006) 'The Multiple Dimensions of Tunnel Vision in Criminal Cases', University of Wisconsin Legal Studies Research Paper, No. 1023.

Fingerprint Inquiry Scotland (2011) 'The Fingerprint Inquiry Report', Edinburgh: APS Group Scotland.

Fisher, H. (1977) 'Report of an Inquiry by the Honourable Sir Henry Fisher into the Circumstances Leading to the Trial of Three Persons on Charges Arising out of the Death of Maxwell Confait and the Fire at 27 Doggett Road, London SE6', London: HMSO.

Foot, P. (1986) *Murder at the Farm*, London: Penguin.

Foot, P. (1997) 'Is this Carl's killer?', *Daily Mirror*, 21 February.

Forensic Science Service (2005) 'DNA Low Copy Number' [online] <http://www.forensic.gov.uk/pdf/company/foi/publication-scheme/communications/DNA_Low_Copy_Number_000.pdf> Accessed 6 May 2012.

Garrett, B. and Neufeld, P. (2009) 'Invalid Forensic Science Testimony and Wrongful Convictions', *Virginia Law Review* 95(1): 1–97.

Geddes, L. (2009) 'Forensic Science "Too Unreliable" Says Report', *New Scientist*, 19 February.

Giannelli, P. (2008) 'Wrongful Convictions and Forensic Science: The Need to Regulate Crime Labs', *North Carolina Law Review*, 86: 163–235.

Gibb, F. (2007) 'Grief-stricken Sally Clark "drank herself to death"', *The Times*, 8 November.

Giddens, A. (1982) *Sociology: A Brief But Critical Introduction*, London: Macmillan.

Gill, P. (2001) 'Application of Low Copy Number DNA Profiling', *Croatian Medical Journal*, 42(3): 229–232.

Gill, P. and Kirkham, A. (2004) 'Development of A Simulation Model to Assess the Impact of Contamination in Casework Using STRs', *Journal of Forensic Science*, 49(3): 1–7.

Gill, P., Brenner, C. Buckleton, J. Carracedo, A. Krawczak, M. Mayr, W. Morling, N. Prinz, M. Schneider, P. and Weir, B. (2006) 'DNA Commission of the International Society of Forensic Genetics: Recommendations on the Interpretation of Mixtures', *Forensic Science International*, 160: 90–101.

Goodhart, D. (2012) 'Stephen Lawrence and the politics of race', *Prospect*, 4 January.

Goodwin, W., Linacre, A. and Hadi, S. (2007) *An Introduction to Forensic Genetics*, Chichester: Wiley.

Gould, J. (2008) *The Innocence Commission: Preventing Wrongful Convictions and Restoring the Criminal Justice System*, New York: New York University Press.

Green, A. (2008) *Power, Resistance, Knowledge: The Epistemology of Policing*, Sheffield: Midwinter and Oliphant.

Green, P. and Ward, T. (2004) *State Crime*, London: Pluto.

Greenhill, S. (2006a) 'Man freed but serial rape accuser remains anonymous', *Daily Mail*, 12 September.

Greenhill, S. (2006b) 'Sex attack liar named by peer', *Daily Mail*, 19 October.

Greer, S. (1994) 'Miscarriages of Justice Reconsidered', *Modern Law Review*, 57(1): 58–74.

Griffin, L. (2001) 'The Correction of Wrongful Convictions: A Comparative Perspective', Pace Law Faculty Publications, Paper 472 [online] <http://digitalcommons.pace.edu/lawfaculty/472> Accessed 22 June 2012.

Griffin, L. (2009) 'Correcting Injustice: Studying How the United Kingdom and the United States Review Claims of Innocence', *University of Toledo Law Review*, 41: 107–152.

Grounds, A. (2004) 'Psychological Consequences of Wrongful Conviction and Imprisonment', *Canadian Journal of Criminology and Criminal Justice*, 46(2): 165–182.

Grounds, A. (2005) 'Understanding the Effects of Wrongful Imprisonment', *Crime and Justice*, 32: 1–58.

Grounds, A. and Jamieson, R. (2003) 'No Sense of an Ending: Researching the

Experience of Imprisonment and Release among Republican Ex-Prisoners', *Theoretical Criminology*, 7(3): 347–362.

Guardian (2002) 'Justice for Downing after 28 years', 15 January.

Guardian (2005) 'Murder bid conviction quashed after 25 years', 25 May.

Gudjonsson, G. (2005) *The Psychology of Interrogations and Confessions: A Handbook*, Chichester: Wiley.

Gudjonsson, G. and MacKeith, J. (2005) 'The "Guildford Four" and the "Birmingham Six"', in Gudjonsson, G. ,*The Psychology of Interrogations and Confessions: A Handbook*, Chichester: Wiley & Sons Ltd.

Gudjonsson, G. and Sigurdsson, J. (1994) 'How Frequently Do False Confessions Occur?: An Empirical Study among Prison Inmates', *Psychology, Crime & Law*, 21(25).

Hale, D. (2002) *A Town without Pity*, London: Century.

Hamer, D. (2011) 'A Dynamic Reconstruction of the Presumption of Innocence', *Oxford Journal of Legal Studies*, 31(2): 417–435.

Hampikian, G., West, E. and Akselrod, O. (2011) 'The Genetics of Innocence: Analysis of 194 US DNA Exonerations', *Annual Review of Genomics and Human Genetics*, 12: 97–120.

Hattenstone, S. (2002) '"I'm dead inside"', *The Guardian*, June 17.

HC Deb (1904) 3 August 1904 vol 139 cc719–20.

HC Deb [1974] 8 April, vol 872 cc45–52.

HC Deb [1985] 29 November, c691–692.

HC Deb [1988] 16 February, vol 127, cc 950–8.

HC Deb [1992] 19 June, vol 209 cc700–1W.

HC Deb [2005] 11 July, c777W.

Henham, R. (1999) 'Bargain Justice or Justice Denied? Sentence Discounts and the Criminal Process', *Modern Law Review*, 62(4): 515–538.

Hicken, M. (2011) 'Glendale will pay man who was wrongly detained in murder probe', *Los Angeles Times*, 18 January.

Hill, A. (2002a) '"I thought it was love. Now I know that I was wrong"', *The Observer*, June 2.

Hill, A. (2002b) '25 years in jail for denying that he's a killer', *The Guardian*, March 3.

Hill, A. (2010) 'Paddy Hill wins trauma counselling for Birmingham Six ordeal', *The Guardian*, 19 October.

Hill, P. (2001) 'The Parole Deal', *Inside Time: The National Monthly Newspaper for Prisoners*, autumn.

Hill, P. J. and Hunt, G. (1995) *Forever Lost, Forever Gone*, London: Bloomsbury.

Hilliard, B. (1990) 'Soldiers of Nothing', *New Law Journal*, 140(6442): 160.

Hillyard, P. and Tombs, S. (2004) 'Beyond Criminology?', in Hillyard, P. Pantazis, C. Tombs, S. and Gordon, D. (eds), *Beyond Criminology: Taking Harm Seriously*, London: Pluto Press.

Hirsch, A. and Sekar, S. (2008) 'Jailing of Cardiff Three witnesses raises questions over law on duress', *The Guardian*, 22 December.

Historic Inflation Calculator (2012) [online] <http://www.thisismoney.co.uk/historic-inflation-calculator> Accessed 22 June 2012.

HL Deb [1974] 27 March, vol 350 cc691–719.

HM Prison Service (2011) 'Resettlement' [online] <http://www.hmprisonservice. gov.uk/adviceandsupport/beforeafterrelease/resettlement> Accessed 24 May 2011.

Home Office (2002) *Justice for All*. Cm. 5563. London: TSO.

Home Office (2012) 'Remissions and Pardons' [online] <http://www.national archives.gov.uk/catalogue/displaycataloguedetails.asp?CATID=7743&CATLN =3&accessmethod=5> Accessed 27 June 2012.

Home Office Circular (1964) (31) London: HMSO.

Home Office Circular (1978) (89) London: HMSO.

Hood, R. and Shute, S. (2000a) *The Parole System at Work: A Study of Risk-Based Decision-Making*, Home Office Research Findings 202, London: Home Office.

Hood, R. and Shute, S. (2000b) *Parole Decision-Making*, Home Office Research Findings 114, London: Home Office.

Hopkins, N. (2002) 'Man wrongly convicted of murder freed after 25 years', *The Guardian*, 14 November.

Hopkins, N. and Morris, S. (2001) 'Why would anybody wish to kill her?', *The Guardian*, 5 May.

Hostettler, J. (2009) *A History of Criminal Justice in England and Wales*, Hampshire: Waterside.

House of Commons Science and Technology Committee (2005) *Forensic Science on Trial*, London: TSO.

House of Lords Constitution Committee (2008) 'Examination of Witnesses (Questions 154–159)', 30 January [online] <http://www.publications. parliament.uk/pa/ld/ldconst.htm> Accessed 26 June 2012.

House of Lords Select Committee on Science and Technology (1993) *Forensic Science*, London: HMSO.

Huff, R. (2002) 'Wrongful Conviction and Public Policy: The American Society of Criminology 2001 Presidential Address', *Criminology*, 40(1): 1–18.

Huff, R., Rattner, A. and Sagarin, E. (1996) *Convicted But Innocent: Wrongful Conviction and Public Policy*, London: Sage.

Hull, L. (2011) 'Female chaplain made false rape claim against Catholic priest after their relationship ended', *Daily Mail*, 14 February.

Human Genetics Commission (2008) 'A Citizens' Inquiry into the Forensic Use of DNA and the DNA Database: Contractor's Report', July [online] <http://www.hgc.gov.uk> Accessed 6 May 2012.

Human Genome Project Information (2009) 'DNA Forensics' [online] <http://www.ornl.gov/sci/techresources/Human_Genome/elsi/forensics. shtml> Accessed 22 June 2012.

Innocence Network UK (2012a) [online] <http://www.innocencenetwork.org.uk> Accessed 24 June 2012.

Innocence Network UK (2012b) 'INUK Symposium on the Reform of the Criminal Cases Review Commission', Norton Rose LLP, 30 March.

Innocence Network UK (2012c) 'Dossier of Cases' <http://www.innocencenet-work.org.uk/wp-content/uploads/2012/05/INUK-Dossier-of-Cases.pdf> Accessed 12 July 2012.

Innocence Project (2007) '200 Exonerated, Too Many Wrongfully Convicted', New York: The Innocence Project.

Innocence Project (2010) '250 Exonerated, Too Many Wrongfully Convicted', New York: Innocence Project.

Innocence Project (2012) 'Eyewitness Misidentification' [online] <http://www.innocenceproject.org/understand/Eyewitness-Misidentification.php> Accessed 20 April 2012.

Irving, H. B. (1921) *Last Studies in Criminology*, London: W. Collins.

ITV Wales (2010) 'Norfolk Police to oversee investigation into the wrongful convictions of the Cardiff three for Phillip Saunders' murder', 13 August [online] <http://itvwalesblog.com/2010/08/13/norfolk-police-to-oversee-investigation-into-the-wrongful-convictions-of-the-cardiff-three-for-phillip-saunders-murder> Accessed 14 January 2012.

James, A. Taylor, N. and Walker, C. (2000) 'The Criminal Cases Review Commission: Economy, Effectiveness and Justice', *Criminal Law Review*, March: 140–153.

Jamieson, A. (2007) 'LCN DNA – Devil in the Detail', *Journal Online: The Members' Magazine of the Law Society of Scotland*, 12 February: 22.

Jamieson, A. (2008a) 'The Philosophy of Forensic Scientific Identification', *Hastings Law Journal*, 59: 1031–1046.

Jamieson, A. (2008b) 'Mixed results', *The Guardian*, 28 February.

Jamieson, A. (2009) 'Teresa de Simone murder: David Lace named as prime suspect after exhumation', *The Telegraph*, 17 September.

Jamieson, R. and Grounds, A. (2002) *No Sense of an Ending: The Effects of Long-Term Imprisonment amongst Republican Prisoners and Their Families*, Monaghan Town, Republic of Ireland: Seesyu Press.

Jamieson, R. and Grounds, A. (2005) 'Release and Adjustment: Perspectives from Studies of Wrongly Convicted and Politically Motivated Prisoners', in A. Liebling and S. Maruna (eds), *The Effects of Imprisonment*, Devon: Willan.

Jeffries, S. (2006), 'Suspect nation', *The Guardian*, 28 October.

Jenkins, S. and Woffinden, B. (2008) *The Murder of Billie-Jo*, London: Blake.

Jessel, D. (2009) 'Innocence or safety: why the wrongly convicted are better served by safety', *The Guardian*, 15 December.

Jessop, B. (1990) *State Theory: Putting the Capitalist State in Its Place*, Cambridge: Polity.

Jinman, R. (2005) 'Jail was brilliant says freed King', *The Guardian*, March 30.

Johnston, P. (1997) 'Pressure mounts on DPP after new court attack', *The Telegraph*, 1 August.

JUSTICE (1989) *Miscarriages of Justice*, London: JUSTICE.

JUSTICE (1994) *Remedying Miscarriages of Justice*, London: JUSTICE.

Kee, R. (1986) *Trial and error: The Maguires, the Guildford Pub Bombings and British Justice*, London: Hamish Hamilton.

Kennedy, L (1961) *Ten Rillington Place*, London: Gollancz.

Kennedy, L. (2002) *Thirty-Six Murders and Two Immoral Earnings*, London: Profile Books.

Kerrigan, K. (2006) 'Miscarriage of Justice in the Magistrates' Court: The Forgotten Power of the Criminal Cases Review Commission', *Criminal Law Review*, February: 124–127.

Kerrigan, K. (2009) 'Real Possibility or Fat Chance?', in Naughton, M. (ed.), *The Criminal Cases Review Commission: Hope for the Innocent*, Basingstoke: Palgrave Macmillan.

Kettle, M. (1979) 'Trying to make the verdicts fit the evidence', *New Society*, 24 May.

Kim, Y. S., Barak, G. and Shelton, D. E. (2009) 'Examining the "CSI-Effect" in the Cases of Circumstantial Evidence and Eyewitness Testimony: Multivariate and Path Analyses', *Journal of Criminal Justice*, 37(5): 1–29.

Krebs, B. (2010) 'Joint Criminal Enterprise', *Modern Law Review*, 73(4): 578–604.

Kyle, D. (2004) 'Correcting Miscarriages of Justice: The Role of the Criminal Cases Review Commission', *Drake Law Review*, 52: 657–676.

Laville, S. (2007) 'Six years on, evidence that helped convict TV presenter's murderer is deemed valueless', *The Guardian*, 21 June.

Laville, S. (2011) 'What price 14 years in jail for a murder conviction that was overturned?', *The Guardian*, 8 May.

Law Commission (1991) *Corroboration of Evidence in Criminal Trials*, London: HMSO.

Law Commission (2001) 'Double Jeopardy and Prosecution Appeals' [online] <http://lawcommission.justice.gov.uk/docs/lc267__Double_Jeopardy_Report.pdf> Accessed 22 June 2012.

Law Commission (2009) 'The Admissibility of Expert Evidence in Criminal Proceedings in England and Wales: A New Approach to the Determination of Evidentiary Reliability' [online] <http://lawcommission.justice.gov.uk/docs/cp190_Expert_Evidence_Consultation.pdf> Accessed 22 June 2012.

Law Commission (2011) 'Expert Evidence in Criminal Proceedings in England and Wales' [online] <http://lawcommission.justice.gov.uk/docs/lc325_Expert_Evidence_Report.pdf> Accessed 22 June 2012.

Law Society (2010) *Defending Rights: Access to Justice Review*, London: Law Society.

Leigh, L. (2004) 'The Criminal Cases Review Commission: Seven Years On', *The Barrister: The Independent Magazine for Legal Professionals* [online] <http://www.barristermagazine.com/archivedsite/articles/issue22/leigh.htm> Accessed 20 June 2012.

Lewis, G. (2002) 'Police meet campaigners over demand for inquiry', *Western Mail*, 4 November.

Liverpool Echo (2000) 'Police must now find out the truth', March 31.

Livingstone, T. (2003) 'Victims call for public inquiry on police: lobby wants miscarriage of justice cases to be probed', *Western Mail*, 4 November.

Loftus, E. F. (1979) *Eyewitness Testimony* Cambridge, MA: Harvard University Press.

Lomax, S. (2003) *Trial and Error: The Case of Barry George*, London: Libertarian Alliance.

Lotter, K. (2007) 'Setback for LCN DNA: Omagh Bombing Trial Outcome – LCN DNA Is Not Reliable as Evidence' [online] <http://dna-trace-analysis.suite101.com/article.cfm/setback_for_lcn_dna> Accessed 26 June 2012.

Lowe, A., Murray, C. Whitaker, J. Tully, G. and Gill, P. (2000) 'The Propensity of Individuals to Deposit DNA and Secondary Transfer of Low Level DNA from Individuals to Inert Surfaces', *Forensic Science International*, 129: 25–34.

McBarnet, D. (1981b) 'The Royal Commission and the Judges' Rules', *British Journal of Law and Society*, 8(1): 109–117.

McBarnet, D. J. (1981a) *Conviction: Law, the State and the Construction of Justice*, London: Macmillan.

McCarthy, T. (2005a) 'Protecting the public', *Inside Time: The National Newspaper for Prisoners*, 78, December.

McCarthy, T. (2005b) 'How Do I Maintain Innocence and Get Parole?' [online] <http://home.vicnet.net.au/~safari/PublicDocs/ParoleBoardReport.pdf> Accessed 12 July 2012.

McCarthy, T. (2006) 'Public body bound by the law', *Inside Time: The National Newspaper for Prisoners*, 82, April.

McCartney, C., Quirk, H., Roberts, S. and Walker, C. (2008) 'Weighed in the balance' *Guardian Unlimited*, 29 November [online] <http://www.guardian.co.uk/commentisfree/2008/nov/29/ukcrime-prisonsandprobation> Accessed 22 June 2012.

McConville, M. (1992) 'Video Interrogations: Police Behaviour on and off Camera', *Criminal Law Review*, August, 532–548.

McConville, M. and Bridges, L. (1994) (eds) *Criminal Justice in Crisis*, Aldershot: Edward Elgar.

McConville, M. and Mirsky, C. (2005) *Jury Trials and Plea Bargaining: A True History*, Oxford: Hart.

McConville, M., Sanders, A. and Leng, R. (1991) *The Case for the Prosecution: Police Suspects and the Construction of Criminality*, London: Routledge.

Mackay, N. (2004) 'We locked you up in jail for 25 years and you were innocent all along? That'll be £80,000 please', *Sunday Herald Scotland*, 14 March.

MacLarty, L. (2011) 'Sheriff critical of teen in false rape claim', *Press and Journal*, 19 January.

McLean, I. (1980) *Criminal Appeals: A Practical Guide to Appeals to and from the Crown Court*, London: Sweet & Maxwell.

McVeigh, T. (2000) '"Corrupt" force in firing line', *The Guardian*, 15 October.

Maddocks, G. and G. Tan (2009) 'Applicant Solicitors: Friends or Foes?', in Naughton, M. (ed.), *The Criminal Cases Review Commission: Hope for the Innocent?*, Basingstoke: Palgrave Macmillan.

Maguire, A. with Gallagher, J. (1994) *Miscarriage of Justice: An Irish Family's Story of Wrongful Conviction*, London: Roberts Rinehart.

Maguire, M. (1988) 'Effects of the PACE Provisions on Detention and Questioning', *British Journal of Criminology*, 28(1): 19–43.

Maiatico, J. (2007) 'All Eyes on Us: A Comparative Critique of the North Carolina Innocence Inquiry Commission', *Duke Law Review*, 56: 1345–1376.

Malleson, K. (1994) 'Appeals against Conviction and the Principle of Finality', *Journal of Law and Society*, 21: 151–164.

Maltoni, D., Maio, D., Jain, A. and Prabhakar, S. (2009) *Handbook of Fingerprint Recognition*, London: Springer.

Mansfield, M. (2009) *Memoirs of a Radical Lawyer*, London: Bloomsbury.

Mathiesen, T. (1974) *The Politics of Abolition: Essays in Political Action Theory*, London: Martin Robertson.

May, J. (1990) *Report of the Inquiry into the Circumstances Surrounding the Convictions Arising out of the Bomb Attacks in Guildford and Woolwich in 1974*, HC 556, 1989–90, London: HMSO.

May, J. (1992) *Second Report on the Maguire Case*, HC 296, 1992–93, London: HMSO.

May, J. (1994) *Report of the Inquiry into the Circumstances Surrounding the Convictions Arising out of the Bomb Attacks in Guildford and Woolwich in 1974, Final Report*, HC 449, 1993–94, London: HMSO.

Meadow, R. (1989) (ed.) *ABC of Child Abuse*, London: BMJ Books.

Mills, H. (1994a) 'Scientist in Birmingham Six case sues TV firm for libel', *The Independent*, 5 October.

Mills, H. (1994b) 'Pub blasts scientist drops libel action', *The Independent*, 18 October.

Ministry of Justice (2006) *Quashing Convictions: Report of a Review by the Home Secretary, Lord Chancellor and Attorney General*, London: Office for Criminal Justice Reform.

Ministry of Justice (2007) 'Service Review: Indeterminate Sentence Prisoners (ISPs)' [online] <http://www.justice.gov.uk/docs/service-review-intermediate-service-prisoners.pdf> Accessed 22 June 2012.

Ministry of Justice (2008) *Compensation for Wrongful Conviction: Notes for Successful Applicants*, London: Office for Criminal Justice Reform.

Ministry of Justice (2009) *Judicial and Court Statistics 2008*, London: TSO.

Ministry of Justice (2010) *Sentencing Statistics: England and Wales 2009*, London: Ministry of Justice.

Ministry of Justice (2011a) *PSO 4700 New Chapter 4: Serving the Indeterminate Sentence*, London: Ministry of Justice.

Ministry of Justice (2011b) 'Incentives and Earned Privilege', PSI 11/2011 [online] <http://www.justice.gov.uk/downloads/offenders/psipso/psi-2011/psi_2011_11_incentives_and_earned_privileges.doc> Accessed 2 July 2012.

Ministry of Justice (2012a) 'Procedure Rules' [online] <http://www.justice.gov.uk/courts/procedure-rules/criminal/rulesmenu> Accessed 22 June 2012.

Ministry of Justice (2012b) 'Offender Behaviour Programmes (OBPs)' [online] <http://www.justice.gov.uk/offenders/before-after-release/obp> Accessed 3 July 2012.

Ministry of Justice (2012c) 'About the Criminal Cases Review Commission' [online] <http://www.justice.gov.uk/about/criminal-cases-review-commission> Accessed 12 July 2012.

Morrish, P. and McLean, I. (1971) *A Practical Guide to Appeals in Criminal Courts*, London: Sweet & Maxwell.

Mortera, J. Dawid, A. and Lauritzen, A. (2003) 'Probabilistic Expert Systems for DNA Mixture Profiling', *Theoretical Population Biology*, 63(3): 191–2.

Morton, J. (2001) 'A Propos', *New Law Journal*, 151(6971): 234.

Moss, L. (2004) 'Study casts doubt on "Meadow's law" of sudden child death', *The Independent*, 31 December.

Mulcahy, A (1994) 'The Justifications of Justice: Legal Practitioners' Accounts of Negotiated Case Settlements in Magistrates' Courts', *British Journal of Criminology*, 34(4): 411–430.

Mullin, C. (1986) *Error of Judgement: The Truth about the Birmingham Bombs*, London: Chatto & Windus.

Mumma, C. (2004) 'The North Carolina Actual Innocence Commission: Uncommon Perspectives Joined by a Common Cause', *Drake Law Review*, 52: 647–656.

National Academy of Sciences (2009) 'Strengthening Forensic Science in the United States: A Path Forward', Washington, DC: National Academies Press.

National DNA Database (2004) 'Annual Report 03/04' [online] <http://www.forensic.gov.uk/pdf/company/publications/annual-reports/annual-report-NDNAD.pdf> Accessed 24 June 2012.

National DNA Database (2006) 'The National DNA Database Annual Report 2005–6' [online] <www.homeoffice.gov.uk/documents/DNA-report2005-06.pdf> Accessed 24 June 2012.

National Policing Improvement Agency (2010) 'The National DNA Database: Basic Facts – FAQs' [online] <http://www.npia.police.uk/en/13340.htm> Accessed 22 June 2012.

National Probation Service (2003) 'OASys: The New Offender Assessment System' [online] <http://www.probation.homeoffice.gov.uk/files/pdf/Info%20for%20sentencers%203.pdf> Accessed 12 August 2005.

Naughton, M. (2003a) How Big Is the "Iceberg?": A Zemiological Approach to Quantifying Miscarriages of Justice', *Radical Statistics*, 81: 5–17.

Naughton, M. (2003b) 'Our shoddy treatment of victims of injustice', *The Observer*, 16 March

Naughton, M. (2004a) 'The parole deal is not a "myth"', *Inside Time: The National Newspaper for Prisoners*, 59, May.

Naughton, M. (2004b) 'Reorientating Miscarriages of Justice', in Hillyard, P. Pantazis, C. Gordon, D. and Tombs, S. (eds), *Beyond Criminology: Taking Harm Seriously*, London: Pluto.

Naughton, M. (2005a) 'The parole deal does exist', *Inside Time: The National Newspaper for Prisoners*, 77, November.

Naughton, M. (2005b) 'Redefining Miscarriages of Justice: A Revived Human Rights Approach to Unearth Subjugated Discourses of Wrongful Criminal Conviction', *British Journal of Criminology*, 45(2): 165–182.

Naughton, M. (2005c) 'Why the Failure of the Prison Service and the Parole Board to Acknowledge Wrongful Imprisonment Is Untenable', *Howard Journal of Criminal Justice*, 44(1): 1–11.

Naughton, M. (2005d) '"Evidence-Based-Policy" and the Government of the Criminal Justice System – Only If the Evidence Fits!', *Critical Social Policy*, 25(1): 47–69.

Naughton, M. (2006a) 'Wrongful Convictions and Innocence Projects in the UK: Help, Hope and Education', *Web Journal of Current Legal Issues*, Issue 3.

Naughton, M. (2006b) 'Parole Board – discredited?', *Inside Time: The National Monthly Newspaper for Prisoners*, March.

Naughton, M. (2007) *Rethinking Miscarriages of Justice: Beyond the Tip of the Iceberg*, Basingstoke: Palgrave Macmillan.

Naughton, M. (2008a) 'Factual Innocence versus Legal Guilt: The Need for a New Pair of Spectacles to View the Problem of Life-Sentenced Prisoners Maintaining Innocence', *Prison Service Journal*, 177, May.

Naughton, M. (2008b) 'Justice must be seen to be done', *The Guardian*, 20 November.

Naughton, M. (2009a) (ed.) *The Criminal Cases Review Commission: Hope for the Innocent?*, Basingstoke: Palgrave Macmillan.

Naughton, M. (2009b) 'The Importance of Innocence for the Criminal Justice System'. in Naughton, M. (ed.), *The Criminal Cases Review Commission: Hope for the Innocent?*, Basingstoke: Palgrave Macmillan.

Naughton, M. (2009c) 'Introduction', in Naughton, M. (ed.), *The Criminal Cases Review Commission: Hope for the Innocent?*, Basingstoke: Palgrave Macmillan.

Naughton, M. (2009d) 'Does the NOMS Risk Assessment Bubble Have to Burst for Prisoners Who May Be Innocent to Make Progress?', *Howard Journal of Criminal Justice*, 48(4): 357–372.

Naughton, M. (2010) 'Can Lawyers Put People before Law?', *Socialist Lawyer*, June: 30–32.

Naughton, M. (2011a) 'How the Presumption of Innocence Renders the Innocent Vulnerable to Wrongful Convictions', *Irish Journal of Legal Studies*, 2(1): 40–54.

Naughton, M. (2011b) 'There's Still Scope for Debate on Miscarriage of Justice Compensation', *Law Society Gazette*, May 19.

Naughton, M. (2012) 'No Champion of Justice' [online] <http://thejusticegap.com/2012/03/no-champion-of-justice> Accessed 12 May 2012.

Naughton, M. and Tan, G. (2010) 'The Right to Access DNA Testing by Alleged Innocent Victims of Wrongful Convictions in the UK?', *International Journal of Evidence & Proof*, 14(4): 326–345.

Naughton, M. and Tan, G. (2011) 'The Need for Caution in the Use of DNA Evidence to Avoid Convicting the Innocent', *International Journal of Evidence and Proof*, 15(3): 245–257.

Naughton, M. with Tan, G. (2010) *Claims of Innocence: An Introduction to Wrongful Convictions and How They Might Be Challenged*, Bristol: University of Bristol.

Naylor, L. (2004) *Judge for Yourself How Many Are Innocent*, London: Roots Books.

Neufeld, P. and Scheck, B. (2010) 'Making Forensic Science More Scientific', *Nature*, 464: 351.

New Scientist (1991) 'In brief: Birmingham Six', 1756, 16 February.

Newburn, T. (1999) 'Understanding and Preventing Police Corruption: Lessons from the Literature', Police Research Paper 110, London: Home Office.

Newby, M. (2009) 'Historical Abuse Cases: Why They Expose the Inadequacy of the Real Possibility Test', in Naughton, M. (ed.), *The Criminal Cases Review Commission: Hope for the Innocent?*, Basingstoke: Palgrave Macmillan.

Newby, M. (2010) 'Investigating miscarriages of justice – thinking out of the box' Keynote Speech to the Innocence Network UK (INUK) Spring Conference 2010, Cleary Gottlieb Steen & Hamilton LLP, London, 12 March [online] <http://www.innocencenetwork.org.uk/communications.htm> Accessed 26 August 2011.

Nobles, R. (2012) 'An Academic's View on the Reform of the CCRC', *INQUIRY: The Newsletter of the Innocence Network UK*, 5: 24–30.

Nobles, R. and Schiff, D. (2000) *Understanding Miscarriages of Justice: Law, the Media, and the Inevitability of Crisis*, Oxford: Oxford University Press.

Nobles, R. and Schiff, D. (2001) 'The Criminal Cases Review Commission: Reporting Success?', *Modern Law Review*, 64 (2): 280–299.

Nobles, R. and Schiff, D. (2002) 'The Right to Appeal and Workable Systems of Justice', *Modern Law Review*, 65(5): 679–84.

Nobles, R. and Schiff, D. (2006) 'Guilt and Innocence in the Criminal Justice System: Comment on R (Mullen) v Secretary of State for the Home Department', *Modern Law Review*, 69(1): 80–91.

Nobles, R. and Schiff, D. (2008) 'Absurd Asymmetry: A Comment on R v Cottrell and Fletcher and BM, KK and DP (Petitioners) v Scottish Criminal Cases Review Commission', *Modern Law Review*, 71(3): 464–472.

Nobles, R. and Schiff, D. (2009) 'After Ten Years: An Investment in Justice?', in Naughton, M. (ed.), *The Criminal Cases Review Commission: Hope for the Innocent?*, Basingstoke: Palgrave Macmillan.

Norman, K. (2001) *Lynch – Mob Syndrome*, Elton, Cheshire: Infinity Junction.

North Carolina Actual Innocence Commission (2012) 'About Us' [online] http://www.innocencecommission-nc.gov/about.html Accessed 17 December 2012.

Norton-Taylor, R. (2000) 'Reginald Dunk', *The Guardian*, 17 April.

Norwegian Criminal Cases Review Commission 'Introduction' (2012) [online] <http://www.gjenopptakelse.no/index.php?id=31> Accessed 22 June 2012.

O'Brien, M. (2005) 'Public inquiry into South Wales Police', press briefing, Norwegian Church, Cardiff Bay, 18 July.

O'Brien, M. with Lewis, G. (2008) *The Death of Justice*, Ceredigion: Ylolfa.

O'Dwyer, E. (2004) 'Barnes cleared of Allen murder', *Illawarra Mercury*, 29 May.

O'Neill, E. (2006) 'Mark of innocence', *The Guardian*, 18 April.

O'Neill, E. (2010) 'Investigative journalism after Watergate in the USA and UK: a comparative study in professional practice', Ph.D. thesis, University of Strathclyde.

Packer, H. (1968) *The Limits of the Criminal Sanction*, Stanford, CA: Stanford University Press.

Padfield, N. (2007) *Who to Release? Parole, Fairness and Criminal Justice*, Devon: Willan Publishing.

Palmer, A. (2006) 'If two people accuse you, then you are guilty. They get compensation, you get jail', *The Telegraph*, 22 October.

Pantazis, C. (1998) 'Inequalities in crime and criminal justice', *Radical Statistics*, 69: 54–63.

Parole Board (2004) 'Denial of Guilt and the Parole Board' [online] <http://www.paroleboard.gov.uk> Accessed 12 February 2004.

Parole Board (2011a) 'History of the Parole Board' [online] <http://tna.europarchive.org/20110206085921/http://www.paroleboard.gov.uk/about/history_of_the_parole_board> Accessed 27 September 2011.

Parole Board (2011b) 'About the Parole Board' [online] <http://tna.europarchive.org/20110206085921/http://www.paroleboard.gov.uk/about> Accessed 27 September 2011.

Parole Board (2011c) 'Annual Report and Accounts 2010/1', London: TSO.

Paton, G. (2006) 'Teacher cleared of rape too late', *Times Educational Supplement*, 21 April.

Pattenden, R. (1996) *English Criminal Appeals 1884–1994: Appeals against conviction and sentence in England and Wales*, Oxford: Clarendon.

Pearce, F. and Tombs, S. (1992) 'Realism and corporate crime' in Matthews, R. and Young, J. (eds), *Issues in Realist Criminology*, London: Sage.

Pearse, J., Gudjonsson, G., Clare, I. C. H. and Rutter, S. (1998) 'Police Interviewing and Psychological Vulnerabilities: Predicting the Likelihood of a Confession', *Journal of Community & Applied Social Psychology*, 8: 1–21.

Peek, L. (2001) 'Prisoner cleared after girl admits rape lie', *The Times*, 15 December.

Peirce, G. (2011) 'The Birmingham Six: have we learned from our disgraceful past?', *The Guardian*, 12 March.

Persuad, R. (2005) 'Meadow is innocent', *Prospect Magazine*, 116, November.

Petherick, W., Turvey, B. and Ferguson, C. (2010) *Forensic Criminology*, Burlington, Massachusetts: Elsevier.

Phillips, C. and Brown, D. with James, Z. and Goodrich, P. (1998) 'Entry into the Criminal Justice System: A Survey of Police Arrests and Their Outcomes', Home Office Research Study No.185, London: Home Office.

Pleasence, P., Kemp, V. and Balmer, N. (2011) 'The Justice Lottery? Police Station Advice 25 Years on from PACE', *Criminal Law Review*, January: 3–18.

Pook, S. (2002) 'Victim of corrupt police freed after 25 years in jail', *The Telegraph*, 14 November 2002.

Price, C. (1985) 'Confession Evidence, the Police and Criminal Evidence Act and the Confait Case Baxter', in Caplan, J. and Koffman, L. (eds), *Police: The Constitution and the Community: A Collection of Original Essays on Issues Raised by the Police and Criminal Evidence Act 1984*, Abingdon: Professional Books.

Price, C. and Caplan, J. (1976) *The Confait Confessions*, London: Marion Boyars.

Punch, M. (2003) 'Rotten Orchards: "Pestilence", Police Misconduct and System Failure', *Policing and Society*, 13(2): 171–196.

Punch, M. and Gilmour, S. (2010) 'Police corruption: Apples, Barrels and Orchards', *Criminal Justice Matters*, 79(1): 10–12.

Quirk, H. (2007) 'Identifying Miscarriages of Justice: Why Innocence in the UK Is Not the Answer', *Modern Law Review*, 70(5): 759–777.

Quirk, H. (2009) 'Re-Thinking Miscarriages of Justice: Beyond the Tip of the Iceberg' by Michael Naughton', *British Journal of Criminology*, 49(3): 418–420.

Ravenell, T. E (2010) 'Cause and Conviction: The Role of Causation in Section 1983 Wrongful Conviction Claims', Villanova University School of Law Working Paper Series, Working Paper 146.

Rawls, J. (1971) *A Theory of Justice*, Cambridge, MA and London: Belknap Press of Harvard University Press.

Raynor, J. (2009) 'Custody nurses at police stations risk "miscarriages of justice"', *Law Society Gazette*, 23 July.

Regan, S. (1997) 'The Bridgewater Catastrophe', *Scandals in Justice*, May [online] <http://www.scandals.org/articles/sr970527c.html> Accessed 30 November 2006.

Reiman, J. (2010) *The Rich get Richer and the Poor get Prison: Ideology, Class, and Criminal Justice* (9th Edition) Boston: Allyn & Bacon.

Reiner, R. (1984) 'Crime, Law and Deviance: The Durkheim Legacy', in Fenton, S. (ed.), *Durkheim and Modern Sociology*, Cambridge: Cambridge University Press.

Reiner, R. (2010) *The Politics of the Police* (4th edn) Oxford: Oxford University Press.

Revill, J. (2003) 'Jailed pair win fight to clear names', *Birmingham Post*, 22 October.

Rhodes, M. R. (2000) *Coercion: A Nonevaluative Approach*, Amsterdam: Rodopi.

Risinger, D. M. (2006) 'Boxes in Boxes: Julian Barnes, Conan Doyle, Sherlock Holmes and the Edalji Case', *International Commentary on Evidence*, 4(2): 1–88.

Roberts, L. and Tozer, J. (2007) 'Sally Clark – wrongly jailed for killing her sons – found dead', *Daily Mail*, 17 March.

Roberts, R. (2004) 'The Royal Commission on Criminal Justice and Factual Innocence: Remedying Wrongful Convictions in the Court of Appeal', *Justice Journal*, 1(2): 86.

Roberts, S. (2003) 'Unsafe Convictions: Defining and Compensating Miscarriages of Justice', *Modern Law Review*, 66(3): 441–451.

Roberts, S. and Weathered, L. (2009) 'Assisting the Factually Innocent: The Contradictions and Compatibility of Innocence Projects and the Criminal Cases Review Commission', *Oxford Journal of Legal Studies*, 29(1): 51–55.

Robins, J. (2010) 'Criminal Cases Review Commission comes under fire', *The Times*, 21 January.

Ronson, J. (2001) 'The fall of a pop impresario', *The Guardian*, 1 December.

Rose, J., Panter, S. and Wilkinson, T. (1997) *Innocents: How Justice Failed Stefan Kiszko and Lesley Molseed*, London: Fourth Estate.

Ross, S. (2006) 'Top QC calls for review of fingerprint cases', *The Scotsman*, 30 March.

Royal Commission on Criminal Justice (1993) 'Report', London: HMSO.

Royal Commission on Criminal Procedure (1981) 'Report', London: HMSO.

Rozenberg, J. (2006) 'Sir Roy Meadow, the flawed witness, wins GMC appeal', *The Telegraph*, 18 February.

Samuels, A. (2003) 'In Denial of Murder: No Parole', *Howard Journal of Criminal Justice*, 42(2): 176–180.

Sanders, A. (2002) 'Prosecution Systems', in McConville, M. and Wilson, G. (eds), *Handbook of Criminal Justice*, Oxford: Oxford University Press.

Sanders, A. and Bridges, L. (1983) 'The Right to Legal Advice' in Walker, C. and Starmer, K. (eds), *Justice in Error*, London: Blackstone.

Sanders, A. and Young, R. (1994) 'The legal wilderness of police interrogation', Tom Sargant Memorial Lecture [online] <http://www.roughjusticetv.co.uk/sander.htm> Accessed 24 June 2012.

Sanders, A., Bridges, L., Mulvaney, A. and Crozier, G. (1989) 'Advice and Assistance at Police Stations and the 24-hour Duty Solicitor Scheme', London: Lord Chancellor's Department.

Sangha, B. and Moles, B. (2011a) 'Why we need a Criminal Cases Review Commission', *Direct Link: NSW District and Local Courts Practice Newsletter*, 8(12): 23–26.

Sangha, B. and Moles, B. (2011b) 'Post-conviction reviews in Australia – "A degree of intellectual isolation"', *Direct Link: NSW District and Local Courts Practice Newsletter*, 8(11): 2–6.

Savage, S. (2007) 'Restoring Justice: Campaigns against Miscarriages of Justice and the Restorative Justice Process', *European Journal of Criminology*, 4(2): 195–216.

Savage, S., Grieve, J. and Poyser, S. (2007) 'Putting Wrongs to Right; Campaigns against Miscarriages of Justice', *Criminology and Criminal Justice*, 7(1): 83–105.

Savill, R. (2009) 'Killer raped woman while on parole', *The Telegraph*, 13 November.

Scheck, B. and Neufeld, P. (2002) 'Toward Formation of "Innocence Commissions" In America', *Judicature*, 86(2): 98–105.

Scheck, B., Neufeld, P. and Dwyer, J. (2003) *Actual Innocence: When Justice Goes Wrong and How to Make It Right*, New York: New American Library.

Schehr, R. (2005) 'The Criminal cases Review Commission as a State Strategic Selection Mechanism', *American Criminal Law Review*, 42: 1289–1302.

Schehr, R. (2009) 'The CCRC as Seen from the United States', in Naughton, M. (ed.), *The Criminal Cases Review Commission: Hope for the Innocent?*, Basingstoke: Palgrave Macmillan.

Schehr, R. and Weathered, L. (2004) 'Should the United States Establish a Criminal Cases Review Commission?', *Judicature*, 88(3): 122–125.

Schiffer, B. and Champod, C. (2008) 'Judicial Error and Forensic Science: Pondering the Contribution of DNA Evidence', in Huff, R. and Killias, M. (eds), *Wrongful Conviction*, Philadelphia, PA: Temple University Press.

Scott, R. E. and Stuntz, W. J. (1992) 'Plea Bargaining as Contract', *Yale Law Journal*, 101(8): 1909–1968.

Scottish Criminal Cases Review Commission (SCCRC) (2012) 'About the Commission' [online] <http://www.sccrc.org.uk/home.aspx> Accessed 24 June 2012.

Seenan, G. (2001) 'Ice cream war duo freed for appeal', *The Guardian*, 12 December.

Sekar, S. (1997) *The Cardiff 3 and the Lynette White Inquiry*, London: Fitted-In Project.

Sekar, S. (2008) 'Wrongly jailed for murder: "Cardiff Three" are finally seeing real justice carried out', *The Voice*, 1346, 11 November.

Sekar, S. (2009) 'The Failure of the CCRC's Review of the Possible Wrongful Convictions Caused by Michael Heath', in Naughton, M. (ed.), *The Criminal Cases Review Commission: Hope for the Innocent?*, Basingstoke: Palgrave Macmillan.

Sekar, S. (2011) 'Still no justice for the Cardiff Three', *The Guardian*, 1 December.

Semikhodskii, S. (2007) *Dealing with DNA Evidence*, Abingdon: Routledge.

Shaw, K. (2009) 'The Quasi-Expert Witness: Fish or Fowl?', *Journal of Criminal Law*, 73(2): 146–152.

Shelton, D. (2008) 'The "CSI Effect": Does It Really Exist?', *National Institute of Justice Journal*, 259: 1–7.

Shorter, L. (2010) 'John Kamara: "What's helped me has been a stable relationship and the kids"', *The Guardian*, 31 March.

Simester, A. P., Spencer, J. P., Sullivan, G. R. and Virgo, G. J. (2010) *Simester and Sullivan's Criminal Law: Theory and Doctrine*, Oxford: Hart.

Slapper, G. and Tombs, S. (1999), *Corporate Crime*, Essex: Pearson.

Smith, L. (2012) 'Mum cried rape because her one-night stand forgot her name', *Daily Mirror*, 8 March.

Soothill, K., Francis, B. and Ackerley, E. (2004) 'Perjury and False Statements: A Criminal Profile of Persons Convicted 1979–2001', *Criminal Law Review*, November: 926–935.

Spencer, J. (1989) *Jackson's Machinery of Justice*, Cambridge: Cambridge University Press.

Spencer, J. (2006) 'Does Our Present Criminal Appeal System Make Sense?', *Criminal Law Review*, August: 677–694.

Spencer, J. (2007) 'Quashing Convictions for Procedural Irregularities', *Criminal Law Review*, November: 835–848.

Spencer, J. (2010) 'Compensation for Wrongful Imprisonment', *Criminal Law Review*, November: 803–822.

St. Johnston, T. E. (1966) 'The Judges' Rules and Police Interrogation in England Today', *Journal of Criminal Law, Criminology, and Police Science*, 57(1): 85–92.

Stanton, K. (2010) 'Wrongful convictions: a role for private law?', Society of Legal Scholars Annual Conference, Southampton, 13–16 September.

Steele, J. (1997) 'Police errors "could not be repeated"', *Electronic Telegraph*, 638 [online] <http://www.telegraph.co.uk> Accessed 12 November 2004.

Steele, J. (2000) 'Bungle by CPS ends murder appeal', *The Telegraph*, 2 August 2000.

Stevenson, R. (2008) 'Colin Stagg wins £706,000 payout over Rachel Nickell murder charge', *The Guardian*, 13 August.

Sweeney, J. and Law, B. (2001) 'Gene find casts doubt on double "cot death" murders, *The Observer*, 15 July.

Tan, G. (2011) 'Structuration Theory and Wrongful Imprisonment: From "Victimhood" to "Survivorship"?', *Critical Criminology: An International Journal*, 19(3): 175–196.

Tan, Y.H. (1993) 'Law report: scientist defamed: Skuse v Granada Television. Court of Appeal (Sir Thomas Bingham, Master of the Rolls, Lord Justice Beldam and Lord Justice Kennedy), 30 March 1993', *The Times*, 2 April.

Taylor, D. (2006) 'Rape victim' rounds on peer who named her as liar', *The Guardian*, 21 October.

Taylor, I., Walton, P. and Young, J. (1973) *The New Criminology: For a Social Theory of Deviance*, London: Routledge & Kegan Paul.

Teed, P. and Cassidy, D. (2006) 'Cleared: the black motorist convicted despite white culprit caught on CCTV', *Daily Mail*, 5 November.

Telegraph (2007) 'Obituaries: Sally Clark', 19 March.

Telegraph (2009) 'Obituaries: Sir Ludovic Kennedy', 19 October.

Thomas, A. P. (2006) 'The CSI Effect: Fact or Fiction', *Yale Law Journal (Pocket Part)*, 115: 70–72.

Thompson, W. Taroni, F. and Aitken, C. (2003) 'How the Probability of False Positive Affects the Value of DNA Evidence', *Journal of Forensic Science*, 48(1): 47–54.

Times (1904) 'Report of the Committee of Inquiry into the Beck case', 26 November.

Times (1999) 'Trevor Campbell', 15 October.

Tozer, J. (2010) '"Wicked" woman who cried rape is jailed for three years despite being seven months pregnant', *Daily Mail*, 16 July.

Travis, A. (2006) 'Anger at legal compensation shakeup', *The Guardian*, 20 April.

Traynor, L. (2006) 'My pledge of justice', *Liverpool Echo*, 18 April.

University of Bristol (2010) 'Why the Conviction of Simon Hall Cannot Stand' [online] <http://www.bris.ac.uk/news/2010/7384.html> Accessed 24 June 2012.

University of Bristol (2011) 'University of Bristol Innocence Project Response to Simon Hall Judgment by the Court of Appeal' [online] <http://www.bris.ac.uk/news/2010/7432.html> Accessed 24 June 2012.

Vasagar, J. (2002) 'End of a nightmare', *The Guardian*, 16 January.

Walker, C. (1999) 'Miscarriages of Justice in Principle and Practice', in Walker, C. and Starmer, K. *Miscarriages of Justice*, London: Blackstone.

Walker, C. and Campbell, K. (2009) 'The CCRC as an Option for Canada: Forwards or Backwards?', in Naughton, M. (ed.), *The Criminal Cases Review Commission: Hope for the Innocent?*, Basingstoke: Palgrave Macmillan.

Walker, C. and Starmer, K. (1999) *Miscarriages of Justice*, London: Blackstone.

Walmsley, R., Howard, L. and White, S. (1992) 'The National Prison Survey 1991: Main Findings', Home Office Research Study 128, London: HMSO.

Ward, J. (1993) *Ambushed: My Story*, London: Vermilion.

Ward, T. (2009) 'Usurping the role of the jury? Expert Evidence and Witness Credibility in English Criminal Trials: Expert Evidence and Witness Credibility in English Criminal Trials', *International Journal of Evidence & Proof*, 13(2): 83–101.

Watson, M. (2002) 'The Prevalence of Perjury', *Justice of the Peace*, 36: 700.

Watson, M. (2005) 'Lying on Oath: New Light on Perjury', *Justice of the Peace*, 29: 548.

Weathered, L. (2007) 'Does Australia Need a Specific Institution to Correct Wrongful Convictions?', *Australian and New Zealand Journal of Criminology*, 40(2): 179–198.

Weathers, H. (2008) '"I've lost three children. Losing another would destroy me," says Terry Cannings', *Daily Mail*, 5 January.

Webster, R. (2005) *The Secret of Bryn Estyn: The Making of a Modern Witch Hunt*, Chilton, Aylesbury: Orwell.

Wells, C. (1994) 'The Royal Commission on Criminal Justice: A Room without a View', in McConville, M. and Bridges, L. (1994) (eds), *Criminal Justice in Crisis*, Aldershot: Edward Elgar.

Wells, G. and Loftus, E. F. (1984) (eds) *Eyewitness Testimony: Psychological Perspectives*, New York: Cambridge University Press.

Wells, G. and Loftus, E. F. (2003) 'Eyewitness Memory for People and Events', in Goldstein, A. (ed.), *Comprehensive Handbook of Psychology: Volume II (Forensic Psychology)*, New York: John Wiley.

West Virginia Supreme Court (1993) 'Investigation of the West Virginia State Police Crime Laboratory, Serology Division' [online] <http://www.truthin justice.org/zainreport.htm> Accessed 12 June 2012.

Wheate, R. M. and Jamieson, A. (2009) 'A Tale of Two Approaches – The NAS Report and the Law Commission Consultation Paper on Forensic Science', *International Commentary on Evidence*, 7(2): 1–25.

Whiteway, K. (2008) 'The Origins of the English Court of Criminal Appeal', *Canadian Law Library Review* 33: 309–312.

Wilson, A. (2010) 'The Law Commission's Proposal on Expert Opinion Evidence: An Onerous Demand upon Judges', *Web Journal of Current Legal Issues*, 1.

Wilson, D. (2001) 'The guilt trap', *The Guardian*, February 1.

Woffinden, B. (1987) *Miscarriages of Justice*, London: Hodder & Stoughton.

Woffinden, B. (2000) 'Extra time for being "in denial"', *The Guardian*, October 16.

Woffinden, B. (2001) 'Prisoners win right to challenge governor', *The Guardian*, 6 August.

Woffinden, B. (2010) 'The Criminal Cases Review Commission has failed', *The Guardian*, 30 November.

Wolitz, D. (2010) 'Innocence Commissions and the Future of Post-Conviction Review', Georgetown Public Law and Legal Theory Research Paper 10-22 [online] <http://scholarship.law.georgetown.edu/facpub/337/> Accessed 22 June 2012.

Woods, R. and Foggo, D. (2008) 'Should Britain have a compulsory DNA database?', *The Times*, 24 February.

Worrall, B. (2005) 'Setting the record straight on case', *Bristol Evening Post*, 13 June.

Worstall, T. (2006) 'Beware Charlie the safety elephant', *The Times*, 21 April.

Zellick, G. (2005a) 'Legal aid', *The Guardian*, 20 June.

Zellick, G. (2005b) 'Facing up to Miscarriages of Justice', *Manitoba Law Journal*, 31: 555–564.

Zellick, G. (2006) 'Oral Evidence to the House of Commons Home Affairs Committee: The Work of the Criminal Cases Review Commission' [online] <http://www.publications.parliament.uk/pa/cm200506/cmselect/cmhaff/1635/6101001.htm> Accessed 24 June 2012.

Index

Abdullahi, Yusuf 27, 30, 63–64
    see also R v Paris, Abdullahi and
        Miller; Cardiff Three
Adams, Andrew 196, 216–217, 219
    see also R v Andrew Adams; R
        (Adams) v Secretary of State
        for Justice; R (on the applica-
        tion of Adams) (FC)
        (Appellant) v Secretary of
        State for Justice (Respondent)
Albert, Joan 192
    see also Hall, Simon
Alejandro, Gilbert 65
Ali, Idris 93
Allen, Kate 101
    see also Barnes, Shane
Allman, Amanda 29
Alverstone, Lord 35
Anderson, George 21, 28, 33
    see also Hewitt, Margaret
Armstrong, Patrick 41–42
    see also R v Richardson, Conlon,
        Armstrong and Hill;
        Guildford Four
Asbury, David 95–96
Atkins, Kelly 55
Attorney-General 49, 52
Attorney-General's Guidelines 51
Avon and Somerset Police 41

Bailey, Kathleen 61
Baldwin, John 80–81
    see also McConville, Mike
Ball, Kenneth 58
    see also R v Spencer and Others
Barnardo's 21
Barnes, Shane 101
    see also Allen, Kate
Barnsley, Mark 121

Beardmore, Roger 61, 233
Beck, Adolf 1–3, 18, 27, 33, 83,
        144–146, 159, 183, 210
Beynon, John 38
Bingham LJ/LCJ 102, 151, 154–155,
        169, 172, 215, 217
Birmingham Six 42–43, 67–68, 77,
        91, 108, 162, 163, 178, 180,
        186, 194
Blackburn LJ 221
Blackburn, Paul 41, 209
    see also R v Blackburn
Blackstone, Sir William 70
Blackwell, Warren 58–59, 181, 184,
        233
    see also R v Blackwell
Blair, Tony 18, 78
Blakelock, PC 92
Brandon, Ruth 91
    see also Davies, Christie
Bridges, Lee 39–40, 47, 80
Bridgewater Four 4, 21–23, 43, 91,
        175, 218, 225
    see also R v Hickey and Others
Bridgewater, Carl
    see under Bridgewater Four
Brown Blakemore, Lisa 104
Brown, David 40
    see also Bucke, Tom
Brown, Robert 28, 31–32, 41, 91,
        115, 126, 138, 195, 209
    see also R v Brown
Buckalew, Jack 66
Bucke, Tom 40
    see also Brown, David
Bulger, James 125
    see also Venables, Jon;
        Thompson, Robert

C3 Division 163, 167–168, 173–176, 178, 186–187, 194, 235
Callaghan, Hugh 2, 42–43, 163
see also R v McIlkenney and Others; Birmingham Six
Callan, Kevin 29, 31–33
Camelo, Joseph 85
see also R v Turnbull and Others
Campbell, Thomas 63
see also Steele, Joseph
Campbell, Trevor 43
Campbell-Savours, Lord 59
Cannings, Angela 73–75, 77, 108, 198–202, 206, 233
see also R v Cannings
Cannings, Terry 202
Cardiff Newsagent Three 48, 93, 222, 224
Cardiff Three 27, 30, 32, 63–64, 80, 137, 154
see also R v Paris, Abdullahi and Miller
Cawood, Ethel 43
see also Campbell, Trevor
Chakrabarti, Shami 5
Chalmers, Robert 135
Charlton, David
see under Dror, Itiel
Charlton, Richard 41
Chatnam House Rules 136
Chindamo, Learco 125
Choongh, Satnam 40
Christie, John 3
see also Evans, Timothy
Clark, Sally 102–104, 108, 198–201, 233
see also R v Clark (Sally)
Clarke, Charles, 17, 211
Clarke, Charles 61
see also R v Maynard and Others
Clarke, Donna 48
see also Hewins, Annette
Clarke, Ronald 171, 181, 183, 207, 232
see also R v Clarke and McDaid; R v Clarke and R v McDaid
Code for Crown Prosecutors 49, 232, 237

Collins J 104
Confait affair 2–3, 38, 49, 51, 183
Confait, Maxwell
see under *Confait* affair
Conlon, Gerry 2, 41–42, 67, 162
see also R v Richardson, Conlon, Armstrong and Hill; Guildford Four
Cooper, Sean 155–156
see also R v Cooper
Cornwall, Michael 61
see also R v Maynard and Others
Coull, Elizabeth
see under Dino
Creighton, Louise 55
Criminal Case Unit 163
Criminal Cases Review Commission 2–3, 6, 10, 17–18, 51, 54, 59, 62, 68, 119, 122, 125, 129, 138, 151–152, 162–188, 191–193, 197–198, 204–205, 207, 213, 218–219, 234–237
Criminal Records Bureau 204
Crocker, Judge John 203
Crown Prosecution Service 22, 49–51, 54, 72, 79, 90, 181, 183, 215, 220,
CSI Effect 95
Cummiskey, John 43
see also R v Cummiskey
Curran, Patricia 93

Dando, Jill 75–77, 219
Daniels, Antonio Eval 132
see also R v Powell
Davies, Michael John 131
see also Davies v DPP
Davies, Christie 91
see also Brandon, Ruth
Davis, Gerald 65
Davis, Michael 152–153
see also R v Davis, Johnson and Rowe; M25 Three
Day, Paul 62–63
de Simone, Teresa 30, 154, 217
see also R v Hodgson; Hodgson, Sean
Devlin Committee 83, 85
Devlin, Lord Patrick 83

Devlin Report 83, 85
Dino 176
Director of Public Prosecution 49
Donovan Committee 147
Dougherty, Luke 83–84
Downing, Stephen 114–115, 126, 138, 195, 209
  see also R v Downing
Doyle, Sir Arthur Conan 144
Dror, Itiel 96
Dudley, Reginald 61–62
  see also R v Maynard and Others
Dunk, Reginald 222
Durham, Timothy 100
Dyson LJ 216–219

Eagles, Maria 68
Easton, Raymond 97, 99
Edalji, George 143
Eddowes, Michael 3
Enhanced Disclosure
  see under Criminal Records Bureau
Enhanced Thinking Skills 114, 123
Epping Torso Case 61
  see also R v Maynard and Others
European Court of Human Rights 176

Fell, Peter 93
Findlay, Keith 76
  see also Scott, Michael
Fisher Report 3
Fisher, Sir Henry 3, 38
Fletcher, Jacqueline 92
Foot, Paul 4
Forbes, William 66
Full Code Test
  see under Code for Crown Prosecutors

Gafoor, Jeffrey 30
  see also Cardiff Three
Garrett, Brandon 65, 106
  see also Neufeld, Peter
Gaunt, Jon 5
Gee, Timothy Darryl 59–60, 233
  see also R v Gee

General Medical Council 103–105
George, Barry 75–77, 219–220, 233
  see also R v Barry George
Giannelli, Paul 107
Glidewell, LJ 51–52
Gordon, Ian Hay 93
Gould, Jon 165
Greater Manchester Police 28, 41
Green, Penny 44–46
  see also Ward, Tony
Greenwood, Margaret 93
Griess tests 67
Grieve, David 96
Griffin, Lissa 164
Grommek, Mark 63–64
  see also Cardiff Three
Gudjonsson, Gisli 82, 91–92, 94
Guildford Four 2–5, 18, 41, 68, 77, 108, 162–163, 180, 186

Hagans, Christopher 44
  see also Wilson, John
Haigh, Victoria 55
Hale, Matthew 56
Hall, Darren 48, 93
  see also Cardiff Newsagent Three
Hall, Simon 180
Hamer, David 71
Hardcastle, Robert Anthony 62
Harris, Leonard 22
Harris, William O'Dell 65
Heath, Gladys 29
Heath, Michael 104–105
Hewins, Annette 48
  see also R v Clarke, R v Hewins; Clarke, Donna
Hewitt, Margaret 21, 28
  see also Anderson, George
Hickey, Michael and Vincent 21–23, 43, 225
  see also R v Hickey and Others; Bridgewater Four
Hill, Paddy Joe 2, 42, 67–68, 194–195,
  see also R v McIlkenney and Others; Birmingham Six
Hill, Paul 2, 41
  see also R v Richardson, Conlon, Armstrong and Hill; Guildford Four

Hill, Peter 115
Hodgson, Sean 30, 32, 137, 154,
      181, 184, 217, 220, 222–223,
      225
   see also R v Hodgson
Hoey, Sean 98
   see also R v Hoey
Holmes, Sherlock 144
Home Office 3–4, 36, 46, 67–68, 91,
      104, 115, 121, 153, 163,
      173–174, 221, 224
Home Office Assessor 224
Home Secretary 2, 17, 84, 143, 145,
      163, 168, 173–174, 194, 211
House of Lords 20, 22, 57–58, 132,
      171, 176, 214
House of Lords Select Committee
      on Science and Technology
      108
Huff, Ronald 164
Hughes LJ 150
Hunter, Gerry 2
   see also R v McIlkenney and
      Others; Birmingham Six
Hurd, Douglas 211

Ibrahim, Leyla 55
Incentives and Earned Privileges
      Scheme 121–122
Independent Police Complaints
      Commission 59
Innocence Commission for Virginia
      165
Innocence Network UK 17, 68, 128,
      179
Interdepartmental Committee on
      the Court of Criminal Appeal
   see under Donovan Committee
Irish Republican Army 2, 4, 18,
      41–43, 51, 67, 92–93, 153,
      162, 187, 194, 215
Irvin, Kenneth 88
   see also R v Irvin

James, Paul 203
Jamieson, Allan 98, 100, 107–109
Jenkins, Billie-Jo 215
   see also Jenkins, Sion
Jenkins, Mechthild 94

Jenkins, Sion 215
Johnson, Margaret 93
Johnson, Randolph 152–153
   see also R v Davis, Johnson and
      Rowe; M25 Three
Jones, Diane 48
   see also R v Clarke; R v Hewins
Jordan, Christine 55
Judge, LJ 74, 200
Judges' Rules 35–38, 41–42, 46–47,
      49
JUSTICE 17, 91, 174
Justice for All 17

Kamara, John 28, 51, 196, 225
   see also R v Kamara (John)
Kane, Patrick 93
Kennedy, Ludovic 3–4
King, Ashley 93
King, Jonathan 134–135
Kiszko, Stefan 137, 154
Krane, Dan 98

Lace, David 218
   see also Hodgson, Sean
Lattimore, Colin 2, 38
   see also Confait affair
Law Commission 108–109
Lawless, Ian 94
   see also R v Lawless
Lawrence, Philip 125
Lawrence, Stephen 18–19
Lawson, Mike 60–61, 233
   see also R v Basil Anthony
      Williams-Rigby and Michael
      James Lawson
Lawton LJ 101
Lee, Ann 93
Leighton, Ronald 2, 38
   see also Confait affair
Liberty 5, 17
Lizar, Robert 209
Long, George 93
Love, Billy 63
Low Copy Number DNA 98
M25 Three 152, 176
   see also R v Davis, Johnson and
      Rowe
McBarnet, Doreen 20, 56

McBride, Ian 68
McCartney, Raymond 219
  see also R (on the application of
    Adams) (FC) v Secretary of
    State for Justice
McDaid, James 171, 181, 183, 207,
    232
  see also R v Clarke and McDaid;
    R v Clarke and R v McDaid
MacDermott, Eamonn 219
  see also R (on the application of
    Adams) (FC) v Secretary of
    State for Justice
McIlkenny, Richard 2, 42
  see also R v McIlkenney and
    Others; Birmingham
    Six
McKenzie, David 92
McKie, Shirley 95–96
Mactaggart, Fiona 221
Maddison, J 65
Maddocks, Glyn 209
Maddox, Wayne 55
Maguire Seven 18, 162–163, 186
Malleson, Kate 150
Managing Indeterminate Sentences
    and Risk 138–139
Mansfield, Michael 5, 74
Mantell LJ 62, 152
Mason, Michael 58
May, Sir John 3, 163
Maynard, Robert 61–62
  see also R v Maynard and Others
Meadow, Roy Sir 73, 102–105,
    199
  see also General Medical Council
    v Professor Sir Roy Meadow
Mental Health Lawyers Association
    41
MI6 153
Miller, Stephen 30, 63–64, 154
  see also R v Paris, Abdullahi and
    Miller; Cardiff Three
Ministry of Justice 68, 114, 138,
    216, 220
Molloy, Patrick 43
  see also R v Hickey and Others;
    Bridgewater Four
Molseed, Lesley 154
  see also Kiszko, Stefan

Morley, Samantha 55
Morton, James 61
Moseley, William 61
Mulcahy, Aogán 82
Mullen, Nicholas 30, 32, 34, 141,
    153–155, 181, 183, 187, 207,
    214–215, 217, 232
  see also R v Mullen; R (Mullen) v
    Secretary of State for the
    Home Department
Mullin, Chris 4, 43, 67

Napper, Robert 223
National Academy of Sciences
    106–108
National DNA Database 22, 31,
    97–99
National Offender Management
    Service 138–139
National Policing Improvement
    Agency 99
Neufeld, Peter 65, 106
Nichols, Patrick 29, 31–32
Nickell, Rachel 223
  see also Stagg, Colin
Nobles, Richard 146, 150, 173
Norman, Ken 73
North Carolina General Assembly
    165
North Carolina Actual Innocence
    Commission 165–166
North, Robert 88
  see also R v North
Norwegian Criminal Cases Review
    Commission 163

O'Brien, Michael 222, 224
  see also R v O'Brien and Others;
    Cardiff Newsagent Three
O'Neill, Eamonn 76
Offender Assessment System
    113
Office for National Statistics 222
Ofsted 203
Ohorodnyckyi, Roman 84
Osborne, Nicola 55
Osbourne, Henrietta 93
Otton LJ 51
Ovasapyan, Edmond 223

Packer, Herbert 184, 187
Panorama 47, 136
Paris, Tony 30, 63
    see also R v Abdullahi, Paris and
        Miller; Cardiff Three
Parole Board for England and Wales
        6, 8–9, 113–139, 234
Pattenden, Rosemary 143, 157
Payen, George
    see under Ohorodnyckyi, Roman
Pearse, John 92
Peirce, Gareth 4
Percival, Kevin 55
Peron, Alisa
    see under Dror, Itiel
Pill LJ 88
Pinder, Barbara 92
Platt, Ward 199
Pleasence, Pascoe 40
Powell, Anthony Glassford 132
    see also R v Powell, R v English
Powell, Richard 64
Power, Billy 2, 42, 67
    see also R v McIlkenney and
        Others; Birmingham Six
Price, Karen 93
Prison Service Order 4700 138–139
Psaila, Angela 63–64
    see also Cardiff Three
Puaca, Steven 104–105
    see also R v Puaca
Puisne Court 147
Punch, Maurice 44–45

Quinn, Joseph 89

Raghip, Engin 92
    see also R v Silcott, Braithwaite
        and Raghip
Rawls, John 25
Raynor, Jonathan 41
Real Irish Republican Army 98
Report of the Departmental
        Committee on Evidence of
        Identification in Criminal
        Cases (Devlin Report) 83
Richardson, Carole 2, 41
    see also R v Richardson, Conlon,
        Armstrong and Hill;
        Guildford Four

Richardson, James 65
Risinger, Michael 3
Roberts, John 93
Roberts, Judith 93
Roberts, Stephanie 157
Robinson, James 21, 43
    see also R v Hickey and Others;
        Bridgewater Four
Roch LJ 22, 156, 218
Rose LJ 153–154
Ross, Marion 95–96
Rough Justice 4, 17
Rowe, Raphael 152
    see also R v Davis, Johnson and
        Rowe; M25 Three
Royal Commission on Criminal
        Justice 3, 10, 80, 108, 163,
        166–171, 174, 177–178, 180,
        182, 184, 186–187, 235
Royal Commission on Criminal
        Procedure 3, 38, 49, 183
Royal Prerogative of Mercy 3, 143,
        168–169, 171, 174, 179, 185,
Royal Statistical Society 103, 199
Royal, Jack 196, 216
    see also Adams, Andrew
Rucker, David 203, 206
Russell, Lin and Megan 63

Salih, Ahmet 2, 38
Sanders, Andrew 39, 79
Sands, Daniel 93
Sankey, Lord 71
Saunders, Philip 48, 93, 222
    see also Cardiff Newsagent
        Three
Savage, Stephen 18
Schiff, David 150, 173
Schlesinger, Alexander 222
    see also Dunk, Reginald
Scott, Michael 76
Scottish Criminal Cases Review
        Commission 163
Second General Multiplex 97–98
Securitas 203
Security Service 153
Sentence Planning Reports 117
Sewell, Wendy 114, 209
    see also Downing, Stephen

Sex Offender Treatment
Programmes 114, 117,
122–123
Sherwood, Ellis 48
see also R v O'Brien, Sherwood
and Hall; Cardiff Newsagent
Three
Shirley, Mark 126
Short Tandem Repeat 97, 99
Silverman, Sidney 3
Simon, Lord 20
Simpson, Thomas 146
see also R v Simpson (Thomas
William)
Skuse, Frank 67–68
see also Skuse v Granada
Television Ltd
Smith, J 85
Smith LJ 89
Soothill, Keith 63
South Wales Police 30, 47–48
Spencer, Alan 58
see also R v Spencer and Others
Spencer, John 160, 217
Stagg, Colin 223
see also Nickell, Rachel
Standard Disclosure
see under Criminal Records
Bureau
Stanton, Barry 90–91
see also R v Stanton
Stanton, Keith 212
Steele, Joseph 63
see also Campbell, Thomas
Steyn LJ 153, 214
Stone, Michael 63
Sudden Infant Death Syndrome
73–74, 102–103, 198–199
Suffield, John Jnr 51, 196
see also Kamara, John
Surrey Police 41, 203
Supreme Court 219–220

Ta Ba, Van 88
Taylor, Edmond 203, 206
Taylor, LCJ 64, 79, 89
Templeton, Emma 55
Territorial Army 76
The Fingerprint Inquiry Scotland 96

The Innocence Project 82–83
Thompson, Emma 4
Thompson, Robert 125
see also Venables, Jon; Bulger,
James
Thornton, Anthony Judge 126
Threshold Test
see under Code for Crown
Prosecutors
Tindsley, Jacqueline 104–105
see also Heath, Michael
Tottenham Riots 92
Treadaway, Derek 43, 91
see also R v Treadaway
Trial and Error 4, 17
Tune, David 55
Turnbull, Raymond 85
see also R v Turnbull
Twitchell, Keith 28, 31–32, 77, 91
see also R v Twitchell
Typology of Claims of Innocence
128, 138
Typology of Successful Appeals
192–193

Udoma, Patrick 55
University of Bristol Innocence
Project 180

Venables, Jon 125
see also Bulger, James;
Thompson, Robert
Vilday, Leanne 63–64
see also Cardiff Three

Walker, Clive 23–25
Walker, Johnny 2, 42
see also R v McIlkenney and
Others; Birmingham Six
Waller LJ 90
Walsh, Annie 28, 209
see also Brown, Robert
Ward, Judith 28, 51–52, 67, 92,
108
see also R v Ward
Ward, Tony 44–46
see also Green, Penny
Watson, Michael 63
Weir J 98

Weir, Michael 22, 31–34, 129, 155, 181, 183, 207, 232
Wertheim, Pat 96
West Midlands Serious Crime Squad 42–47, 67
West Yorkshire Police 42
Wheate, Rhonda 107–109
    see also Jamieson, Allan
White, Lynette 30, 63
    see also Cardiff Three
Widgery LJ/LJC 85, 155–156
Wild, Anthony 61–62
    see also R v Maynard and Others
Wilkins, Alfred 94
    see also Lawless, Ian
Williams, Alan 198
    see also Clark, Sally

Williams-Rigby, Basil 60–61, 233
    see also R v Basil Anthony Williams Rigby and Michael James Lawson
Wilson, David 115
Wilson, Gary 93
Wilson, John 44
    see also Hagans, Christopher
Woffinden, Bob 4, 176
Wolitz, David 165
Woodall, Glen 65
World in Action 67–68
Worstall, Tim 211

Zain, Fred 65–66, 86
Zellick, Graham 178, 185
Zirag, Laszlo 83

Printed and bound in Great Britain by
CPI Antony Rowe, Chippenham and Eastbourne